The Tolpuddle Six

the Hammett relative

S R McMahon

ISBN: 978-1-291-82562-6

PublishNation, London

www.publishnation.co.uk

CONTENTS

DEDICATION

To all those who paved the way for future generations in the struggle for better working conditions and wages

To my husband Kevin and daughter Emma for their patience during the construction of this book

To all the new relatives and friends I have discovered and made along the journey of compiling this literature

THANK YOU ALL

ACKNOWLEDGEMENTS

Angela McCormick
Becky Stares and the Gibbons Family
Dawn Stewart
Donna King
Enid McEvoy
Hazel Werner
Irene Howgate (R.I.P.)
Kevin McMahon – for creating and producing all artwork and most photography
Len Ruffell
Marjorie Spencer
Moria Andrews
Mrs Freda Wade (Dorset Memories, Dorchester Age Concern and additional information)
Mrs Morland (Wilton information)
Nari Fairbanks (the Australian connection)
Pam Collins
Ancestry web site
Bank of England: The Inflation Calculator
BBC Archives
British Library and newspaper archives
Commonwealth War Graves Commission
Coors Brewers Ltd (Bass & Co)
Dorset History Centre, Dorchester
Findmypast web site
FreeBMD web page/certificates – birth, marriage and death
Hampshire Record Office
Modern Record Centre The University of Warwick
National Probate Wills
On-line Dorset Parish Clerks
The Latter Day Saints
The National Archives, Kew
Trade Union Congress and The Tolpuddle Martyrs' Trust
Various Internet Sites
And any other person(s) or organization(s) I have omitted to thank or acknowledge.

THE TOLPUDDLE MARTYRS

They were six honest family working men
Hoeing the land but possessing knowledge of paper and pen
Employers repaid them with exploitation
The public supported the Six with a march and petition
Over the seas and far away they were sent
Leaving their families back home with more poverty and rent
Pardons well overdue many years later they would secure
United the men stood in what they had had to endure
Dispatched to their homeland for a few years
Determined to put behind them all their fears
Loveless (x2), Standfield (x2), Brine and Hammett were their names
Emigration to Canada for all but Hammett also known as James
Many years have since passed those days of old
All over the world to many their story is still told
Remembering the Tolpuddle Six stood up for the working classes
Treated so badly by the ruling elite; to the Martyrs we raise our glasses
Yearly in Tolpuddle we celebrate and give thanks to those brave fellows
Remember all they had wanted was a fair wage for their working day
Shame on all who instead rewarded them with transportation for pay.

S R McMahon 2013
1st cousin 4x removed
to James Hammett TM

1

HOW ALL THE TOLPUDDLE MARTYRS WERE RELATED

The marriage of Elizabeth Hammett and Stephen Loveless links all six Tolpuddle Martyrs together by blood and marriage lines. This union also links back again into the Hammett family.

Elizabeth Hammett was sister to James Hammett TM (Tolpuddle Martyr).

Stephen Loveless was son of John, born 1783, who was first cousin to brothers George and James Loveless (both TMs). He was also uncle to Loveless sisters Judith, born 1809, and Elizabeth, born 1814, whose father was his brother William, born 1775. These two Loveless sisters married two Hammett brothers William, born 1819, and John, born 1823, who in turn were first half-cousins to James Hammett TM.

**

The six Tolpuddle Martyrs were related thus:-

Thomas Standfield TM wed Dinniah Loveless sister of George and James Loveless TMs. They had a son, John Standfield TM, and a daughter, Elizabeth Standfield, who married James Brine TM (after the return from transportation). James Hammett TM's sister, Elizabeth Hammett, married Stephen Loveless, as mentioned above.

**

CENSUS DATES

The census was taken every ten years and noted all types of useful information on individuals, with the earlier ones containing less personal information than the latter ones. At the time this would have been used to gather knowledge on the population for the Government, but later it was to become a very necessary tool for those wishing to trace and gather information on people from bygone times. Most notably those researching their family ancestors and relatives would first use this source. Listed below are the years with the earlier one being taken in a summer month, then subsequent ones being noted in the springtime.

1841, 6TH JUNE

1851, 30TH MARCH

1861, 7TH APRIL

1871, 2ND APRIL

1881, 3RD APRIL

1891, 5TH APRIL

1901, 31ST MARCH

1911, 2ND APRIL

INTRODUCTION

Situated approximately seven miles east of Dorchester in the county of Dorset on the northern banks of the River Piddle is to be found the village of Tolpuddle, previously known as Tolpiddle, and even further back in time Pidele. The sun rising over the hill each morning in the east lit up the dewy water meadows and the village inhabitants in their homes. A place once owned by childless Tola, wife of Orc, a servant of King Canute, later passing into the hands of the monastery at Abbotsbury, with the Doomsday Book mentioning the Abbot had a manor called Pidela. The manor came under the Hundred of Puddletown, as did nearby Southover which came under the Tolpuddle parish. The twelfth century church of St John the Evangelist in Tolpuddle also served Southover where there was not one. At the other end of the village far away from the church was a barn. This served as the first Methodist Chapel built in about 1818. It would not be until 1862 that a second larger one was constructed, this time out of bricks.

The main industry of the village was farming, with some having more than one string to their bow to make ends meet for their families. A few others within this community had a trade, masons, carpenters, thatchers and so on. Housing was overcrowded containing large families, and made of poor quality construction and conditions. The pathways and road infrastructure were not much better, and quickly becoming unusable in the wet conditions.

Over the years many illness and diseases would cast black clouds over the village inhabitants, smallpox being no exception in the year 1791. This fell within the watch of Reverend Dr Bernard Hodgson, vicar of Tolpuddle. Upon his death in 1805 Reverend Dr Thomas Warren would fill his shoes, and in time be known as a man who went back on his word regarding the Tolpuddle Martyrs.

But really from 1834 history will remember the village of Tolpuddle forever being associated with the Tolpuddle Martyrs or, as they were known in their day, The Dorchester Unionists. For it was these six men who projected the village into the spotlight, not only within their own country but, in time, the rest of the world. If not for

4

them, Tolpuddle would have probably remained a quiet, pretty village joining the ranks of similar ones to be found in modern times in Dorset. Today Tolpuddle is firmly on the global map due to these six men. All they and other members of the village had wanted was to be able to work and be paid adequately for their services, as did the agricultural labourers elsewhere in the country. They formed a Friendly Society whereby all members vowed not to work below a certain level of money a week. For this they were punished with transportation to the other side of the globe, well six names on that members' list were. This punishment served as a lesson to the others left behind. It could quite have easily have been them.

Many books have been written and published on the story of these men, with one famous local author Thomas Hardy knowing their home village well. In his works he referred to it as Tolchurch.

As was the case with many rural villages in times gone by where people did not move around very far, it was not uncommon for many to be related to each other either by blood or marriage. The Tolpuddle Six were no exception to this, with their immediate and outer families all suffering the transportation sentence too, back home in Tolpuddle. Now for the story to unfold.

PART I

Chapter 1

BACKGROUND AND AN EARLY MORNING CALL

Across the English Channel in France the French Revolution came to an end in 1799 after a decade. This violent social upheaval disturbed those in power in England and they now viewed with suspicion and fear any sort of workers' association or trade union. These organisations had the potential to influence society, especially workers, who could then make demands, dictate to their betters and so forth. No longer would the ruling elite be able to control the much-needed workers without questioning on their lands. With support and advice behind them from any such societies, they could all rise up together in unison and be troublesome. These facts were very much talked of in hushed tones within the various corridors of power, country estates and those who held all the purse strings of society from the top to the bottom.

The ordinary working people were in real poverty with the newly invented machines taking over some of their jobs. Machines did not require or demand a weekly wage, did not complain or were slack and idle. They also could do the job of more than one man and were therefore quite favourable, and profit making for the landowner or farmer. In addition to this the build up of the various Inclosure (Enclosure) Acts over the years, particularly in the 1770's, gradually squeezed, tightened and almost strangled the ordinary people with regards to being able to use the common lands for the various previous purposes which had been allowed to them.

Fuelled by the discontent among the rural working-class, the year 1830 saw the Swing Riots spread through the southern counties in England, including Dorset. Within these areas the land workers would have initially felt the frustration rise within themselves once the impact of these changes in work conditions were felt. Emotions of anger and outrage would soon take over with many uniting together and resulting in the smashing of farm machinery and rick-burning. Captain Swing had arrived. Who was this person? An anonymous leader of this uprising, with probably a number of people using this pen name to sign off threatening anonymous missives in relation to their loss of jobs and so forth. Five hundred of these land workers were transported to far off shores, with many others seeing their end by the noose. This was supposed to serve as a warning to those who would dare to ever again follow the ways of Captain Swing. But these actions did not deter many, who had been awakened to improving their working life.

Life in those times at Tolpuddle, would have been a daily challenge, especially if you were an agricultural labourer. In other parts of the country, and even the county, these workers were paid more than those in Tolpuddle, who were starting to see their weekly wage reduced. The nine shillings a week they received was gradually reduced to seven. With the threat in the air of a further reduction to their already meagre weekly income the situation could not continue. Already they were finding it hard to put food in the mouths of their families, which could be large. Children often went barefoot for lack of shoes and clothes were far from Sunday best. Their homes would have been extremely basic, even with dirt floors. These people were getting desperate. How much longer could they reasonably be expected to put up with the way things were?

Amongst those in Tolpuddle was a local man with a moral conscience, namely George Loveless. An educated man, able to read and write, and with the gift of oration, George was the ideal man to lead those wanting to better their working lot. He was already well known, being the local Wesleyan Methodist preacher with vast family connections within the village. The obvious pillar of this community to hear their plight was Dr Warren, the Church of England vicar. It was him George initially approached to use his influence in aiding the labourers when their wages in Tolpuddle first started decreasing. Dr Warren heard what he had to say and local farmers promised payment the same as those of others in the county of ten shillings a week. Were they all just agreeing to appease George and the rest of the labourers? What was certain was that a promise would be broken. These men had no feeling or sympathy for the plight of the workers for they were far removed from their world. No empty larders for them, or purses without coins. So it was that, instead of an increase in their weekly wage rates, the decrease continued. A man of the Church was one of those who badly let them all down, and did not stand up for them in their hour of need. If one could not trust a church representative, then who could be trusted?

The labourers, led by George Loveless, then went to Mr Pitt, a nearby magistrate. Here was a man who represented the law and all that was honourable and right. He would surely assist them. They were only asking for equality to other workers of the soil. So it was a subsequent meeting was held in Dorchester. Representation of the agricultural labourers and farmers appeared, with James Frampton, the local rich landlord from Moreton, being the Chair. Here, at this very meeting, the Tolpuddle vicar denied all knowledge of a promise of equal pay for the Tolpuddle men, putting them on a level with the rest of the Dorset agricultural labourers. Instead at the end of this meeting free hand had been granted to the local farmers and landowners, with wages set at seven shillings a week, and six being introduced in the very near future. These were wages of starvation.

What was left for George and these men to do? Literature and correspondence has noted that George was supplied with the information and rules for the society by his brother John, a flax draper, who lived at Burton Bradstock in Dorset. John had obtained them from the Flax Drapers' Trade Union in Leeds. Then contact was made with The Grand National Consolidated Trade Union, with a subsequent visit to Tolpuddle by a couple of their members. The Friendly Society of Agricultural Labourers was then born in Tolpuddle. This was certainly not to prove popular with the local ruling classes and employers. George Loveless kept a book (British Library Frampton Papers Add MS 41567 L:30 Jan 1834 – 3 May 1834), noting the names of the members of this new society along with their monetary contributions. This he kept under lock and key in a box in his home, safe from the eyes of those who would not want to support them. Their meetings were held in fellow member Thomas Standfield's home, with the adoption of swearing a secret oath, and again kept secret from those non-supporters, for very good reasons.

Unions were not illegal, but the swearing of an oath, and a secret one at that, was to seal the fate of this Friendly Society, especially six of the members there. These six would come to be known as the Dorchester Labourers, The Tolpuddle Martyrs, or as in this literature, The Tolpuddle Six. They would be brought to trial and convicted under the 1797 Mutiny Act, which forbad the swearing of any illegal oaths.

News of this newly formed society in Tolpuddle reached the ears of the local squire and magistrate James Frampton, who had been keeping an eye on the unrest with the agricultural workers of Dorset, and not forgetting the riots of 1830. He was most concerned with his area and used his position to plant a spy or two in the community to gather evidence. Frampton feared there was a rapid movement of membership to these Societies in the local area, which would continue to grow. The manners and behaviour of the labourers had changed considerably, with restlessness and signs of not being settled. He wanted their minds returned to that of order and stillness. In other words total obedience was what he required. Frampton circulated a notice, which is recognised as The Caution, dated 22nd February 1834. This stated anyone joining societies or showing allegiance to illegal oaths would be transported for seven years. Clearly this was to discourage membership. Later, upon his arrest, a copy of this notice was to be found on George Loveless. This was indicative of his knowledge regarding the local influential gentry and the attempt to break his newly formed society.

The likely spies magistrate James Frampton recruited were John Lock and Edward Legg, both of whom would be called as witnesses at the trial. Recruiting such persons, in the climate of starvation wages in the Tolpuddle area, would not have been impossible. Individuals would have most probably feared for their own employment and living accommodation. The latter usually came as part of their employment package, or possibly family connections. So, not wanting to put either themselves or their families out of a job and home, just the suggestion of it would have been enough for some individuals to relay information and observations in the direction of magistrate James Frampton.

The world of James Frampton was very different from that of his tenants and workers. Living in his big house at nearby Moreton, he was well looked after and catered for. During the transportation of the Tolpuddle Martyrs his faithful housekeeper Maria Jones would most likely have been privy to and have overheard certain conversations. By all accounts her loyalty and service was in high regard for on her headstone in the nearby churchyard of St Nicholas it states she was a most faithful and attached servant for fifty years to James Frampton Esq. Having departed this world on the 17th January 1875, aged 91, she lived to a ripe old age. Could she have forewarned the Tolpuddle men of what was planned for them, or did she, as others had done, value her job and home more?

Frampton had previous knowledge from a local farmer, who lived about one mile from Tolpuddle, that brothers George and James Loveless had supported the riots of November 1830, and tried to get labourers to join those who had assembled at Piddletown (Puddletown). But with the threat of names being noted of those who did so, this did not happen, and the Tolpuddle labourers went back to work. Obviously since that time all was not at ease with the workers in his parish, and understandably so, but magistrate Frampton did not want a replay of what had happened on the French shores, albeit the shoots of growth of one. Therefore he would nip it in the bud.

Even if the sun was shining brightly upon the village of Tolpuddle on the morning of 24th February 1834, a huge dark cloud had already descended upon the community. Certain abodes there had already been selected to receive a knock on their door, with individuals to be taken away from them.

The person responsible for these early morning calls was the parish police constable, also a resident of Tolpuddle. He went by the name of James Brine and, although he shared the same surname as one of the Tolpuddle Martyrs, there appears to have been no known family connection.

These selected doors were opened by the occupants, surprised by their early wake up call, and wondering what the matter could be. The homes of George and James Loveless, Thomas and John Standfield, James Brine and James Hammett were the chosen ones. George Loveless and James were brothers, Thomas Standfield was the future father-in-law of James Brine and brother-in-law of George and James Loveless, and James Hammett would later link in with this Loveless family via his own and sister's marriage. These families would be torn apart and never be the same again.

As they all knew the police constable and thought they had nothing to fear for they had done no wrong, each man went willingly with him. Although he told each man he had a warrant for his arrest, not one of them attempted to escape or refused to accompany him. Instead each walked with him to the next man's home and then all seven of them walked the seven miles to Dorchester. They went of their own free will with Constable Brine and were unshackled. Their warrants were for taking part in an illegal oath. What they all spoke about on that journey, one can only assume. The men never thought events would turn out as they did. They sincerely believed they had done no wrong, and therefore had nothing to be fearful of.

Firstly they were taken to Wollaston House in Dorchester, the home of magistrate Charlton Byam Wollaston, half-brother to magistrate James Frampton. One would like to think they were given some refreshment after their long walk from Tolpuddle and they probably had not even had time for a small bite to eat for breakfast, but somehow it is doubtful. Here the six men were questioned by both magistrates in the presence of Edward Legg, one of their informers, who was known to them. Clearly this had all been planned in advance, yet nothing had leaked out to the unknowing Tolpuddle Six.

Once the questioners were satisfied for the day, it quickly became obvious to the selected men from Tolpuddle that they would not be returning home, that day or any day soon. Instead the cells at Dorchester Prison awaited them, with all the unpleasant and uncomfortable conditions it could throw at them, including having their heads shorn and clothes stripped off. Shocked to the core they must have been, never envisaging at the start to their day they would end up here. Their families back home worried that they had been taken in the first place and now had not come home. Locked up in a prison and not knowing what the future held for them or themselves. That night no peaceful sleep would come for all concerned, and the village of Tolpuddle would never again be the same.

11

At the time of their arrest the six men of Tolpuddle were:-

James Brine 1813-1902, aged 20, unmarried but would later marry Thomas Standfield's daughter.

James Hammett 1811-1891, aged 22, married father with one child. Later his sister Elizabeth would marry Stephen Loveless, whose father was first cousin to George Loveless. In the future through his second wife, James linked into the other Tolpuddle Martyrs via his father-in-law who was first cousin to siblings George, James and Dinah Loveless, the latter who was wife and mother to Thomas and John Standfield (Tolpuddle Martyrs), and also mother to Elizabeth Standfield who would marry James Brine another Tolpuddle Martyr.

George Loveless 1797-1874, aged 37, married father with three children, leader of the Tolpuddle Martyrs and brother to fellow member James Loveless.

James Loveless 1808-1873, aged 25, married father with two children, brother to George Loveless who was leader of the Tolpuddle Martyrs.

John Standfield 1813-1898, aged 21, unmarried son of fellow Tolpuddle Martyr Thomas Standfield, and nephew of both George and James Loveless, Tolpuddle Martyrs. (He would later marry in the September quarter of 1841 at St Saviours, Southwark to Elizabeth Thurgood).

Thomas Standfield 1789-1864, aged 44 and the oldest Tolpuddle Martyr, married to the sister of fellow Tolpuddle Martyrs George and James Loveless, and father of six.

It is also worth mentioning that apart from James Hammett, all were Methodists, with George Loveless being a Methodist lay preacher. This religion was not popular with the establishment, as it leaned towards the working classes and poor.

These prison cells were to be their home for several weeks until two days before their trial on Monday 17th March at the Crown Court in Dorchester, when they would be moved to the dark, damp cell beneath that Court.

PART I

Chapter 2

JUSTICE THROWS A LOADED DICE

Finally, after weeks of being locked up in miserable prison-cell conditions, the six men of Tolpuddle must have thought today is the day when all will be revealed. We are all innocent and a terrible mistake has been made regarding our arrests. For today, Monday 17th March 1834, is our trial day at the Crown Court in Dorchester. Freedom will be not far away for us six hard-working men.

With the six men of Tolpuddle standing in the dock, to the front and either side of them sat those who would decide their fate. All of these were male and are listed below.

The Hon Sir John Barnard, the Hon John Williams, Edward Doughty, Henry Mooring Aldridge, and Joseph Stone were the judges, High and Under Sheriffs and County Clerk. One of the above was a Knight and all were from the gentry.

The next tier down was the Grand Jury starting with the foreman the Hon William Francis Spencer Ponsonby, Henry and William John Bankes, Thomas Bowyer Bower, John Bragge, Samuel Cox, James and Henry Frampton, James Chamness Fyler, Augustus Foster, John Hussey, William Hanham, George Thomson Jacobs, Benjamin Lester Lester, George Colby Loftus, John Michel, Richard Augustus Steward, Charlton Byam Wollaston, Humphrey Weld, Thomas Horlock Bastard, James Henning, John Hesketh Lethbridge and Thomas Banger. All these were esquires, otherwise squires.

Lastly there was the jury themselves, comprising of William Bullen from East Pulham, Edward Bennet from Cerne Abbas, William Booby from Godmanstone, John Case from Bathenhampton, Thomas Cox from Corscombe, Elias Duffett from Stalbridge, Matthew Galpine from East Pulham, Samuel Harris from Stalbridge, Joshua Lambert from Hazelbury Bryan, John Morgan from

Fordington, Joseph Tucker from Stoke Abbott and George Tulk from Weston. All, apart from Thomas Cox who was a farmer, were yeoman.

With such members of the judging team and both juries, they were unlikely to be sympathetic to the agricultural labourers and their wages of starvation. Not to mention the various connections to these upper classes. Both magistrates James Frampton and Charlton Byam Wollaston were half-brothers, Henry Frampton being their nephew and son. The foreman William Francis Spencer Ponsonby was the Whig MP for Dorset, son of the Earl of Bessborough and Lord Melbourne's brother-in-law. The prosecutor was Edward Gambier and Mr Bartstow. Gambier would later be made a Knight. The defence was George Medd Butt and Mr S Derbyshire. Butt would later become a QC and the Tory MP for Weymouth. These latter promotions, one cannot help but think of as rewards for the outcome of the trial. From the start, this trial was not a fair and just one for the six men from Tolpuddle. Instead, justice would throw a loaded dice in their direction to achieve the desired outcome.

Meanwhile, behind the six men, sitting or standing in the elevated area of the courtroom were the public. Many of these people were the family and friends of the men standing below them in the dock. Watching and listening in heightened awareness to every detail, praying and hoping their loved ones would be released and come home with them.

John Lock of Affpuddle was called to the witness box. Here he stood before the men on trial that day. He was no stranger to them. For he too had been a member of the society in Tolpuddle, paying his fee to George Loveless just as the others here on trial today had. He stated he initially went with James Brine, James Hammett, Edward Legg, Richard Percy, Henry Courtney and Elias Riggs. The fee was one shilling, then a weekly penny.

John Lock's background was thus, he was baptised on the 20th October 1809 at Affpuddle, the son of Robert and Mary. An agricultural labourer, he had married in Tolpuddle on the 22nd April 1829 to Rebecca Riggs, who was baptised in Tolpuddle on the 20th January 1805 of parents Richard Riggs (of Tolpuddle) and Mary Randle. Her parents had married at Moreton on the 10th December

1798, and John's wife Rebecca had a brother called Richard, probably so named after their father. This brother had previously been charged with James Hammett for stealing iron. Now either this father or son were noted as paying members in the book George Loveless kept so safely in the box in his house. No mention of this fact was brought up at the trial. This book was essentially an item of evidence, only parts of which were used and revealed to suit the prosecutors. Magistrate Frampton was well aware of the entire contents of that members' book, along with all the names contained within it, for he had previously instructed that this book be brought to him after the arrests. He subsequently was then able to view it before the trial, giving him ample time to plan his course of action. Further background information on John Lock showed that with Rebecca he had had nine known children - Sarah 1829, Elizabeth 1832, Mary 1834, Ann circa 1836, Matthew 1836, Jane 1839 (died aged six weeks), Priscilla 1840, Charles 1842 and Robert 1846. All were born in Affpuddle where John lived with his family until his death aged 73 with his burial being held on the 2nd June 1883 at St Lawrence, Affpuddle.

John Lock's father was the gardener at Moreton House where Magistrate James Frampton resided. Again at the trial there was no mention of this connection either. Perhaps there was a threat of John Lock's father losing his position and home if his son did not co-operate in the downfall of the Tolpuddle Friendly Society of Agricultural Labourers. John himself had a young family to feed and look after. With Affpuddle and Tolpuddle being in the same region, did John Lock and James Hammett's paths ever cross again once James had returned to Dorset from transportation? The probability is yes, but it is a question which will never fully be answered.

Next to be called to the witness box was Edward Legg who told how James Hammett and James Brine had called upon his home, on the 9th December 1833, and asked him to come with them to Tolpuddle. Once there they took him to Thomas Standfield's house where he was sworn in to the society. On oath he said both Hammett and Brine were there, along with George and James Loveless and Thomas and John Standfield. This was the same Edward who had previously identified the six men at the Dorchester home of

Magistrate Charlton Byam Wollaston, a member of the grand jury of this trial. Edward was a man known to the six on trial, and they must have felt betrayal was surrounding them that day, just as the air they breathed was.

Background details for Edward Legg were that of also being an agricultural labourer, born in about the year 1798 at Milborne. He had married Sarah (Salley) Lawrence (born Briantspuddle, buried in 1874 aged 79 at Affpuddle, of Wareham Union), in 1820 at Affpuddle. They had ten children - Eliza 1822, William 1826, Lawrence 1828, Henry 1830, Thomas 1832, Richard 1834-37, Ann 1834-35, Elizabeth 1837-43, Harriett circa 1843-72 and Herbert 1843. Edward Legg also would have had a young family to feed and look after at the time of the arrests and trial, as did John Lock. No evidence of monetary bribes has been uncovered, but one cannot rule this action out, and in any case who would have known. Edward's son William went on to become a prison officer at Dorchester, with another son Henry becoming a drill-sergeant instructor in Dorchester. I have not been able to locate a death for Edward post 1871, but that is not to say there is not one.

Edward's wife Sarah/Sally Lawrence had a brother Sergeant William Lawrence, who was an interesting individual of the 40th Foot Regiment (1790-1869). He had seen service in South America, the Peninsular War and Waterloo, retiring from the army in 1820. In 1844 he took over a public house in Studland called the New Inn and renamed it the Wellington Arms, in honour of the Duke of Wellington whom he had served under. Retiring from this pub in 1856, he moved into a nearby cottage in Manor Road, and died in 1869 aged 80. He is buried in the churchyard at St Nicholas, Studland with his wife. Their headstone is a very detailed and interesting one, having their inscriptions on both sides, and gives an account of his military service history. But before he departed this world he had the insight to write his autobiography, which was published after his death, in 1886. Within that publication a mention is made of his sister Sally's husband Edward Legg, and also his other sister Elizabeth and her second husband Henry Courtney (first husband John Ridout buried 25th April 1826 Affpuddle, aged 32 of Briantspuddle). Both of his brothers-in-law were agricultural labourers with growing young families to feed and keep. Money was tight with threats of pay cuts sailing on the breeze.

The story within that literature concurred with that of Edward Legg's whereby James Brine and James Hammett called upon his property with the invite to Tolpuddle. Apparently they told him his brother-in-law Henry Courtney would also be attending, so he had agreed to go with them. Henry Courtney was also listed as a member paying fees in the book George Loveless kept. But there was no mention of that at the trial either. Again as with John Lock, did Edward Legg who lived in Affpuddle, ever bump into James Hammett after his return from transportation? Questions which will never be answered, and the answers to them taken to the graves of those involved at the time.

The closest one can get is via recollections of descendants of the informers, which have been passed down in their families. Such a case appeared in a local Dorset paper in 1934 (Daily Echo 01/09/1934 – Trade Union Congress Library) when Andrew Legg of Weymouth claimed a connection to the Tolpuddle Martyrs. Andrew Legg was born circa 1855/57 and possibly died in 1941, aged 86, in the Dorchester area. His father was William Legg, a warden at HM prison in Dorchester, whose father had indeed been Edward Legg, one of the informers of the Tolpuddle Martyrs. According to Andrew Legg, Edward's wife Sarah had demonstrated compassion towards the families of the Dorchester labourers by way of giving food to the Loveless children when they were in need, and in return their mother gave her a chair and they regarded her with affection. The said chair was passed down to Andrew Legg. One can either believe stories such as this or not.

The above-mentioned pieces of information are a diversion from the trial of 1834, but a much needed one to keep the reader informed of the shadowy dark dealings being manipulated in favour of those individuals throwing the loaded dice, which they called a fair trial. Other witnesses were called upon and both the prosecution and defence teams had their say. The Jury returned a verdict of guilty.

Sentence would not be passed for a few days, until the 19th March. In the meantime, the men, their family and friends all lived on tenterhooks, wondering what would happen. Their lives shattered on the lip service of a whole spider's web of lies, so interwoven and pre-planned, that really the six men did not stand a chance.

Two days later, on Wednesday 19th March 1834, the sentence was handed down. Transportation. The maximum term available under the law. Seven years for each man.

Their destination was to be New South Wales (Australia). This was an extreme sentence for the men, none of them had stolen goods or murdered anyone. No, this sentence was supposed to have been harsh, and to serve as an example to any others attempting to form or belong to any kind of society which would unite them, and potentially cause trouble for their employers and betters. What a shock for not only the six Tolpuddle men but also their family members, friends and supporters who had been sitting in the packed courtroom throughout the trial. All of these folks would have had to make their journeys back and forth to Dorchester with their lives on hold too. Now the wives would be left husbandless, and their children fatherless for years.

The six men from Tolpuddle had all been found guilty under the Mutiny Act of 1797, as they had partaken of an illegal oath when they joined the society George Loveless headed up in Tolpuddle. As stated previously, the members' book George kept locked in a box in his cottage had been collected from his house two days after his arrest by constables James Brine and John Toomber, as they had the key which George was asked to give them. What a gem of evidence for the prosecution. Apart from the six Tolpuddle Martyrs listed therein, no others named were brought to account. George Loveless had made it clear on more than one occasion that James Hammett had not been present at the meeting of the 9th December 1833. It was his brother John Hammett who was present. But this made no difference. James Hammett had a previous conviction in 1829 for stealing iron jointly with one Richard Riggs, for which he was imprisoned at Dorchester, with four months hard labour. This fact only gave more ammunition to the prosecutors, with informer John Lock probably keeping quiet about the fact that the said Richard Riggs was his brother-in-law.

A totally unfair, unjust and fixed trial was that for the Tolpuddle Six. Now they were to be thrown to the mercy of the seas to be taken far away.

PART I

Chapter 3

TO THE BOTTOM OF THE WORLD

George Loveless was not faring too well after the trial, and was quite ill. Not surprising given what he had just gone through with the other five men from Tolpuddle. They were all used to being out in the fresh air every day working, but instead these last few weeks they all were locked up in unhealthy cells. Then there was the stress of the whole unbelievable situation, not to mention the worry of how their families would cope. Now they were out of the way, would they be picked on, excluded, shunned, oh the worries were endless. When would they see their loved ones again, what terrors awaited them when they reached their transported destination? The questions and worries going around in their heads must have been never-ending. But at least they had had each other during part of that confinement period.

Now George would be split up from the other five Tolpuddle men, as he was far too ill to be moved. Instead George would travel later without them, setting sail in the May of 1834 on the convict ship the William Metcalf. His destination would also be different from the other five, Van Dieman's Island (now Tasmania). George would arrive there in the September of that year.

So it was James Brine, James Hammett, James Loveless, John and Thomas Standfield said their goodbyes on the 27th March to George and were taken from Dorchester to the prison hulks (floating prisons) at Portsmouth. Deposited there on the York (an old battleship) until the 29th March, then transferred to a lighter (flat bottomed boat used for loading/offloading and transporting goods to port/other ships), they were taken to Spithead to be boarded on the awaiting Surrey convict ship. This vessel would then take them all the way to the bottom of the world as far as they were concerned.

But before sailing entirely off home shores, the next stop would be Plymouth to collect more convicts. From here the Surrey set sail on the 11th April, with the final destination of New South Wales (Australia) not being reached until 17th August 1834.

Conditions on board were bad, and not surprisingly, James Hammett appears on the ship's sick register (The National Archives ADM/101/70/5) under the watchful eye of Surgeon John Smith. He suffered first a simple fever, then severe head pains with aching limbs. From his admittance on the 23rd May, for almost a week he lay in the sick ward. Sometimes even the soldiers who were the convict guards fell ill and would also end up there. Once recovered, James was back to those terrible convict conditions alongside the other men. On board this vessel there were two hundred and sixty male prisoners, thirty-one men who were their guards (i.e. soldiers) and their wives and children. For the latter two no numbers were noted.

Arriving at the intended destination on the 17th August, they had spent some one hundred and eleven days at sea on the waves, but now Sydney harbour was in sight. There the Surrey convict ship docked in Sydney Cove, Sandy Beach, but the men would not get to enjoy land legs again for another three weeks. On the 4th September, they finally got to go ashore. One cannot begin to imagine the conditions experienced on that journey, nor what lay ahead. This new land would certainly be a very different place to what they were used to, with a climate at times being far too hot. In addition, some of the people in their new surroundings were just as harsh. Perhaps they were always that way, or moulded so in time being surrounded by the life of hardship.

Once on the soil of this new land, the convicts were at the mercy of the Governor and, as was the law, he had the say so of where they would work, for either the government or the settlers there. Convicts could only hope they would be given work, or assigned to a fair and good master, which sadly was not always the case. In most cases they just became little more than slaves. In addition to these two avenues, for those who attempted to escape or misbehaved, sometimes for even the most smallest of deeds, there were the penal settlements. The ones most dreaded and terrible were within the area of Van Diemen's Island, namely Macquarie Harbour, Port Arthur and Norfolk Island.

The fate of James Brine, James Hammett, James Loveless, John and Thomas Standfield had already been determined before they ever arrived ashore, for their new places of work and abode had already been agreed with their new masters. After leaving the ship they had to go to the Hyde Park Barracks, then one by one they would go their separate ways, only for some of them to meet up again.

John Standfield witnessed his fellow Tolpuddle men leave, until he was the only one left there from their home village. He initially did not have far to go. He was assigned to Mr Jones in Sydney. But this new master had farms elsewhere and John was sent to the one at Balwarra on the Hunter River, a few miles from the town of Maitland. His father Thomas had been assigned to Mr Nowlan which was just a couple of miles away from where John now was. Therefore John was able to visit his father over a period of months, which was of some comfort to Thomas who was in a bad way, covered with sores and weak. But then Thomas was transferred elsewhere miles away, where his son John was unable to visit him.

After a period of time, John Standfield was imprisoned at Maitland and upon being taken to the courthouse there he found himself once again in the company of his father Thomas. Both were then returned to where John had been imprisoned, and along with others were a few days later taken to Morpeth situated along the Hunter River. Then a few days later the father and son along with a few other prisoners were transported to Sydney by boat. Once again they were put in prison, housing many more poor souls. A couple of days afterwards they appeared in the courtroom with others, only to later be handcuffed to a chain connecting them all, and paraded through the Sydney roads for all to see.

During the whole of this movement from one place to another, many days the father and son went without food, a bed to sleep on or blankets at night to keep them warm, with the added attire of handcuffs, irons or chains. No reasoning had been forthcoming as to all this cruel treatment of the father and son, apart from Home Government orders to remove them from their masters, to only work on Government projects. The Stanfield men were to be locked up again in Sydney after their forced participation in the chained and shamed walk through the streets. Enduring this for a few days, they were then to be joined by some familiar home faces, those of James Brine and James Loveless.

James Loveless had been living some three hundred miles away from Sydney at Strathallan where his master resided. It was a journey he had had to walk when they had all first landed in New South Wales and dispersed in different directions to their new masters, a journey taking some fourteen days through the bush weighed down with his provisions and bedding. Thrown to the elements and wild animals, one cannot begin to imagine what it was like for him (and the rest of the men). Arriving there he had stayed nineteen months, and then in the November of 1835 he was told he had to go to Sydney. James like the other two was not informed why and was once again joined in unison with the two Standfield men and James Brine there for three months.

James was asked if he wanted his wife and family to be brought out to him, as if he did he would receive a pardon. In response to this he said he would prefer the pardon first and was told he had a couple of days to think it over. James still did not change his mind and, when sent to be locked up at Sydney, would meet up with the Standfields, namely his brother-in-law and nephew, and James Brine.

James Brine meanwhile was initially sent to Glindon along the Hunter River to work on a farm. He too had had to make that journey by foot, carrying not only a blanket but also a small bed some clothes and money. Unfortunately for him he was robbed one night as he slept out in the bush whilst making that journey, leaving him in just his old rags of clothes. Starved for days, he finally arrived at his destination to meet his new master Magistrate Robert Scott, who did not believe his story of being robbed.

This master had already made his mind up about him. He not only called him a liar but said he was a machine breaker from Dorsetshire and should be flogged. James was not given any food, so was starved for another day. In addition his feet were bleeding as a result of having had to walk barefoot with the threat of a beating if he did not work. This was all the welcome he had received on his first day, with the added addition of having to do heavy manual work.

For half a year James Brine had no new clothes or bedding, including a bed. Working sometimes in cold damp conditions for days on end in water washing sheep, he eventually became ill. This new master had already demonstrated how cruel he could be, which appeared to be a normal part of his character. For even now he was still totally unmoved with total lack of compassion for the condition James found himself in and refused solidly to give him any warmth by way of bedding. He also was questioned about the union, but unable to deliver what his master wanted to hear, was rewarded with the threat of violence towards him.

By the end of the year 1835 James was taken to Maitland and locked up for a few days with just a little water and bread. The last night he was chained to other prisoners. With them he had to sleep like that in the open, in readiness to be put on a boat for Newcastle. Once there he saw no court or magistrate, and must have felt totally confused to say the least, for he had committed no crime.

So it was James Brine was to find himself put on board another nautical contraption, this time bound for Norfolk Island, cited by some as hell on earth. This knowledge was known to James, and what made it all the more tragic was that this time those in authority knew the conditional pardon had been given for Hammett, Brine and the Standfields, the notice having appeared in the New South Wales Government Gazette on Wednesday 22nd June 1836. This stated they had to live in New South Wales for a period of two years from the date they had arrived, though in the case of James Loveless, his term was three years, as he was considered a more senior player in the troubles back in Dorset alongside his brother George.

Luckily for James there was hope on his horizon in the shape of an imminent sea gale, which forced the journey to Norfolk Island to return to Sydney. He found himself once again locked up. This time it was more bearable as he was reunited there with father and son John and Thomas Standfield, and later James Loveless.

Once these four Tolpuddle men had been reunited, it was not long before they were informed that a conditional pardon for them was going to be granted. But for now they were to go about one hundred miles north of Sydney to another penal settlement called Port Macquarie for the next year, until the King of England decided further their fate. Not liking the sound of this, John Standfield sent a petition to the governor for them to be returned to their masters instead, an act which paid off in his favour.

Both the Standfields were sent to Mr Nowlan's property in the Maitland area, with Thomas the father falling very ill for many weeks, but at least he had his son with him. After being there for nearly three quarters of the year, John Standfield discovered George Loveless was in Van Diemen's Land. So he immediately sent him a letter, with a reply forthcoming a couple of months later. George informed him he was setting sail homeward bound with instructions for all of them to do likewise, as they had all been granted a full pardon. This was news to them, as no one had mentioned this, but of course knowledge the masters and keepers must have been aware of at that time.

Meanwhile, both James Brine and James Loveless had been sent to a farm about twenty miles from Sydney at Prospect, belonging to Mr Brennan, the Superintendent. James Loveless would only stay here a while and then be moved to another at Kurryjung a little further away. It was while he was here that he was to learn from another the newspapers contained a full account of their pardons. Immediately James Loveless left for Sydney to seek out the truth, towards the end of January 1837. Although it was indeed confirmed, the employer of James said the men would not get free passage home, and have to remain there. So back to his farm James went for a few months, only to be told they would have free passage home after all. James had had his work cut out with this difficult employer, but eventually he managed to secure the free passage home for the four of them. Setting sail to winds that would carry them home from Sydney aboard the John Barry on the 11th September 1837.

The story for George Loveless was thus, that along with his fellow convicts aboard the William Metcalfe, all were instructed to leave the ship on the 12th September 1834 just as the sun was rising. They had arrived at their designated place of transportation, Van Diemen's Island, taken to the prison there to be inspected and allocated their place of abode and work. Since the trial back in Dorchester, George had been questioned many times on his connection with the unions, but each time demonstrated that he knew not the replies to their questions. This questioning that had followed with him over the seas. Loveless had made an impact on the Governor there, Colonel Arthur, whose farm he would be sent to at New Town, but not before spending a week working on the roads with a chain gang, and sleeping on the floor of the barracks at night. New Town was a little better, but with a shortage of beds only a few men enjoyed that luxury.

Attempts were made to get George to bring his family over from Dorset, which he did not want to do so long as he was a convict. Veiled threats were made, then eventually the hint of freedom if his wife came over. Finally George gave in and wrote to his wife on the 27th January 1836, with a free passage being granted for the journey over. On the 5th February 1836 George was given a ticket which excluded him from compulsory labour, and permitting him to work for himself.

Although this sounded good, George was alone, without connections and the foundations by which to support himself. Work was hard to find, and finding himself in Hobart he advertised his services. It paid off as in the spring of 1836 he found work at Glenayr, near Richmond, with Major de Gillern, where he would remain whilst still at the bottom of the world. George eventually received a letter from his wife in the December of 1836 stating she did not wish to come out there, but instead for him to come home, as by then he was free to do so. This he did aboard the Eveline on the 30th January 1837. One man was still missing though, unheard of and seemingly forgotten. That was James Hammett.

Back in Dorset some forty-one years later during a public address (The Dorset County Express and Agricultural Gazette 23/03/1875), James Hammett would give an insight into his transportation years. But firstly said how it had indeed been his brother John who had attended that meeting on the night in question back in Tolpuddle before the arrest. Although he was a member of the union, he had not attended that night. Once the convict ship he was on docked in Sydney, they were all kept on board for a further three weeks. Then off to the barracks they were all taken, only for him to be greeted with a scene of a man being stripped and put across a barrel and flogged. This man received twenty-five lashes on his back, twenty-five on his backside and twenty-five on the calves of his legs. Then James along with the other men there were all sold for one pound each with their names having been put on bits of paper with the various agents then drawing them out.

An agent took James off to the town where he was distributed with rations for twenty-two days including his bed, and told to go to another part of the country some four hundred miles away. Finding himself all alone with no money, he had to sleep out rough travelling on feet which were sore from his time spent on board ship. Eventually he arrived at his destination with the rations long gone. James made no mention of his time being ill on that sea voyage out there, nor of anything else, with further information having had to be gleaned from the official records or hearsay for a fuller picture.

James had been assigned to Edward John Eyre (1815-1901), born at Whipsnade, Bedfordshire, the son of a vicar, with the family then moving to Yorkshire. He had set sail aboard the Ellen from London on the 19th October 1832 under the watch of Captain George Dixon. This vessel carried cargo and passengers, and arrived the next year at Hobart on the 4th March. It then set sail again on the 20th, Sydney bound, with additional passengers being six aborigines. Eyre had well over a thousand acres at Molonglo Plains, near Queanbeyan farming sheep.

Later after James had left, Eyre would cross Australia from east to west exploring with his aborigine friend Wylie, and become Resident Magistrate and Protector of the aborigines in the River Murray area. Then, leaving Australian shores, became Lieutenant Governor of New Zealand, Acting Governor in the West Indies of the Leeward Islands, and in 1865 became Governor of Jamaica. Here the ex-slaves found themselves in never ending poverty alongside natural disasters, which had an impact on their crops and farming. Wanting to better themselves, Eyre feared an uprising and when the Morant Bay Rebellion appeared, he squashed it with brutal force, with divided feelings back in England.

Luckily for James Hammett he had been under Eyre's wing in much earlier times and appears to have been well looked after and not flogged, a punishment meted out by other masters and overseers to their charges. So it was here on the Woodlands estate James would stay, unlike his fellow Tolpuddle men who were shunted from this place to that, locked up, and at times denied food, water and basic human comforts. On this vast estate James worked as a shepherd, not an easy job, but at least he was out in the fresh air and not chained up. James learned of his pardon via a newspaper left aside by his master, Edward Eyre.

By the May of 1836 James was at the Hyde Park Barracks in Sydney on the orders of the Governor of New South Wales, and in the September of 1837 James was on an assault charge at Windsor, Australia (no records are available/have survived for further clarification). Then in the February of 1839 James (or a representative on his behalf) wrote to the new Governor for New South Wales, pointing out that James was granted a free pardon in 1836. But due to his circumstances at that time of being charged with an assault, was unable to join his fellow Tolpuddle men when they made their voyages home to England.

The Governor responded by making an urgent authorization of the passage homebound for James Hammett. Sailing on board the Eweretta on the 8th March 1839 bound for England, James this time was a truly a free man, presumably able to enjoy the benefits of the sea air and voyage home.

PART I

Chapter 4

THOSE LEFT BEHIND - TOLPUDDLE CAME TO LONDON

The transportation of the six men from Tolpuddle to New South Wales and Van Diemen's Island had left a huge hole not only within their families, but the whole community back in Tolpuddle. Within this location it may not have been uncommon then to catch whispers in the wind of it could have been my husband, brother, son or any member whose name had appeared on the list George Loveless had kept. The whole episode, from the arrest to the trial to the sentence and transportation, had been widely followed courtesy of the newspapers of the day and of course by word of mouth. Feelings had been running high with a huge public outcry and utter shock at their sentence of transportation. These men were not thieves or murderers.

Back in their home village of Tolpuddle, the Parsonage house windows had been broken during the night of the 31st March or in the early hours of the morning of the 1st April 1834. In addition to those, windows at the home of a local shepherd, who had refused to join the union there in Tolpuddle. These acts did not go unnoticed by the local squire and Magistrate, namely James Frampton (The National Archives Dorchester Labourers Papers 30/69/1382.)

The family relatives and associates left behind in Tolpuddle, along with those whose names had appeared as members of the Union in the book George Loveless kept, would also experience hardships, and even be marked out. Local farmers would not feel inclined to employ any of them. Frampton had refused to order parish relief for the families of the six Tolpuddle convicts, an act based on their jailer in Dorchester informing him that the wives had supplied the men with more food than they could want for during their stay there before conviction. Also as their husbands had signed up to a union whose leaders stated they would look after them and their families whilst being unemployed, therefore it should be in the direction of those leaders support ought to be pleaded.

Frampton had quietly said to the Overseer that he was not to provide relief to them, but to watch over them and if they needed it, to do so, but as if it had come from him and not Frampton. Therefore this would prove to the labourers that if they were not supported in this way, i.e. from the unions, then they had been deceived by the union leaders. However, if they were to support them, then this would relieve the Parish of their support. Additionally, no one whose name appeared in the said union members' book, which was used in evidence at the trial, was to receive parish relief. The reasoning being, as mentioned above, that the union could support them. Also as they previously could afford the payment of a shilling to join the union with subsequent weekly payments, then they were obviously financially in a sound position. If they received parish relief, then this payment to the union would continue out of that pot, and therefore be supported by the Parish. Frampton was mindful that at no time any concerned had acknowledged the error of their ways. In any case, outside financial donations and help had been given to them. Even the Reverend Warren was in receipt of some outside donated funds for them.

Along with the other Justices from the trial, Frampton had advised the local farmers to be generous to the labourers who did not join the union. This was in the form of wage increases and their being given work which would enable them the best financial rewards. These actions were their rewards and set them apart from those who did join the union.

Frampton did, however, acknowledge that some of the wages of the union members were low, but they had been in regular work, with others earning good wages, and even had abodes with gardens and their own property. Perhaps at times there had been some grievance towards the farmer, but in return he had had to have dealings with a certain set of individuals, who proved more than hard to work with. The speedy result of the trial of the six men from Tolpuddle had, according to Magistrate Frampton, brought to the whole of the upper classes a great satisfaction.

As if to further justify himself, after the trial Magistrate Frampton conveyed to Viscount Melbourne, the then Home Secretary, the following on the six men from Tolpuddle (I have omitted some of their ages and marital status as this was mentioned previously):-

James Brine Was aged about 17 in 1830 when the riots took place, was of good behaviour and attempted to keep away from them. But is now very idle and in the company of James Hammet(t). Refused winter work whilst walking about looking for work the whole time, and suspected of working for the Loveless and Stanfield families along with James Hammet(t).

James Hammet(t) Spent four months in prison with hard labour for stealing iron. Very idle and ready for mischief.

George Loveless Methodist Preacher, first to instigate the Union in Tolpuddle, very active in the 1830 winter riots, had information about the Flax and Hemp Trade on him, along with the Book of Rules and members list in his home.

James Loveless Methodist Preacher, very active in the 1830 winter riots.

John Stanfield Ready for disturbance and very saucy.

Thomas Stanfield Owner of the house where the Union meetings took place, and the Methodist Meeting House. To be found where there is a disturbance and very discontented. He also has a namesake son who was also a union member.

Frampton had also furnished Melbourne with the names from the list of members and explained relationships. He had done his utmost to rid his area of this union with the conviction and the making an example of these six men.

Life for those families and friends of the Tolpuddle Six left behind was far from easy with them also having the added worry as to their loved ones' lives across the seas. Two missives gave a glimpse into that world. Firstly, Elizabeth Loveless, wife of George, along with the wives of the other Tolpuddle Martyrs had sent a letter to a Mr Goode of Butts Lane in Coventry in 1834. Within that correspondence it described how their children along with themselves had known hard times since the departure of their husbands. Also conditions in Tolpuddle had been for a long time despotic and, since the member's list had been taken, some names on that list had been suffering since. William Hamet (Hammett) was noted as being out of work, due to his refusing to work for four shillings a week for a whole year with the farmer, and was aged 21.

In another letter from Mr Brine, Overseer of Tolpuddle, a William Hammett was listed as a Unionist and described as very idle young man, who if they can help it, nobody would want in their employ. This William was related to James Hammett, for he was his first cousin, and no doubt with sharing the same surname and being on the members' list, would have been an easy target for making an example of.

So it must have come as a little comfort for those left behind in Tolpuddle to know that outside folks also felt their pain and gave their support by way of signing a petition and taking part in what would later to be known as the Grand Demonstration. This took place in the London area on the 21st April 1834 (an event remembered on numerous anniversaries since, but particularly one hundred and seventy-five years later and called Tolpuddle KX). This resulted in pardons for the Tolpuddle Martyrs but not without them first experiencing the hardships over on the other side of the world.

As dawn broke across London on the morning of the 21st April 1834 none of the occupants there could have envisaged the importance that day would come to signify in history nor the vast crowds their roads would have to accommodate. Stretching from the northern side of Kings Cross, in an area known as Copenhagen Fields, all the way to south of the river at Kennington Common, this was the planned route for what would become an historic gathering and procession. Already by seven o'clock upon that morning people began to appear with their Trade Union banners and signatures representing their various lodges. Alongside them were ordinary people who also wanted to give their support and join the procession for the day. They must have made for a colourful sight and drawn much interest. This gathering would become known as The Grand Demonstration, an event strongly attended with support of between thirty thousand and one hundred thousand people, who all had one purpose and aim in common, which was to demand the release and return of the Dorchester Labourers, better known as The Tolpuddle Martyrs.

The plan was to proceed from Copenhagen Fields to Whitehall and deliver to the Home Secretary (Lord Melbourne) a huge petition consisting of some half-a-million signatures in support of the men's plight. Fear of public disorder with this march was anticipated by those in power. Along with the Life Guards, Household Troops, detachments of the 12th and 17th Lancers, a couple of troops of the 2nd Dragoons and some battalions of infantry and arms, in excess of five thousand special constables were sworn in.

All these individuals would protect London from any disorder this procession might create. Yet somehow all this protection was to be kept out of sight and therefore along the route hardly a soldier or policeman was to be seen. The Committee hosting the event was headed by Robert Owen (1771-1858 who formed the Grand National Consolidated Trades' Union) and the Reverend Dr Arthur S. Wade (Vicar of St Nicholas, Warwick, Cambridge educated, and supporter of reform movements). By seven o'clock that morning, this Committee and managers had gone to Copenhagen House and used the long room there as a council room. At nine-thirty that morning they had all gathered in the tennis ground where the petition was brought to the decorated car attached by poles to be carried upon the shoulders of twelve supporters.

A rocket was fired and this started the procession off led by Robert Owen and Dr Wade (whose weight was twenty stone, one could pity the horse that carried him) who both rode on horseback. They were orderly and peaceful, and there was no requirement to use heavy-handed tactics with them. The route moved from Copenhagen Fields, King's Cross, Gray's Inn Lane, Guilford Street, Russell Square, Keppell Street, Tottenham Court Road, Oxford Street, Regent Street, the Quadrant, Waterloo Place, Pall Mall, Charing Cross and then Whitehall. The streets were lined with well-wishers cheering the procession on their way. Businesses and shops appeared to have shut, or temporarily ceased for the event.

Once at Whitehall the petition was taken to the office of Lord Melbourne who, from his window, had watched it arrive along with the huge procession. This petition he would not accept, for Melbourne refused on the basis of the manner in which it had been delivered. He also did not wish to meet or see anyone from the representing body. On another day, in a better fashion, he would have accepted and presented it to the King, but not this day.

The petition was therefore taken back by the representing body and the procession proceeded along Parliament Street, crossing Westminster Bridge, along St George's Road, passing the Elephant and Castle and along Kennington Road to Kennington Common. Near the Toll House there was a rest with a few speeches as many had been on their feet since seven o'clock that morning. As it was now four-thirty in the afternoon many of the crowd had broken up and gone their separate ways.

Three days later, the petition was presented to the King. There was wide Press coverage at the time and The Pioneer stated, on the 26th April 1834, "Last Monday was a day in Britain's history which long will be remembered, for labour put its hat upon its head and walked towards the throne".

On the 14th March 1836 the powers that be all agreed the six men, the Tolpuddle Martyrs, should all receive a full and free pardon. Without a doubt the pressure from such a public demonstration must have sent shock waves through the Government and ruling classes resulting in this outcome.

PART I

Chapter 5

FREEDOM – ENGLAND, ESSEX AND CANADA

The Tolpuddle Martyrs, as previously mentioned, all returned from transportation at different times. George Loveless being the first, having departed on the Eveline at Hobart on the 30th January 1837, arrived in London on the 13th June 1837, to a welcome by the London Central Dorchester Committee.

Next to arrive were Thomas and John Standfield, James Loveless and James Brine whose ship the John Barry(*) arrived in Plymouth on Saturday 17th March 1838 (one newspaper report stated it was on the Friday – British Library Newspapers - The Hull Packet 23/03/1838). Here their first steps on home soil were where the Pilgrim Fathers took their last strides onto the Mayflower in 1620, taking them to the New World. Today many plaques line the wall there, including one for these four Tolpuddle Martyrs. The people of Plymouth welcomed them, including Charles Morgan, landlord of the nearby Dolphin Inn. He possibly accommodated them with their first night's rest on land. For the next day, on the eighteenth, it was to the home of local resident James Keast, a trade unionist of the building trade to whom they would retire.

There in Plymouth on the 22nd March the four returning men attended a welcome by the Committee of Trades at the Mechanics Institute in Princes Square. The following day, they travelled by coach to Exeter, attending another gathering. From there they progressed to Dorchester, arriving at the Antelope Inn on Monday 26th March, this being a day before they were expected and therefore the intended welcome of music and flags was missing.

However, the returning men must have been a vista to behold, for they were dressed in their new smart attire. With not much of a welcome in Dorchester and longing to see their family and friends, off home to Tolpuddle they went where they were greeted by their families. This reunion was to be short-lived as they could not stay for long, with the expectation of being in London by Monday 16th April, Easter Monday, to be guests of the London Dorchester Committee. There was to be a procession followed by dinner at the White Conduit House, with George Loveless joining them (British Library Newspapers – The Ipswich Journal 07/04/1838).

(*) I was unable to find either the ship's log or surgeon's journal for HMS hired convict ship the John Barry for 1838 when the four men arrived at Plymouth. However, I did find the surgeon's journal for it between the period of 21st October 1838 to 26th March 1839 on the outward bound voyage to Sydney, New South Wales (The National Archives ADM/101/38/5). The surgeon was Mr Campbell France and the ship carried three hundred and twenty male convicts who came on board at Woolwich and Sheerness in the November. Previously, on the 31st October a guard of thirty-one soldiers and two officers of the 50th and 51st regiments came on board for the trip, along with six women and seven children (presumably their wives and children, often selected from lots drawn to accompany their husbands). There were also three government officials. On that voyage two hundred and one names appeared in the surgeon's journal, but the women and children were excluded. Therefore, there is no way of knowing if they suffered from any ailments for the duration of the sailing.

Two deaths would occur on this voyage. One of those was from diarrhoea on the 11th March 1839, the victim being convict Andrew Blythe, aged 40, who was apparently in an emaciated state due to a habit of exchanging food with other prisoners for his addiction to tobacco.

Another surgeon's journal I came across for this ship was previous in time to when the four Tolpuddle Martyrs sailed on it, and for the period from the 14th August 1835 to the 4th February 1836 (The National Archives ADM/101/38/4). James W Firman or Turman (hard to read) was the surgeon. Convict William Lus died on the 4th February 1836 at Sydney at seven o'clock in the morning. Apparently as he came up the ladder of the main hatchway, he fell into the main hold. He was removed to the Colonial Hospital immediately for an inquest by the coroner. There were another two deaths on that trip, but his was the only one caused by an accident.

This surgeon noted how the convicts were put into seven divisions, each having a specific morning to be mustered on deck at day break, in their bare feet. They were to wash the decks, pumping and filling the bathing tub buckets for their own use. Arms and legs bare for examination, along with their blanket and pillow for inspection too. Another division would be employed cleaning the water closets, mid-sails and stoves. This had a double purpose. Firstly to give the men exercise and secondly to keep things clean which reduced infections. I make mention of the above facts to give an insight as to how life on board might have been for the Tolpuddle men.

Lastly James Hammett sailed aboard the Eweretta on the 8th March 1839, arriving in the August, and meeting up with his wife in London. Earlier reports in the Press stated the other Tolpuddle Martyrs had been unable to find him, otherwise they would have all returned together. James met the Dorchester Labourers' Committee for the first time in Holborn on Wednesday 21st August 1839. Here they would learn it was not his fault that he had been detained for so much longer than his Tolpuddle companions, (but not expanded on any further).

This delay was probably due to the fact that James Hammett had been on an assault charge and was possibly in the Windsor prison system in Sydney as in the September of 1837 James had been on an assault charge. Having missed the welcome the others received in London on the 16th April 1838, James would later attend jointly with some of the others a benefit performance at the Victoria Theatre (Old Vic) in Waterloo Road, London.

Preparations had been already planned and laid, before the six Tolpuddle men had returned home, by the Dorchester Committee in London. They foresaw problems returning sooner or later for the men if they settled back into their old lives in Tolpuddle. What they needed was a completely fresh start elsewhere. If the men had their own farms to work they could be their own bosses and be self-sufficient.

When the returning Tolpuddle men, apart from Hammett who was still missing, attended their honorary dinner in London, on the Easter Monday of 1838, their intended futures were revealed to them. This was something they were more than happy to embrace, so long as they were all kept within a close radius of each other.

The next month the Dorchester Committee set up a fund for this project of acquiring farms along with the required equipment to make it viable, called the Dorchester Labourers' Farm Tribute, following on with leases established for two farms in Essex. One at New House Farm (now Tudor Cottage), Greensted Green not far from Chipping Ongar, located on high ground with views and consisting of around eighty acres of arable and pasture land along with the farm house and associated outbuildings.

The other farm was located about four miles away at High Laver near Harlow, and consisted of around forty-three acres. The former farm and the larger of the two was occupied by the Loveless family and James Brine and the latter one by the Standfields.

It was to the New House Farm in 1839 that James Hammett and his wife Harriett would go, briefly joining the Loveless family there at their abode. Previously, whilst James was still missing, his wife Harriett had agreed for his share of the monies to be used towards the lease of New House Farm (British Library Newspapers – The Charter 04/08/1839). Given this, they probably felt they had a stake there, and a logical place to settle. Whilst James was still missing and had not returned, Harriett had not been forgotten and given some funds to help tide her over.

Here in their new home of Essex, the Reverend Philip W Ray, the local parson at St Andrew's Church, Greensted Green, was not very welcoming to the Tolpuddle men, whom he regarded as convicts and out of favour as followers of the Methodist religion. His complaints and disapproval continued as, once settled in their new homeland, the Tolpuddle men formed a local Chartist group. This action additionally caused concern for local landowners and gentry, all of whom must have been aware of the background of these Dorset men. They certainly would not want a repercussion of what happened in Tolpuddle here in their neighbourhood, not to mention having made global news at the time.

Despite all the ill-feeling towards them in this new county they were to call home, James Brine, Tolpuddle Martyr, married on the 20th June 1839 to Elizabeth Standfield, daughter of fellow Tolpuddle Martyr Thomas Standfield, at the local church of St Andrew's, with the ceremony performed by Reverend Philip W Ray. Both bride and groom signed their names, were single, residents of Greensted, with James aged 26 and noted as a farmer, and Elizabeth aged 21. They had four witnesses who were John Standfield, Charity Standfield, Joseph Brine and Susan Standfield.

St Andrew's Church is reported to be the world's oldest surviving wooden church built between the ninth and eleventh centuries. In the churchyard the oldest grave is believed to be that of a bowman from the twelfth-century crusades. Also laid to rest there is the Reverend Phillip W Ray, and the local innkeeper who died in 1842. Whilst under the influence of drink, he took on a bet which involved using a scythe. No doubt the local residential Tolpuddle folks would have heard of this terrible accident.

John Standfield on the other hand did not marry at St Andrew's Church, Greensted Green, or indeed anywhere else in Essex. No, instead he married in 1844 at Southwark, London to Elizabeth Thurgood. Perhaps they lived for a while in this area of London. From researching other twigs in my family history unrelated to Tolpuddle ones, I found the surname of Thurgood is popular around the Harlow area of Essex. Some of those Thurgoods from Harlow also ended up in the Southwark area with family events in St Saviours there in the 1840's.

The 1841 census finds living at New House Farm, Greenstead Green, Ongar, Essex:-

James Loveless 30 farmer, Sarah 35 and Eli 10, all not born Essex.

George Loveless 40 farmer, Elizabeth 40, George 15, Robert 10, Thomas 10, Louisa 2 and Louisa 7 months. Apart from the youngest two who are born in the county of Essex, the others are not.

James Brine 25 farmer, Elizabeth 20, Mary Ann 1, Joseph Brine(*) 20 shoemaker. Only the youngest is born in Essex.

(*Joseph Paracott Brine was born 1819 in Tolpuddle and was brother to TM James Brine. He married in 1845 within the Ongar

38

district to Charity Standfield, daughter and sister of Tolpuddle Martyrs Thomas and John).

Maximum Smith aged 26 a tool maker not born in Essex is also living here.

The 1841 census finds living at High Laver, Ongar, Essex:-

John Standfield 25 farmer, Thomas Standfield 50, Thomas 20, William 10, Dianna 50, Charity 15, all not born in Essex.

On the 4th July 1841 at the Parish Church, Christ Church (Southwark) Surrey, John Standfield married by banns to Elizabeth Thurgood. He was a carrier, his father Thomas a cooper. Elizabeth's father was John Thurgood a farmer. The young couple were both were of full age, single and lived 18 Thurlow Street. Their witnesses were Joseph P Brine and Charity Standfield (a couple who would later marry each other). The name of Thurgood/Thorogood/Thergood occurs in Essex for many generations, many being farmers. Possibly Elizabeth Thurgood was baptised on the 10th May 1829 at High Laver of John and Elizabeth, although born 1821, not uncommon.

In 1844 a few of the Tolpuddle Martyrs had decided to move to Canada, due to the tenancies on the two farms expiring and their unwanted presence by the local people of influence. Life could not have been easy for them in such a community, and no wonder they were such a close-knit one themselves.

By 1846 all of the group, apart from James Hammett, were living in Canada with their wives and children, settling in the London area of Ontario to make a fresh start. None of them would ever return to England again, let alone Dorset. In this new country they quietly carried on with the rest of their lives. It would only come to light after their deaths, the story of their transportation, an unknown tale recounted to their descendants purposely uneducated about it by their ancestors. Back in Tolpuddle the year 1912 would witness the newly erected Memorial Arch in honour of the men, an event which transmitted over to Canada. Perhaps the actions of their ancestors had been one born out of protection, for fear of what they had experienced both in Tolpuddle and Essex, and maybe not wanting their descendants to be labelled either.

The journey out to Canada could not have been an easy one, and they would have had to endure the harsh winters. A vast area of a country, with only a few developed areas, accessing roadways in those early times must have been difficult to say the least. A good job it was then that these Dorset folks were a hardy bunch for, once settled, they were quite a productive lot. With all the seeds sown, they would be able to watch their next generation develop and grow. This country was a fresh start for all of them, offering opportunities they could only have dreamed of back on their birth soil.

George Loveless was still very much part of the Methodist Ministry and preached, built a house and assisted in the building of a church with his wife at his side just outside London, at a place called Siloam. His brother James became a sexton in a Methodist church at London Town. John Standfield ended up running first a store at Bryanston, then an hotel. He also set up a choir and became Mayor at East London, with his parents Thomas and Dinniah spending their twilight years with him. James Brine with his wife ran a farm near Clinton and Bayfield, with moves later to London and St Mary's. Who knows what James Hammett might have accomplished out there if he had joined them with his family.

Every year in May, at the Peace Garden in London, Ontario, Canada, a picnic is held by the local Labour Council. Here they present the Tolpuddle Award to Trade Union Activists, with a Memorial Service. There is a Tolpuddle Housing Co-operative in London Ontario, and in 2011 a new artwork was installed in the Peace Garden which took the format of two hands, in honour of the Tolpuddle Martyrs.

Some could say as the law had let these six Tolpuddle men down in 1834, Parliament too would suffer. In the October of 1834 a great fire occurred, quite innocently. The Exchequer needed to dispose of the accumulated tally sticks, which were once used in the old system of accounting in 1826. The basement of the House of Lords had two under floor coal stoves, which heated the premises, an ideal way of disposing of them.

On the sixteenth of that month, the Clerk of Works, Richard Whibley, instructed Patrick Furlong and Joshua Cross of this duty which needed to be carried out. By that afternoon, other sources had noted that the flooring to the House of Lords was hot with smoke rising through it. The stoves were not put out until five o'clock in the evening and by an hour later the House of Lords was on fire, as was the rest of the Palace. Soldiers were called in and had to keep the ever-growing crowds of onlookers at bay.

Despite all efforts having been made, most of the buildings were destroyed, apart from Westminster Hall and a few other areas, which were only saved by the change of wind and the brave attempts by some to put the fire out. It would later be deduced that chimney flues overheating were the main cause of this fire. This would be the biggest fire London had seen since 1666. The eyes of artist Turner viewed it, later transferring that image to canvas. Author Charles Dickens would make mention of it.

By 1844 the Palace of Westminster had been rebuilt in the Gothic Revival fashion. Quite by coincidence, the year 1844 also witnessed the first wave of the Tolpuddle Martyrs' permanent move to Canada.

One modern day point of interest is that in Tasmania, where George Loveless was transported, is a Tolpuddle Vineyard. So named after the Tolpuddle Martyrs, located in the Coal River Valley, near Richmond, and close to another vineyard called Glen Ayr. George Loveless it is said lived in a cottage at Strath Ayr farm, which is where the Glen Ayr wines hail from. That very cottage is now the vinery's office. The vineyard at Glen Ayr was planted in 1975 and the one named Tolpuddle in 1988.

PART II

Chapter 6

JAMES HAMMETT – TOLPUDDLE MARTYR

It may seem a little unfair on the other five men to have researched and covered more information for James Hammett, and not to have done the same for them. But essentially it was James Hammett who first led me to discovering the Tolpuddle Martyrs. Through tracing my family history I discovered both James and myself shared ancestry as he was first cousin to his younger namesake, who in turn was my two times great-grandfather. Therefore I have somewhat of a soft spot for this Tolpuddle Martyr and through years of researching I have gathered knowledge on our shared family history. The earliest joint ancestral roots of which I have included within the chapter for his paternal grandfather, who was also my ancestor.

James Hammett was born on the 11th December 1811 and baptised on the 3rd May 1812, both events having taken place in Tolpuddle. The Regency Period began in the year of his birth, as did the Luddite Movement in Nottinghamshire (machine breakers and supporters in the textile industry who against the bleak economic backdrop of the Napoleonic wars feared for their jobs).

James died on the 21st November 1891 aged 79 at the Dorchester Union Workhouse, of cerebral softening, was almost blind and stated as a former mason's labourer of Tolpuddle. His burial was three days later on the 24th in the northwest corner of the churchyard of St John's Church of England parish church in Tolpuddle. A headstone was not forthcoming for him until some forty-three years later when the TUC (Trade Union Congress) erected one, carved by Eric Gill. This headstone reads *1834 James Hammett Tolpuddle Martyr pioneer of Trades Unionism Champion of Freedom born 11 December 1811 died 21 November 1891.* James is the only one of the six Tolpuddle Martyrs to be buried in England, with the other men all being laid to rest in Canada where they settled. James entered the workhouse, it is said, because he did not want to be a burden on his family.

James was 5ft 7¼" tall (sorry I still work in imperial measurements), blue-eyed, with dark brown hair and a fair complexion. He had a pockmark on his right cheek and a cut diagonally on the right side of his forehead. These were all descriptions taken of him at the time of his arrest on the 24th February 1834. Although this was not the first time he had been arrested.

On the 2nd March 1829, aged just 18, he was jointly charged for stealing iron from William Brine the elder, with Richard Riggs (brother-in-law of John Lock who later was an informer of the Tolpuddle Martyrs). James received hard labour of four months and was bailed by his father. From this arrest his physical description was 5ft 6" with brown hair, dark blue eyes, of fair complexion, he had a cut on the middle of his forehead, on the back of his left hand a burn mark and a cut on the bottom part of a forefinger.

Upon his return from transportation in 1839, James and his small family lived for a short time at the New House Farm in Essex, with some of the other Martyrs. For whatever reasons this did not work out for them, with some suggesting his wife Harriett was homesick for Tolpuddle. So James and Harriett returned to Tolpuddle in time to appear there on the 1841 census.

Confirmation of this suggestion is supported in earlier reports before James had returned (British Library Newspapers –The London Dispatch and People's Political and Social Reformer 26/08/1838). It was noted that Harriett had expressed a wish to be allowed to stay in Tolpuddle with her friends if James was not to return and for their child and herself to receive his share of the funds from the Committee. However, a newspaper article from early August 1834 made mention of some extracted information from a circular issued by the London Central Dorchester Committee. This implied that Harriett along with the Standfields had agreed to nearly all their share of the funds being secured for New House Farm where the Loveless brothers and James Brine would reside. The committee had placed the two Standfield men at High Laver. It would appear

43

that James did not receive monies directly, presumably his share going towards the farm in Essex, which he did not reside at for long with his return to Tolpuddle. Later at his 1875 presentation in Dorset it was recognised that he had missed out in this respect.

On Tuesday 10th March 1875 in a field at Briantspuddle near Tolpuddle, James was presented with an Illuminated Address, an inscribed silver watch and purse of ten gold sovereigns by Joseph Arch on behalf of the National Agricultural Labourer's Union. It was the occasion of the forty-first anniversary since his conviction. The Times newspaper of 24th March 1875 (British Library Newspapers) reported that James said he was associated with the General Society of Labourers and told how he was sold for a pound, just like a slave, and the cruel times he had endured. The Dorset County Express and Agricultural Gazette revealed James said he had belonged to the union but was not there at the time the men at his trial had said he was but that it was his brother John, with said brother agreeing nearby in the crowd. The oath their own men agreed to was only not to work whilst the strike was on and he was absent when it was taken.

The Address had been written and illuminated by Master R R Rose of Blandford, and it was to be glazed and framed. In 1929 the Illuminated Address was in the possession of his daughter-in-law and niece Mary Ann (Polly) Hammett who kindly allowed it along with the original photograph of James, to be photographed by Harry Brooks, and later published in his book *Six Heroes in Chains*.

The watch, Illuminated Address, photograph of James and a book (*Morning Light; or waking thoughts for every day in the year*) belonging to his son Samuel were donated by the family, possibly all being on display at the Dorchester County Museum. Certainly the Illuminated Address was on display there in 1955 when a family relative viewed it. Later in 1984 at the museum in Tolpuddle the Illuminated Address, watch and photograph of James were on display there. Sadly the watch was stolen from Tolpuddle in 1989 and has never been recovered, despite the TUC having put up a reward.

The People's History Museum in Manchester does have in their archives a framed address with a copy of a photograph of James.

Although it states it is the original, it is possibly the original draft, but not the one presented to James, which was on one vellum page and beautifully decorated with the various signatures of the presenting parties.

I had for a long time been in search of these remaining original family pieces connected to James, as the Museum in Tolpuddle was no longer in possession of them. Eventually it transpired they were at the Trade Union Congress Library in London where I could make an appointment to view them (apart from the photograph). Inside his son Samuel's book is a written inscription presumably in Samuel's hand dedicated to his father (I have left the original spelling in). *In affectionate remembrance of James Hammett who died November 21st 1891 aged 79 years and was this day interred in Tolpuddle Church yeard with the family and kind regards Tolpuddle November 24th 1891. Adieu dear Father short farewell what thou has suffered none can till. But thou art gone to endless rest to be ever with the bless. How much he suffered Heaven knows, but now he's freed from all his woes he's passed through Jordon swelling floods and landed safe with Christ his God.*

An agricultural labourer for most of his life, James seems to have changed professions, somewhere between the 1861 and 1871 census, to that of a journeyman bricklayer. This would be indicative of someone who although had learned their trade, was not yet a master of it, and probably working for a fully qualified other party. James may have assisted with the building of the new Methodist Chapel at Tolpuddle in 1862 but certainly would not have had the experience or expertise to do it alone.

With the Depression in the 1870's perhaps it made better financial sense to change professions. Also there had in the 1860's been a growing trend for Unions, which saw a backlash in the 1870's. Unions wanted better pay and conditions for members and farmers often felt it was in their best interests not to employ Union members. If they had such employees they might be tempted to throw them over for non-members, which could see a member not only out of work but out of their tied cottage too. So, perhaps with this in mind, silence was the best policy or a different trade for James.

From the various records of his life he left behind there was a question as to whether he could read and write. Well, he certainly was able to read when he viewed his pardon in that newspaper left by his master back in Australia and thus learned of his freedom. Furthermore, it is almost certain he could write or at least was able to sign his name. This theory only arose from some certificates having him sign his name with an X as his mark. Perhaps certain people dealing in these matters automatically presumed upon his educational limits or he himself at the time was unable to sign or did not want to.

From his Tolpuddle Martyr or, as it was known, Dorchester Unionists/Labourers fame James was described as being always very idle and ready for mischief. But then again the powers that be would hardly have described him in a positive light.

One press publication of the 24th November 1891 (British Library Newspapers – Daily News) had a small piece, *Death of the Dorset Martyr*, but as usual the press stated erroneous facts. James had died the day before which would have been the 23rd (his death certificate said the 21st). He had expired of old age, was once of national interest, the leader in Dorset of the agricultural labourer's revolt against the machinery being introduced, those riots were violent and serious. After returning back to his native village became a labourer once more, had little fire left in his being and thus sinking lower and lower, had in the end sought refuge at the workhouse in Dorchester. No change with the times and newspapers then, even back in those days the press would do their utmost to grab attention for a story, even if it meant a little fabrication.

The truth was James was never the leader and he had had family around him in his old age but did not want to be a burden so was admitted to the workhouse. Little wonder he was known as the silent one out of the Tolpuddle Martyrs, hardly ever talking about his experiences. It also must be taken into account that as the only one who remained in England, in the very village where it all happened with the same community and prominent figures still around, he must have felt he had to be careful not to send any sort of ripples out, especially later in the Depression period of the 1870's. Keeping a low profile, no one could blame him.

According to the above-mentioned publication by Harry Brooks the burial of James posed a likely influence on the local agricultural workers. The local squire of the time made an appearance in the churchyard that day to ensure there were no Trade Union speeches at his graveside. Once again reinforcing the image that life in Tolpuddle after transportation could not have been easy for James.

James must have been a loving man for he married three times and had quite a few children. Some printed works have suggested he might have been a ladies' man due to the fact that he married three times. The hard facts are that he outlived all his wives and many men of that period were married more than once. This was mainly due to the high death rates of women associated with childbirth and the many illnesses and diseases, nowadays easily cured by medicine not readily available then.

The first marriage was to Harriet Gibbons at the parish church in Tolpuddle on the 1st November 1832 by Vicar Thomas Warren, witnesses Samuel Bullen and John Mitchell (his brother-in-law), both were single and Harriet put an X as her mark. Harriet was baptised in nearby Affpuddle on the 3rd February 1811, possibly a baseborn child of Ann Gibbons. Harriet bore James five children before departing this world on the 27th June 1860 aged 49 from cancer of the womb with James by her side. She was buried in Tolpuddle on the 1st July, with James stated as being an agricultural labourer.

The second marriage took place a little over two years after first wife Harriet had died, on the 6th September 1862, again at the parish church in Tolpuddle, this time by Vicar George Nash, to Charlotte Daniels. Both were of full age and of Tolpuddle, with James a widower and mason (builder) and Charlotte's father noted as William Daniels, a labourer. Their witnesses were John Hammett (could be either the father or brother of James) and Ann White who made her mark of an X.

Charlotte was baptised in Tolpuddle on the 21st June 1832 the child of William Daniels and Jane Loveless. Jane Loveless had two sisters Judith and Elizabeth who each married a Hammett brother. Judith married William and Elizabeth married John. These brothers were the builders of the Methodist Chapel in Tolpuddle, with

William being a Methodist preacher for many decades. There is a plaque in his honour housed there. Also these two Hammett brothers were half-cousins to James Hammett as their fathers were half-brothers. There was also a further connection with the families of Charlotte and James as Charlotte's two aunts and mother's first cousin Stephen Loveless married Elizabeth Hammett who was the sister of James Hammett. What a tangled lot these Tolpuddle Hammetts are.

It would also appear from the members' book list, which George Loveless kept, (which was subsequently seized on the orders of Magistrate Frampton and was to play a vital role on convicting James and the other five Martyrs), that Charlotte's father William Daniels was also a listed member. Although he was not the father-in-law of James at that time, but in later years he would be.

Again James was to be the surviving spouse with the death of Charlotte on the 5th July 1870 in Tolpuddle aged just 38 from paralysis. Once more he was with a wife when she died and oddly enough put his mark of an X (it is known he could read and write before this time period, perhaps again it was just assumed he could not or was in shock from her death). He was noted as a journeyman bricklayer. Charlotte bore James two children, although one died as a very young baby.

The third marriage for James took place just over five years after the death of his second wife Charlotte, on the 11th September 1875. This time not at the parish church in Tolpuddle but in the Registry Office in Dorchester. James was 64 now, a widower and bricklayer, whilst the bride was Ann Frampton aged 60 and a widow. Their witnesses were Richard Spicer and Amelia David, both of whom put an X as their marks as did the bride Ann. Both Ann and James were of Tolpuddle, so very strange not to be married in the parish church there. They were free to marry in a church as both had been widowed and this was a third marriage for both of them.

Ann was born circa 1817 at (Nether) Kingcombe, Dorset, and baptised on the 20th December 1818 at Toller Porcorum of parents Joseph Green, an agricultural labourer, (later a carpenter) and Anne. Ann had first married as Eliza Ann in Tolpuddle on the 7th August 1839 to Giles Daniel, a widower, whose father had the same name.

She was a spinster of Burleston, father Joseph Green a labourer. They had two issue in Tolpuddle who were Matthew baptised on the 20th November 1841 and Charles Albert on the 19th October 1845. Giles died aged 75 and was buried in Tolpuddle on the 5th February 1862. Ann appears as Elizabeth aged 25 on the 1841 census in Tolpuddle with Giles being 50 and an agricultural labourer and her brother George Green aged 30 is also with them and Mary Ann Loveless aged 22. On the 1851 census Ann appears as Eliza aged 37 born Kingcombe in Tolpuddle with Giles 64, Charles 5 and Matthew 9. The 1861 census shows Ann is 45, born Kingcombe in Tolpuddle, with Giles 76, Matthew 18 and Charles 14.

Ann married for a second time in 1866 within the Dorchester district to John Frampton (born circa 1797 Charlton Marshall). In the 1861 census he is aged 65, a widower living in Tolpuddle as a lodger to Mary Way. His wife Edith died in 1855 Blandford district. This second marriage for Ann was to be short-lived as John died aged 72 and was buried in Tolpuddle on the 6th December 1869. On the 1871 census Ann is living in Tolpuddle, a widow aged 56 born Kingcombe, and has a lodger (her stepson) John Frampton aged 16 born Dewlish, a baker's assistant.

This third marriage for James was to be his shortest yet, as again he out-lived another wife, with Ann dying on her husband's birthday, which was the 11th December 1877, in Tolpuddle. She was 60 and once again James was with a wife when she died and was listed as a bricklayer journeyman. James would not marry again. Due to both James and Ann's ages there were no children from their very brief marriage.

Some family have said James was not popular in the village due to the Tolpuddle Martyr connection. Possibly, not wanting to be known by association, some may have feared work, and the often housing opportunities that came with it, closed to them by those prominent local figures who may have disapproved of the Tolpuddle Martyrs.

In the days well before the popularity of the event held each July in the village of Tolpuddle by the Unions, it is possible there was still some resentment by locals. Family rumour (source his niece/daughter-in-law, herself once a pupil teacher) suggests he ran a night school for the local children to learn to read and write. As previously stated, he could do both. I believe there was a school in the Church Hill area of Tolpuddle. Perhaps this was it (Modern Records Centre The University of Warwick – MSS.292/1.91/50 JW/EG/618).

This same source also suggested he once lived in the cottage next to the one she resided in. Almost certainly not during the same time period, as she lived at "Hoad Cottage", 27 Dorchester Road, which was next to the Church View/Hill Cottages. Today his suggested cottage would be "Sweet William Cottage", 29 Dorchester Road, a Grade II listed cob cottage.

James Hammett appears on the various censuses throughout the years:-

1841 living Tolpuddle James is 30, an ag lab, wife Harriet is 30 and son George is 8.

1851 living Tolpuddle James is 39, an ag lab, Harriet is 40, born Affpuddle with children Harriet 9, Emily 7 and a visitor James Mitchell unwed aged 24, an ag lab born Woolbridge. Next-door is Daniel Mitchell nephew of James, visiting the Legg family who are his future in-laws.

1861 living Tolpuddle James is 49, an ag lab widower with children Emily 17 and unwed, James 9 and Samuel 6.

1871 living No 1 Church Close Place, Tolpuddle (possibly the site where Hammett Close is today, near the newly completed Methodist Chapel, his neighbours are mostly all in the building trade, and many are his kinsfolk) James is 59, a bricklayer journeyman widower with sons Samuel 18 and William 5.

1881 living White Hill, Tolpuddle, James is 69, a journeyman bricklayer widower with sons Samuel 26 and William 15.

1891 living Dorchester Union Workhouse, Fordington, Dorchester, James is 80, a pauper and widower.

Children for James Hammett and Harriet Gibbons:-

1) George baptised 31st March 1833 Tolpuddle, died 6th January 1855.

2) Harriet baptised 12th September 1841 Tolpuddle, died 1869.

3) Emily born 20th April 1843 and baptised 22nd April 1843 Tolpuddle, died 15th February 1871.

4) James baptised 23rd August 1851 Tolpuddle, died 14th June 1870.

5) Samuel George baptised 16th July 1854, died 1925.

Children for James Hammett and Charlotte Daniels:-

6) Jane baptised 24th February 1863, buried 9th March 1863 an infant, both events in Tolpuddle.

7) William baptised 12th November 1865 Tolpuddle, died 1940.

PART II

Chapter 7

JAMES HAMMETT'S CHILDREN AND DESCENDANTS

Seven children were fathered by James with two of his three wives in Tolpuddle. These were four boys and three girls. Sadly some were to die young, with none of the boys having children of their own. To trace descendants of James, one has to look to the lineage of his daughters, where of course usually the Hammett name is taken over by another, unless there are baseborn children. Now to have a look into the lives of his children:-

George 1833-1855
George was baptised in Tolpuddle on the 31st March 1833, which was the same year as the Slavery Abolition Act. This meant that within the British Empire all slaves were free and their owners compensated, which amounted jointly to some £20 million. The slavery abolitionist William Wilberforce died that year too.

Having joined the Royal Marines on the 5th July 1851 at Plymouth, George enlisted at Dorchester aged nearly 19½ years old. From the description given he had black hair, light brown eyes, a fair complexion, and was a labourer. Sadly George was to die young serving his country during the Crimean War in the Black Sea Theatre, at approximately eleven-thirty in the evening of Saturday 6th January 1855 (The National Archives ADM/54/260, ADM/38/8962, ADM/58/232). No marriage or children have been traced for him.

George died on board H.M.S. Sans Pareil, which was anchored at Balaklava, with his body being interred on the Sunday after midday, presumably into the water, as was the custom then. This ship was taken from the French in 1794 and used in the Crimean War, and from January to April 1855 it was engaged in the Black Sea Theatre of war, which is where George passed away. This vessel carried seven hundred and fifty men, many of whom would also lose their lives or be wounded on this ship, some who caught my eye were:-

Frederick Baggage, Joseph Bouncehall, William Bytheway, Nicholas Cudlip, Swafren Hicks, Thomas Shirewell, Edward Skillicorn to name but a few.

This part of the world must have been very different from George's beginnings in life. In the census for 1841 George is aged 8 and living at home in Tolpuddle. The census for 1851 finds him living at the Royal Marine Barracks, East Stonehouse, Plymouth, Devon aged 19, unwed, Private Marine, born Tolpiddle. (Years earlier in 1838 four of his father's comrades from Tolpuddle Martyr fame, landed close to this region in Plymouth. The first English soil they would touch since their banishment to New South Wales. George may have been aware of this fact.)

Harriet 1841-1869

Born after her father's return from transportation, Harriet was baptised on the 12th September 1841 in Tolpuddle. That same year saw the first census being recorded which listed all the names within a household or institution, and *The Old Curiosity Shop* by Charles Dickens also entered the world. Harriet was probably named after her mother and, like her elder brother George, she too would die young aged just 28 in the last few months of 1869.

Harriet married Alfred Battrick/Batterick in the early part of 1859. He was born to Alfred and Charlotte in 1839 at Bere Regis. Harriet lived her entire short life in Tolpuddle, with one census entry showing her in-laws living next door to them early in her marriage.

Alfred would need his parents close at hand after Harriet's death, if only to help out with the children. It would be many years later after Harriet's untimely early death that Alfred would take another wife, and this he did in 1874 with the marriage of Emma Mary Rideout. This union produced one child namely Alice Martha Battrick in 1876. She grew up and married in 1901 to Alfred Ernest King. When Alice died in 1941, she was laid to rest with her elder half-sister Sarah at Bincombe. Her husband Alfred was witness at her half-sister Sarah's husband's second marriage in 1903, so relations between the families must have been close after Sarah's death in 1898.

Harriet and Alfred had five children all of whom were born in Tolpuddle, and were George 1859, Samuel 1860, Angelina in either 1861 or 1862, William 1864 and lastly Sarah 1866.

George Battrick married Lydia Robbins in 1885 and they lived in Dorchester with their children Alfred George 1886, Frederick Thomas 1887, Annie Florence 1892, Daisy Maud 1896, James William 1899 and Reginald Percy 1905.

Samuel had died in 1861 and was probably no more than one year old.

Angelina married James Trevis in 1881, but they appear to have had no children.

William died aged 7 in 1871 and was buried in Tolpuddle.

Sarah married Thomas Trevett in 1885. His father David is buried in Tolpuddle churchyard, the headstone reads *In loving memory of David Trevett who died July 21st 1906 aged 79 years. "Rest in the Lord."* Sarah was to die young just as her mother Harriet had done, and passed away on the 29th March 1898 aged just 33. She is buried Holy Trinity Church, Bincombe with her younger half-sister Alice King. Their headstone reads *In loving memory of my beloved wife Alice Martha King who fell asleep Feb 6th 1941 aged 64 years. Until the day-break and the shadows flee away. Also Sarah Trevett beloved sister of the above who fell asleep March 29th 1898 aged 33 years. They will be done.*

In the same churchyard in 1801 two German-born soldiers are buried who belonged to the York Hussars, and were shot for desertion. They were both buried on the 30th June and aged 22 respectively. One was Corporal Matthew Tina born Sarrbruk, Germany, the other Christopher Bless born Lothaargen, Alsatia. With the threat of invasion by Napoleon at this time, the King, George III spent most of the summer at Weymouth, with the troops camped on Bincombe Down. The writer Thomas Hardy may have known about these events and been the inspiration for one of his works, 1890 *The Melancholy Hussar of the German Legion.*

Thomas Trevett married a few years after Sarah's death in 1902 to Jessie with one of their witnesses being Alfred Ernest King, who was Sarah's half-sister Alice's husband. Sarah and Thomas had children who were William Alfred 1886, Daisy Alice 1888, Alfred George 1889-1916 (died whilst serving his country in WW1 on 7th October 1916 aged 26 as Rifleman 4501 with the London Regiment 8th Bn (Post Office Rifles, as he was a postman in civilian life) and is buried in Grave I.C. 29 at Warlencourt British Cemetery, Pas de Calais, France (The Commonwealth War Graves Commission), Percival Thomas 1892-1928 (one of his children married a man who was an active member of the National Union of Agricultural Workers attending the rallies at Tolpuddle, with them living and raising their children in a tied cottage on the Frampton estate at Moreton where he was a worker), Frederick 1893 and lastly Elsie Sarah 1895.

Emily 1843-1871

Emily was born on the 20th April 1843 and baptised a few days later on the 22nd April in Tolpuddle. That same year Nelson's Column in London's Trafalgar Square makes an appearance, also in London, Sir Henry Cole prints the first Christmas cards. Although Emily is listed in the 1861 census as living at home in Tolpuddle with the family, later that year in September, she was in the Union Workhouse in Fordington (Dorchester). Here she gave birth as an unmarried mother, putting X for her mark. The child born out of wedlock was named after her mother Harriet, who sadly had died the previous year in 1860. This same workhouse over the years housed other Hammett relatives of Emily's, including her own father James. There is no indication as to who the father was of Harriet, the baseborn child of Emily.

A few years later in 1865 at Dorchester, Emily married Thomas Lester. They both were aged about 22, and the Lesters being a Fordington family which was an area of Dorchester. Along with Emily's daughter Harriet Hammett who had been born in 1861, Emily and Thomas had their own two children Jane born in 1866 and Thomas James in 1867.

Unfortunately, Emily would join her older siblings in dying young, for she passed away on the 15th February 1871 at Fordington aged just 30 of organic disease of the heart. Her daughter Harriet was present at her death and the named informant, Thomas, was listed as the husband, an agricultural labourer.

Thomas now found himself in the position of raising his step-daughter Harriet Hammett along with her younger half-siblings who were his daughter and son at their home in Mill Street in Fordington. Later that year Thomas married Elizabeth Bowring who was a much older woman than himself. He was aged 29 whilst the bride was aged 44 a laundress who also had been a widow. His father was noted as James Trevett, but I have not been able to ascertain if there was a connection to this Trevett family and that of Emily's niece Sarah whose father-in-law was David Trevett. Elizabeth had first married John Bowring in 1846 and he had probably died in 1870. Whilst Elizabeth was some fifteen years older than Thomas, she outlived him for he died aged 54 in 1898.

Emily's baseborn daughter **Harriet Hammett** married Henry Collis with her father on the marriage certificate being noted as Thomas Lester Hammett, perhaps to avoid the stigma of being baseborn. They had children Alice Emily 1882, Frederick Edwin 1887, Nora Frances 1887 (not twins), Walter Charles, John Richard 1892-1893, Fanny Rose 1894 and Lily Annie 1897.

Jane sadly would die young just as her mother and grandmother before her had, aged 26 years old in the latter part of 1892.

Thomas James would have a path in life which would also be cut short resulting with his death aged 17 in 1884. He was buried in Fordington.

James 1851-1870

James Hammett was baptised on the 23rd August 1851 in Tolpuddle. This year also bore witness to the first time the census listed the full location of birth details, Buckingham Palace in London would be without Marble Arch as it was moved to where it is now located. The New York Times newspaper also made an entrance. Clearly James was named after his father and during his short life, was an agricultural labourer too. He died of sequele of scarlatina aged just 18 years at home in Tolpuddle on 14th June 1870 with his father by his side. He was buried the next day on the 15th in Tolpuddle churchyard.

In his brother Samuel's book *Morning Light; or waking thoughts for every day of the year*, and presumably in Samuel's hand is written *In affectionate remembrance of James Hammett who died June 14th 1870 aged 18 years and was this day interred in Tolpuddle Church yard with the family and kind regards Tolpuddle June 17th 1870. Adieu dear brother a short foray. What thou hast suffered none can tell but thou art gone to endless rest to be ever with the bless. How much he suffered heaven knows but now he's freed from all his woes. He's passed through Jordon's swelling floods and now landed safe with Christ his God.* (Note the burial date differs from that which appeared in the parish records.)

Samuel George 1854-1925

Samuel George was born in 1854 and baptised that year in Tolpuddle on the 16th July 1854. That year also saw the end of the Chartist Movement, and in the March the commencement of the Crimean War as Britain declared war with Russia. Later Samuel would become a soldier in the Dorset 39th Regiment of Foot, Private No. 40, with him being sent out on detachment to Nowgong, Bundeland, East India, after having first landed at Bombay. His name appeared on the musters out there from 1st October 1877 until 31st March 1879 (The National Archives WO/16/1702, WO/334/82).

Back on home soil, for over twenty years he worked at the Dorset County Lunatic Asylum near Dorchester as a mason and attendant on the insane. His building skills most probably initially drew him there, with him living in one of the various staff cottages nearby. He is noted as living there on the 1891, 1901 and 1911 censuses. The 1901 census showed there were eight hundred and ninety-five people at the Asylum, of which seven hundred and twenty-three were patients, seven officers, eighteen were of officer's families, seventy-two nurses/attendants, fifty-one were of attendant's families, sixteen domestic servants and eight were of trade and industry.

The Dorset County Asylum, Herrison Hospital opened in 1863 and closed in 1992, initially accommodating three hundred and twenty patients, comprising one hundred and sixty male and one hundred and sixty female. There was a growing need for additional beds, with the increase of pauper patients. Various building projects also were carried out there. In about 1891 the existing building was enlarged, a water reservoir followed two years later, installation of electric lighting in about 1894, a new chapel the next year, a female annex was added in the years 1895 to 1896, and a private patient block in 1903. Samuel's building skills more than likely would have been used in some capacity regarding these various projects. His boss would have been Dr Peter William MacDonald, a surgeon born in Scotland.

Samuel married late in life, aged 64 years on the 2nd April 1919 at The Prebendal Church of St George in Fordington, Dorchester to Mary Ann Loveless who was his first cousin. His father and her mother were brother and sister. In some quarters this liaison may have been frowned upon, but it probably was a marriage of companionship. Samuel was noted as a bachelor, mason and asylum attendant of Charminster, father James Hammett deceased, a bricklayer. Mary Ann was 58 a spinster of 3 East Parade, Fordington, father Stephen Loveless, a labourer. Their witnesses were Hannah White and Stephen Loveless (most probably her brother, as her father by the same name had died in 1899 which she failed to mention on her marriage certificate).

Mary Ann was born in Tolpuddle and baptised there on the 25th December 1859. She was about five years Samuel's junior, and therefore no children would be blessed from this union. Mary Ann was also known in the family as Polly. This marriage was to be short-lived, as about six and half years later Samuel died at home in the Church Hill area of Tolpuddle during the Christmas period on the 21st December 1925. He was buried aged 70 years on Christmas Eve, the 24th December 1925 at Tolpuddle, like so many of his kinsfolk before him.

This event would have put the festive season on hold somewhat for the Hammett relatives, and no doubt came as a shock. Some relatives would have had a journey to make to Tolpuddle for the burial, not easy given the transport of the time and winter road conditions, along with it being the festive season.

Samuel had the good sense to make a will in favour to his wife and first cousin Mary Ann. The gross value of estate was £460.5.9 (in 2012 would roughly equate to £23,682) and the net value of personal estate £240.5.9 (in 2012 would roughly equate to £12,355). The solicitors were Messrs Thomas Coombs & Morton Solicitors in Dorchester, with Samuel Loveless a carrier, and Albert Miles a baker, both of Tolpuddle being the sureties. These Tolpuddle men made sure his will and wishes were carried out, and were also relatives of Samuel and Mary Ann's.

Samuel Loveless, who also went by the surname of Riggs and had a wooden leg, was a nephew of Mary Ann and a first cousin once-removed to Samuel. Albert Miles was the son-in-law of Samuel Loveless mentioned above, as he had married his daughter.

Amongst Samuel's possessions was a book by the Society for promoting Christian knowledge called *Morning Light or waking thoughts for every day in the year*. Relevant for Samuel therein *40 Pte Samuel Hammett A. Company 39th Regt Nougong Bundeland East India*. As mentioned above, this relates to his army career, and at the back appears his name alongside that of either his father or brother James and Tolpuddle Dorset. This item was donated by the family and is in the possession of the TUC Library in London.

Jane 1863-1863

This poor child was baptised and buried in less than a month, and noted as an infant, so probably just a month or so old. Obtaining the death certificate would reveal more information regarding the cause of death. Infant mortality could be high in those times, with the lack of medicine, sanitation and so forth. She was more than likely named after her maternal grandmother Jane Daniels, nee Loveless.

William 1865-1940

William Hammett, also known as Billy, was born 1865 Tolpuddle and baptised 12th November 1865 in the parish church there. That same year was the birth of writer Rudyard Kipling, in Whitechapel, London the Salvation Army was formed by husband and wife William and Catherine Booth, and in the United States of America the Civil War ended. William was the second child born to the second wife of James Hammett. He was the only one to survive from that marriage and the last child James fathered. It is probable he was named after his maternal grandfather.

Through his mother Charlotte Daniels, William also shares blood links with the other Tolpuddle Martyrs. Charlotte's mother was Jane Loveless whose sisters had married the first half-cousins of William's father James, who were William and John Hammett. The father of the Loveless girls was William who was first cousin to Tolpuddle Martyrs George and James Loveless, and also their sister Diniah. Diniah was wife and mother to two further Tolpuddle Martyrs who were Thomas and John Standfield, and she was also the mother of Elizabeth Standfield who married another Tolpuddle Martyr, James Brine. So, all in all, William Hammett was very well connected and blood related to all of the Tolpuddle Martyrs.

He attended the Centenary Commemorations of the Martyrs in Tolpuddle alongside his sister-in-law and first cousin (Polly) Mary Ann Hammett. This event was widely covered by the Press of the time, with both William and Mary Ann being mentioned in the likes of the Times Newspaper.

Information gleaned from a newspaper of the relevant period gave a brief mention of William's 70th birthday (Dorset County Chronicle 1935), which was spent visiting his cousin in Tolpuddle namely Mrs Hammett, her home being situated near the church where his father is buried and acknowledged William had been practically blind for four years. That would place William losing his sight aged about 66 years old.

The Press in 1938 stated he was living in poverty, his home a small abode at the Eastern side of Dorchester and he was almost blind (as was his father in his later years). Aged 71 he was the only surviving child of any of the Tolpuddle Martyrs (he certainly was the only surviving child of James Hammett then). Memorials had been made for his late father and his comrades, but William had seen little benefit, and was described as a cheerful, if pathetic little man (from photos he was small in stature and wore dark glasses due to his failing eye sight). It went on to say, apart from a niece and a nephew he was alone in the world, (not strictly true, there were other nieces and nephews, but he may not have been aware of them due to their parents dying young). The article closed saying he was unwed and the last of the Hammetts.

This would suggest the journalist was drumming up sympathy and support for William. The likely root cause being that prior to this time in Tolpuddle, the Trade Union Congress (TUC) had constructed the Martyrs Memorial Cottages. These were to be occupied by retired poor agricultural labourers, who were union members. William had never been a union member and therefore did not qualify.

Consideration in 1934 was given by the TUC as to whether William needed assistance, but local agricultural trade unionists were strongly opposed to anything of the kind being done for him. As they all knew he had never been a union member during his working life it was very difficult for the TUC to help him further.

In late 1938 a Mr James of the National Union of Agricultural Labourers gave William 2/6 whilst he was looking into his living arrangements, due to a false rumour circulating that his landlady was moving. At the time William lived in Dorchester with said landlady whom I discovered was a Mrs Roberts,. William paid her £1 (in 2012 equates to £56.46) per week to look after him (Modern Record Centre The University of Warwick – MSS.292/1.91/57). Further evidence of where and with whom William lived in 1934 came in the shape of the contribution a Mrs Freda Wade made via the Dorchester Age Concern's Dorset Living Memories. She recalled how during the Centenary Commemorations in Dorchester between the 30th August and the 2nd September 1934, each evening at the Corn Exchange in Dorchester, a play was put on re-enacting the story of the Tolpuddle Martyrs.

One afternoon during this time period, aged nearly ten, Mrs Freda Wade recalled walking with her grandmother Mrs Edith Vincent down the Holloway Road in Dorchester. They stopped to talk to an elderly near blind man who was standing in the doorway of Mrs Roberts' cottage. Her grandmother, knowing of his connections, enquired whether he had been invited to the celebrations being held at the Corn Exchange. He said he had not and was totally unaware of what was going on there. Holding rank of son of James Hammett, one of the Tolpuddle Martyrs, they found this quite extraordinary. Although William was present at the unveiling of his father's headstone in Tolpuddle, and spoke to the Press and dignitaries, it does seem odd that he was not included in the events held at the Corn Exchange then.

From the electoral lists of the time it would appear William lived at 48 Holloway Road, Fordington with a residence occupation status. Mrs Elizabeth Roberts was also noted there with the same status and also occupation qualification, she was the main head there, indicative to her being the landlady. Also living there with the same status as William were Earl Bowering and Charles Gould (Dorset History Centre – QDE (R) West 1935).

Mrs Freda Wade was invited to a Tolpuddle Hammett and Loveless family history gathering one Saturday before the rally/festival in Tolpuddle. She was kind enough to show myself along with the other relatives this property William had resided in, as it was not far from our gathering. But now it is noted as being number 46 (next door is 46a, supporting my theory that re-numbering at some stage had occurred).

This property was a semi and did not look that large, so probably a squeeze housing four separate individuals. Mrs Wade informed me that one of the men (possibly one of the ones previously mentioned from the electoral lists) was a widower whose little girl also resided there. This little girl of course would not have shown up on those lists. She further said that Mrs Roberts was a widow herself with little money. One must be mindful that this time frame fell within the Great Depression period, with money being very tight for all concerned and many living hand-to-mouth.

Apparently William would sit on a little stool in the doorway with his dark glasses on, not being able to read through his blindness, and apart from those he lived with, this was most probably the only activity/contact he had on a daily basis with the outside world. Little wonder then that some noises had been made on his behalf regarding the Memorial Cottages.

One person who did talk to William at Tolpuddle in 1934 was David Lloyd George (Prime Minister 1916-1922 and a major participant at the Paris Peace Conference which drafted the Versailles Treaty of 1919). He told William that he would rather have been descended from his father (James Hammett) than from William the Conqueror. It is not known how William reacted to this, but it is probably safe to assume it made him feel very proud of his parentage.

William died aged 75 in 1940 within the Dorchester registration district. According to an Australian newspaper report of 1956 (The Age 07/04/1956) Charles Boyt a former branch secretary of the Tolpuddle Agricultural Workers' Union who lived in one of the Memorial Cottages at Tolpuddle, said William is buried alongside his father James in Tolpuddle. He went on further to say that he buried William (more than likely would have been assisted) and knew his brother Samuel.

Unfortunately I cannot check the records for this, as I have been unable to locate or find the burial plot map for St John's graveyard in Tolpuddle. From the burial information available I did not find a burial there for William either. I am not suggesting for one minute that Charles Boyt was making this all up, but simply that I have been unable to verify this information.

It is quite feasible that William was brought back to Tolpuddle to be laid to rest, as others had done who lived elsewhere. This included his cousin and sister-in-law Mary Ann (Polly) Hammett who died some four years after him in what was once the old Dorchester workhouse where his father had died. In more modern times it was known as Damers House and part of the hospital complex. Mary Ann was buried in Tolpuddle and appears in the records, but again frustratingly I am not able to locate her grave plot.

From the various photographs taken at the 1934 centenary celebrations, William along with other relatives have been captured, and from those viewed, he appeared to be a very small man. Although in advanced years, he would probably have been that size all his life.

Before leaving this chapter, it is worth mentioning Mrs Freda Wade again. When she met William Hammett on that day in 1934, she was not only residing with her parents in the same road as him which was Holloway Road in Fordington, but in the very house one of his relatives had lived in back in 1901. That property was 21 Harvey's Buildings, which is now Harvey's Terrace. The relative was William's first cousin Henry Hammett who was the baseborn son of Sarah Hammett who was the sister of James Hammett,

William's father. Next door to Freda and her parents at number 20 lived her grandmother Edith Vincent. Freda later would inform me, her grandmother had said to her on that afternoon back in 1934 when they stopped to speak to William, "Now you can say you have spoken to a son of one of the Tolpuddle Martyrs".

Part II Chapter 7

FAMILY TREE

James Hammett 1811-1891
Marriage 1:
Harriet Gibbons 1811-1860

George 1833

Harriet 1841

Emily 1843

James 1851

Samuel 1854

Marriage 2:
Charlotte Daniels 1832-1870

Jane 1863-1863

William 1865

Marriage 3:
Ann Frampton 1817-1877
No children

65

Part II Chapter 7

FAMILY TREE

Harriet Hammett 1841-1869
wed
Alfred Battrick 1839-poss 1908

George 1859	Samuel 1860	Angelina 1861/62	William 1864	Sarah 1866
wed	died 1861	wed	died 1871	wed
Lydia Robbins		James Trevis		Thomas Trevett

George 1859 children:
-Alfred George 1886
-Frederick Thomas 1887
-Annie Florence 1892
-Daisy Maud 1896
-James William 1899
-Reginald Percy 1905

Sarah 1866 children:
-William Alfred 1886
-Daisy Alice 1888
-Alfred George 1889
-Percival Thomas 1892
-Thomas Frederick 1893
-Elsie Sarah 1895

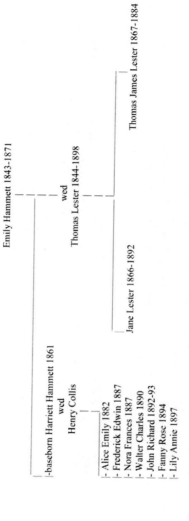

Part II Chapter 7

FAMILY TREE

Emily Hammett 1843-1871

wed

Thomas Lester 1844-1898

Thomas James Lester 1867-1884

Jane Lester 1866-1892

-baseborn Harriett Hammett 1861
wed
Henry Collis

- Alice Emily 1882
- Frederick Edwin 1887
- Nora Frances 1887
- Walter Charles 1890
- John Richard 1892-93
- Fanny Rose 1894
- Lily Annie 1897

Part II Chapter 7

FAMILY TREE

LINKING *WILLIAM HAMMETT 1865
TO ALL THE TOLPUDDLE MARTYRS

John Loveless 1731 wed Thomasina Gould

John Loveless 1751 wed Judith Hibbs

Thomas Loveless 1761 wed Dinah Stickland

William Loveless 1774
wed
Jane Hoare

John Loveless 1783
wed
Elizabeth Gover

Diniah Loveless 1789
wed
Thomas Standfield **TPM**

George Loveless 1797
TPM

James Loveless 1808
TPM

Stephen Loveless 1816
wed
Elizabeth Hammett
sister of James Hammett **TPM**

John Standfield
TPM

Elizabeth Standfield
wed James Brine **TPM**

Jane Loveless 1803
wed
William Daniels

Judith Loveless 1809
wed
William Hammett

Elizabeth Loveless 1813
wed
John Hammett

Charlotte Daniels 1832
wed James Hammett **TPM**

|- *WILLIAM HAMMETT 1865

brothers and ½ cousins to James Hammett **TPM**

68

Part II Chapter 7

FAMILY TREE

LINKING *WILLIAM HAMMETT 1865
TO LOVELESS FAMILY

William Loveless wed 10/03/1796 Jane Hoare

| Edward 21/11/1796 | William 1798-poss died 1798 | Ann 08/09/1801 wed 01/08/1828 William Bartlett | Jane 19/10/1803 wed 10/07/1826 William Daniels (witness Edward Loveless) (Tolpuddle by Rev Richard Wadding) | William 1806 wed 01/05/1831 Hannah Pierce (Tincleton) | Judith 1809 wed 02/11/1840 William Hammett | Elizabeth 1813 wed 25/12/1843 John Hammett | Martha 1813-1876 never wed |

brothers & ½ cousins
to James Hammett **TM**

- baseborn Edward Daniel Loveless 09/07/1826
- Ann Daniels 01/06/1828
- Jane Loveless Daniels 26/12/1830
- Charlotte Daniels 21/06/1832
  wed 06/09/1862 James Hammett **TM**
  - Jane Hammett 24/02/1863-09/03/1863
  - *William Hammett 12/11/1864
- Harriett Daniels 08/05/1834 -02/05/1835
- William Daniels 26/02/1837
- Emily Daniels 13/03/1840
- Martha Daniels 24/06/1842 – 16/09/1843

PART II

Chapter 8

JAMES HAMMETT'S PARENTS, SIBLINGS AND THEIR OFFSPRING

James was the seventh child of thirteen born to parents John Hammett and Elizabeth Foot. They had married in Wareham on the 24th June 1799, where Elizabeth hailed from, with her being aged 18 and John 24. John was born in Tolpuddle in 1775 and baptised there the same year on the 1st of March and, like his father before him, was a mason by trade. From Elizabeth's age at her marriage, she was born in about the year 1781.

Elizabeth would not live to see ancient bones, for she died aged 55 and was buried in Tolpuddle by Vicar Thomas Warren on the 8th November 1835. As this time period falls before the registration of certificates (which commenced from the third quarter of 1837) I was unable to obtain a death certificate for her to ascertain her cause of death. An educated guess might point in the direction of the associated stress and strain of the year 1834 which had engulfed the family and village of Tolpuddle, when one of her sons was transported to the other side of the world in New South Wales. A mother never ceases to worry about one of her brood, no matter how old they are. So upon his return James would have not received his mother's welcome, but that of a stepmother, as his father remarried less than two years after Elizabeth's death.

On the 29th July 1837 in Tolpuddle, John Hammett married by banns to Elizabeth Green, a spinster, and their witnesses were John Hammett (his son) and William Bullen. There would be no children from this union. Her birth details have been gleaned from the various census entries, but I favour 1796 as it ties in with her death at the Charminster Asylum on the 2nd September 1870 aged 74 years.

This asylum opened in 1863 and was situated about one mile from Charminster, which is about two miles from Dorchester. Perhaps Elizabeth's problems were more of the mind, as one can only speculate as to why she did not go to the Dorchester workhouse in Fordington, perhaps the former catered more for her needs. More than likely her date of entry would have been sometime between the opening in 1863 and her death in 1870. I have not been able to find a baptism for her, but perhaps her parents were Thomas Green who was buried in Tolpuddle in 1827 aged 58 and Susannah Green buried 1830 aged 65 in Tolpuddle.

John was not to outlive his second wife and was buried in Tolpuddle on the 10th April 1857 aged 82. Siblings for James from his father's first marriage were Honor 1800-post 1871, Sarah 1802-1896, Dennis 1803-1804, Henry 1804-1893, Dennis 1808-? Ursula 1809-1810, Ursula 1813-post 1881, John 1815-1892, Elizabeth 1816-1907, Maria 1818-1818, Anna 1822-1886 and Daniel 1826-1826. Not all these children lived with some being named after their deceased siblings and all born and baptised in Tolpuddle.

Honor 1800-post 1871

Sister Honor was born on the 25th May and baptised on the 15th June 1800, with the ruling monarch of the time being Mad King George III. He was so called due to his mental instability, which probably resulted from the medical condition of Porphyria, an unknown illness of the time. The same year saw the invention of the lathe by Henry Maudslay. Aged 17 or 18, Honor became an unmarried mother with the birth and subsequent baptism in Tolpuddle of her daughter Rebecca Lucas Hammett on the 3rd October 1819. This parish event was recorded as being the daughter of Honor Hammett and William Lucas an agricultural labourer of Tolpuddle.

Their liaison was not to be, for he went on to marry by banns a short time later to Sarah Way. This event took place on the 11th November 1819 and produced a daughter for them called Martha Winter Lucas. She was baptised in Tolpuddle on the 18th August 1822. One can only imagine how Honor must have felt about this abandonment with no marriage, or perhaps she was relieved, something we will never know.

Little Rebecca had a short life being buried in Tolpuddle aged 2 on the 15th May 1820, which means she was probably aged about 1½ when baptised. Samuel Pope Hammett was Honor's second baseborn offspring and baptised in Tolpuddle on the 29th February 1822. An educated guess would suggest the father was a Mr Pope, which was later confirmed when he married and named his father as Samuel Pope, a cooper.

Samuel Pope Hammett 1822 was possibly not part of his mother's new life when she married, for aged 15 in the 1841 census he is in Tolpuddle with his grandfather John Hammett. Samuel at some point left Dorset as he married in 1850 to Rebecca Bawcock at St Mary's Cheshunt, Hertfordshire. Both were noted as living in Crossbrook Street, Cheshunt, his father Samuel Pope a cooper and her father James Bawcock a blacksmith. Like his mother Honor, Samuel's wife Rebecca had two baseborn children both born at Ware. They were Jane Bawcock born 1846 and George Henry Draper Bawcock born 1849.

Samuel and Rebecca do not appear to have had their own children, although Samuel took on the role of father to Rebecca's two. This little family appear to have moved around eventually settling in Islington, London where Samuel died in 1884 aged 62, and Rebecca in 1887 aged 64.

Honor married as Hallett instead of Hammett. It is worth remembering many could not read or write back in those days. In addition, with their different accents and pronunciation of words, which often were the only method of transcribing the census information, often by people in parishes and places far from their native Tolpuddle roots, it is no wonder errors such as this occurred.

Some might say William Daniels, by making her his wife on the 7th February 1826 by banns at the Church of St Mary in the village of Tarrant Rawston, Dorset, made Honor a respectable woman at last. William Daniels was baptised on the 11th September 1803 at Tarrant Keynestone and was therefore a few years younger than Honor. He was buried aged 72 on the 5th December 1875 at Tarrant Tawston, with Honor dying sometime after 1871.

Their surname of Daniels is sometimes spelt as Daniells and they appear to have lived most, if not all of their time, in Tarrant Rawston. They had children George 1825, James 1829, William 1831, John 1883, Alfred 1835 and Elizabeth 1839.

George Daniels 1825 married Hannah Gilbert in 1850 at Tarrant Rawston. They had a son William James baptised 13th May 1855 Tarrant Rawston. Then he married Elizabeth (born circa 1824 Wiltshire) and they lived in 1881 at Lambeth, Surrey.

James Daniels 1829 in 1851 was still unmarried and living at home.

William Daniels 1831 I have not been able to trace since 1841 when he was aged 10 at home.

John Daniels 1833 married Emma Mary Muston in 1857. They moved around in Dorset and Wiltshire and had children Isabella Susan 1858, William John 1859-1860, John Muston 1860, Anna Maria 1862-1862, Frederick 1865-1865, Alfred William 1863, Clara 1866, Edwin born 1872, Ellen Matilda 1873 and Emma Rosetta 1876.

Alfred Daniels 1835 apart from being at home in 1841 and 1851, nothing else is noted for him.

Elizabeth Daniels 1839 married John Ball Roberts in 1857. They moved around living in Derby, Wales and Shropshire where he was noted as being a groom, gardener and parish clerk. Their children were Mary Jane 1865, John Owen 1867, Sarah Ann 1871 and James Guppy 1873.

Sarah 1802-1896

Sister Sarah was born on the 1st November 1802 in Tolpuddle with her birth year witnessing in London the opening of the wax museum of Marie Tussaud, and the suggestion of a Channel Tunnel. Sarah lived to see very old bones indeed, as she died aged 94, seemingly spending her entire life in or around Tolpuddle and nearby Southover. She married by banns in Tolpuddle on the 20th October 1828 to John Mitchell, an agricultural labourer. Both were single, of the parish and their witnesses were Henry Hammett (her brother) and Samuel Bullen. John Mitchell was baptised in Tolpuddle on the 15th

August 1807 of Thomas (his first wife was Elizabeth Vincent) and Ann Mitchell.

John Mitchell was more than likely the same one noted on the member's list of The Friendly Society of Labourers found in the box belonging to George Loveless. He had made membership payments on the 16th November and the 14th December 1833 and also on the 8th February 1834, just before the arrests on the 24th of six other members on this society's list.

This was the very list used by Magistrate Frampton as evidence to convict and transport the six men, who later became known as either the Dorchester Labourers or the Tolpuddle Martyrs. With one of these men being Sarah's brother James Hammett and therefore John's brother-in-law, it could have easily have been John Mitchell who was transported.

John was not as fortunate as his wife Sarah in living a long life, for he was buried in Tolpuddle aged just 33 in 1841. Sarah never married again with John seemingly popular with her siblings, as he was witness at three of their marriages – James in 1832, Elizabeth in 1837 and John also in 1837. Sarah and John had children Daniel 1829, Ann 1830, John 1833-1833, Dennis Hammett 1834, Elizabeth (Lizzie) 1837 and John 1840.

Daniel Mitchell 1829 married in 1851 to Jane Legg, who was baptised in 1830 at Puddletown of David and Mary Legg. After living in and around Tolpuddle, Daniel and Jane moved to Wales, with their children who were:-

1) Mary Jane 1853

2) John (Jack) 1855

3) George 1858, by 1881 was married to a lady called Elizabeth who was born in Buckland, Dorset.

4) James (Jim) Legg 1864. He married Marian Salter 1890 Newport, Isle of Wight where she hailed from. When he died there in 1934 aged 70, the Times newspaper of 26th September 1934 (British Library Newspapers) mentioned he died on the evening of the 25th and was an Alderman having been Mayor of Newport on the Isle of Wight for the last two years of his life and previously headmaster of the local council school. Gleaning various census entries his occupation was indeed schoolmaster and in 1891 his wife was a

schoolmistress. Their children were Millicent Mary S 1892, George James S 1894 and Arthur John Salter 1903-1903.

Ann Mitchell 1830 was last noted in the 1841 census at home aged 11.

Dennis Hammett Mitchell 1834 married in 1885 to Jane Ann Vincent who was born in 1842 of George and Mary Vincent. Dennis appears to have lived his entire life with his mother Sarah, even when he married, and does not appear to have had any children.

Elizabeth (Lizzie) Mitchell 1837 married in 1860 to George Riggs who was baptised in 1836 at Tolpuddle, the son of Amy Riggs. Elizabeth died young aged 37 in 1875. Left with a young family George married again. Elizabeth and George's children were:-

1) Sarah Ann 1861-1867
2) Emma Jane 1862
3) Mary Louise 1864
4) John 1866
5) George Dennis 1868, married Mary Ann Bennett.
6) Sarah Ann 1870-1872
7) Frank 1872, married Annie Hibberd Wheeler. They had children George 1892, Bertrum 1893, Louisa 1894, Edwin 1896, Charles 1897 and Edith 1900.

John Mitchell 1840 married Ann Clark in 1867. They lived in the Wareham area and later moved to Bromyard in Hereford with their son John Oliver.

Henry 1804-1893
Brother Henry was born in 1804 and baptised on the 30th January 1805 in Tolpuddle. His birth year witnessed Spain instigating war with his birth country and Richard Trevithick constructed the first steam locomotive. Henry like his elder sister Sarah lived to a ripe old age, as he died aged 93 on the 15th April 1893 at the Union Workhouse in Fareham, Hampshire with his surname changed to that of Hannett. His cause of death was that of senectus, which means old age or dementia. The master of the Union, Daniel Johnson was listed as the informant with Henry being noted as a general labourer from Titchfield.

Henry was witness at his sister Sarah's wedding in 1828 Tolpuddle and put an X for his name, so one would assume he could not sign his name or write. He did well to live to such a grand old age given a portion of his life was spent as a tramp living outdoors and exposed to the elements.

He had married Mary Ruffell (baptised 19th January 1813 Avington, Hampshire, parents William Ruffell and Sarah Page) on the 4th September 1834 at Winnall, Winchester. They both received parish relief from Avington Overseers of the Poor for this event, which was by Licence and paid for by them.

In 1832 both had spent three months in Winchester prison for vagrancy and one wonders if this is where they had met. Henry was noted in the various censuses as a rag-gatherer, pedlar and, when aged 90, a bricklayer. Mary was noted as a bark scraper, rag and bone collector, pedlar and live hawker. No children for this couple have been found. Mary died as Hamett in 1886 aged 72 in the Fareham area.

Dennis 1807-?

Brother Dennis was baptised in Tolpuddle on the 30th August 1807, the same year slavery was abolished within the British Empire (although it continued until 1833) and the first gas lighting appeared in London's Pall Mall.

Family rumour has suggested that Dennis was stationed with the military at the Sydney Barracks in New South Wales during the year 1834, which was the same time his brother James was transported and imprisoned there. Apparently they were able to see each other and met up. So far I have not been able to verify this with documented evidence.

However, I did find him listed as serving with the Dorset Militia at Dorchester from the 11th May to the 7th June 1825. He was listed as living at Affpuddle and enrolled at Elwell near Upwey (The National Archives WO/13/578). No census details were found for him, suggesting he could have been abroad or dead. Family rumour also suggested he died in India, again something I have not been able to prove.

Ursula also known as Persila or Priscilla 1813-1896

Sister Ursula was born in 1813 and baptised in Tolpuddle on the 18th September 1814. Her birth year was also that for the explorer David Livingstone, and *Pride and Prejudice* by Jane Austen. Like her elder sister Honor, Ursula had a baseborn child the year before she married, called Elizabeth Hammett. Ursula married as Priscilla to William Stroud, who was born circa 1811 in Puddletown, parents John and Fanny, on the 1st February 1844 at Tolpuddle, making her about two years older than him.

In some of the censuses she appears as Persila or Priscilla with William either being stated as a labourer or mason. Both their fathers were masons and, with the villages of Tolpuddle and Piddletown (Puddletown) so close to each other, it is possible the two families knew each other. William died first in 1889 aged 78 and Priscilla in 1896 aged 81.

At some point in her life Ursula must have suffered from some sort of mental illness for in the 1871 census she is to be found being noted as Priscilla, a lunatic invalid/patient in the Dorset County Asylum. She is married but her husband William is living in Piddle Hinton with their youngest son Henry aged 12.

She obviously made a recovery, as the 1881 census finds her reunited with William and living in Puddletown, and 1891 she is managing on her own as a widow there. The census for 1861 finds her living in Puddletown with the family, but her husband William and son John are both living in Charminster, near Dorchester as boarders, with William's occupation being that of bricklayer journeyman, and another boarder William Holland also being a bricklayer journeyman.

The construction of the Dorset County Lunatic Asylum could have commenced round about this time period as it opened in 1863, so perhaps this was the reason William and other bricklayer journeymen were living in that location then. If that was the case, how ironic Ursula's husband William assisted in the construction of this institution, and a place where her nephew Samuel Hammett was employed many years later. Perhaps Ursula was even admitted in 1870, and met up with her stepmother Elizabeth who died there later that year. Ursula and William had children:-

1) John 1844
2) Sarah 1846
3) Jane 1848
4) Fanny 1849
5) Priscilla/Persila 1851
6) Lucy 1853
7) Henry/Harry 1859

Elizabeth Hammett 1843 although baseborn could have been the natural daughter of William Stroud, her mother's husband, but with no supporting evidence, it can only be assumed. In the 1851 census she does adopt his surname. I have not been able to locate her after this time.

John Stroud 1844 married in 1865 to Charlotte Saint and, like his father, was a bricklayer journeyman. They had a daughter in 1868 named Ursula Mary.

Sarah Stroud 1846 is at home in the censuses for 1851 and 1861 with no more information researched for her.

Jane Stroud 1848 along with her younger sister Priscilla appear to have been adventurous and headed off to the East End of London, perhaps as a result of attending a local hiring fayre. This is where the 1871 census finds them. Jane is living in Oakfield Road, St John Hackney and working as a general servant for a timber merchant and his family.

Fanny Stroud 1849 married George Sargent in 1874. I do like some of the names of the addresses they resided at which were in 1881 Holloway Row, near *Mushroom Bridge* in Fordington. This Holloway Row being an address where other Tolpuddle Hammett relatives lived at over the years. In 1891 *Bleak House*, Cuckolds Row, Fordington, with Cuckolds Row also being another place where Tolpuddle Hammett descendants had lived. This couple do not appear to have had any children.

Priscilla/Persila Stroud 1851 in the 1871 census is found living at Hackney Green, St John Hackney, a domestic servant for a merchant. As she is in the same area as her older sister Jane they most probably left Dorset together in search of work in the London area.

Lucy Stroud 1853 is at home for the 1861 census and in 1871 is residing at Piddletrenthide as a servant housemaid.

Henry/Harry Stroud 1859 is at home for the 1861 census, and in the 1871 one with his father in Piddle Hinton and noted as a bricklayer's labourer.

John 1815-1892

Brother John was born in 1815, and baptised on the 15th October in Tolpuddle. That year Wellington defeated Napoleon at the Battle of Waterloo bringing victory home to England, the miners' safety lamp was invented by Sir Humphrey Davy, and the Corn Law was passed which banned the importing of foreign grain, thus causing the increase of bread prices.

John would end his days just as his older brother James had in the Dorchester Union Workhouse and likewise was buried in the churchyard at Tolpuddle on the 20th February 1892 aged 76, having died on Tuesday the 16th.

Much has been written over the years of his famous older brother James who was one of the six Tolpuddle Martyrs. This includes a suggestion that it was John himself, and not his brother James, who was at the meeting in Tolpuddle on that infamous night which sealed the fate of the Tolpuddle Martyrs. This could be true as there was a John Hammett on the list of names of the members found in a box belonging to George Loveless at the time of the arrests. Also when James gave his 1875 public speech he did say that it was his brother John and not himself who had attended the meeting on that fateful night, with John in the crowd agreeing.

But there is one repeated published fact, which is wholly incorrect, that John was newly married with a baby on the way at the time of the arrests and that is why James took his place. The real truth is John married quite a few years after the Tolpuddle Martyrs were transported in 1834, on the 3rd December 1837, in the parish church at Tolpuddle. It states quite clearly he was a bachelor, of full age, a labourer living in Tolpuddle, his father John a mason. The bride was Elizabeth Brown, a spinster of full age, also of Tolpuddle, her father Christopher Brown a labourer. Their witnesses were William Bullen (possibly the parish clerk as he is the witness at quite a few other marriages in Tolpuddle) and the mark of John Mitchell (presumably John's brother-in-law, who married his sister Sarah, and quite possibly also a member with his name noted in the book belonging to George Loveless). I suspect the source for the story of John having been married at the time of the arrests and with a baby on the way came from William/Billy Hammett, son of James and nephew of John. This is based on an interview he gave to a newspaper whereby he said it was his Uncle John who had been at the meeting in question instead of his father, and whose wife was with child. Therefore his father James took his Uncle John's place in chains. The chain reference probably being a figure of speech, as the six men went freely with the constable to Dorchester, but thereafter were in chains (Daily Herald 29/08/1924 – Trade Union Congress Library).

No previous marriage in the parish records has been found for John, nor any child born previous to this marriage, stating his paternal interest. If his future bride was with child in 1834 she would have been around 16 years old. It is possible she could have miscarried or had a stillborn and thus no recorded entry was made, but this is only speculation. The most likely reason was that James being older never thought for one moment the events would turn out as they did and after a telling off things would go back to normal, but of course they did not.

John's wife Elizabeth Brown was born in 1818 at Athelhampton and died nearly six years before him on the 30th September 1886 aged 69. Her burial in Tolpuddle took place on the 5th October.

Her bible is in the Museum at Tolpuddle with the inscription and notation *In loving memory of John Hammett who died at Tolpuddle Tuesday February 16th 1892 aged 76 years. "I will give you rest" – Matt XI 21. Elizabeth Hammett her book April 1862 Tolpuddle. Prepare to meet thy God.*

John was for the main of his life a bricklayer, with one later census showing him to be a carrier and grocer. This couple spent their years in Tolpuddle raising their family of which eight were born and they were:-

1) Henry 1838
2) Daniel 1840

3) Elizabeth 1842
4) John Christopher 1845
5) Jane Brown 1848
6) Martha Ann 1850-1851
7) Martha Ann 1852
8) Sarah 1855

Henry Hammett 1838 had a short life as he died aged 27 with his burial in Tolpuddle on the 14th April 1866. But before then he did manage to enjoy a few brief years of married life, marrying on the 2nd November 1863 in Tolpuddle to Isabella Riggs (who was baptised in *Tyneham on the 25th December 1840, but born Whitewash, Dorset of Joseph and Mary Ann Riggs). Both Henry and Isabella were noted as being single, he a mason, and her father listed as Joseph Riggs a labourer, witnesses being John Hammett (possibly his father) and Jane Hammett (probably his sister). Isabella was to die young too aged 32 some seven years after Henry, and was buried on the 5th July 1873 in Tolpuddle.

(*The village of Tyneham, not far from Lulworth in Dorset, would later gain fame for being the village which in late 1943, the War Office (MOD – Ministry of Defence) commandeered, along with all the surrounding area for training troops during the Second World War. Some two hundred and fifty-two people were removed and settled elsewhere in the belief that this arrangement was only temporary. In 1948 a compulsory purchase order was made by the MOD and to this day military training is still carried out there. From 1975 the village and pathways were opened up to the public at certain times of the year. The old schoolhouse and church are still intact, with other buildings in various states of disrepair. This ghost village was the setting for Tolpuddle in the 1986 film *Comrades*, which recounts the story of the Tolpuddle Martyrs. Those who have seen the film and are familiar with Tyneham village will recognise the buildings.)

Henry and Isabella do not appear in any censuses together given their brief marriage, nor appear to have had any children. Gleanings from the censuses show Henry mainly lived in Tolpuddle, apart from in 1861 when he lodged with the Grant family in Poole's High

81

Street. After his death, and the last census Isabella appears on, she is living in the Tolpuddle area with her parents.

Daniel Hammett 1840 shared the same birth year as another Dorset lad; the author Thomas Hardy. Daniel married Esther Sansom in 1866. This was to be a fertile liaison with eleven children all born in Winfrith Newburgh, but by 1901 only seven were still alive. They were:-

1) Ada 1867-1868

2) John (Jack) Sansom 1869, married Christine (Cissie) Roberts. No children blessed this marriage. He was a plasterer and builder, lived Weymouth and in later years owned the boats and floats/pleasure boat proprietor at Preston Beach.

3) Frederick 1869. It is possible for a woman to have had two children separately during one year, as I suspect was the case with John (Jack) Sansom and Frederick. Frederick first married Amelia who sadly died in childbirth with their first child Eveline who survived. He then married Louisa Sabina Miles with their children being Hettie Louisa 1905 who lived to be 100, and Esther (Nellie) Ellen 1908.

4) Amy 1871, a domestic cook in 1901 to the Wanhill family in Poole.

5) Beatrice 1873, was a dressmaker.

6) Edith 1874, sadly died young aged 2.

7) Agnes 1876, a domestic servant and still unwed in 1911.

8) Ellen 1877, died young aged 23.

9) William George 1879, known as George. Married Louisa Maria Crumbleholme and within months they were on board The Empress of Britain at Liverpool sailing second class to Saint John in Canada where he put his carpentry skills to use and built a house for them to live in. Within seven years they were back in Weymouth where he too had boats on the seafront like elder brother John. They had two children; William George who died aged 31 and Marjorie who was a tax inspector.

10) Gertrude (Gertie) Fanny 1881, married James Arthur Loosemore. They lived on the Isle of Wight and had daughters Esther Alice and Christine Gertrude.

11) Alice Esther 1885, married Alfred Enos Pike. Sadly she died young, aged 22, possibly in childbirth as in the same quarter of that year in 1907 Hilda Emily Pike was born, possibly her daughter.

Daniel died on the 18th December 1922 in Weymouth, a retired bricklayer who left a will worth £737 14s (in 2012 equated to about £35,464.53). His son John Samson Hammett carried out the administration.

Elizabeth Hammett 1842 never married and like her older brother Henry also had a short life as she died in 1867 aged about 25 and was buried in Tolpuddle.

John (Jack) Christopher Hammett 1845 married Jane Lane in 1870 at Bere Regis, with him being noted as a bricklayer from Tolpuddle and Jane from Shitteron (yes that really is a place not far from Bere Regis). Between the years of 1871 and 1881 they moved from Tolpuddle to the Bournemouth area. Perhaps even at the same time as his second half-cousin John Hammett who was born in 1822, and his son Francis who was born in 1851. All three were in Tolpuddle in 1871 and in 1881 were living in Wyndham Road, Bournemouth as either bricklayers or carpenters. John and Jane do not appear to have had any children and just over thirteen years later (unlucky for some so the saying goes), John died in 1883 aged 38, and was buried at St Clements, Bournemouth on the 9th August 1883.

Jane Brown Hammett 1848. The April of that year saw, in Kennington Park, London, a Chartist rally held with Parliament receiving their petition. Jane's middle name is her mother's maiden name, which was a custom some adopted and when used can make researching family history much easier. She married George Pride Cox in 1867 who had been born in 1843 at Tolpuddle. He appears to mostly have been a miller and a baker, but in later life a porter. From information gleaned on their various census returns they appear to have moved around the country, living in Tolpuddle in Dorset, Norwood and Southall in Middlesex, Slough in Buckinghamshire (in later years it changed coming under Berkshire), and in various places on the Isle of Wight. The 1901 census notes they had eleven children but only nine were alive, and these were the only ones I have been able to account for:-

1) Annie Beatrice born 1868 Tolpuddle.

2) John Henry born 1870 West Cowes, IOW (Isle of Wight).

3) Joseph born 1873 Tolpuddle.

4) Martha Florence born 1875 Tolpuddle.

5) Frederick George born 1877 Norwood.

6) Frank born 1880 Norwood.

7) Catherine Barbara born 1883 Southall. Married Arthur Norman Girling in 1905. 1911 finds the couple out in The Orange Free State in South Africa where he is a Lance Sergeant with No 24 Company Royal Medical Corps as a cook. With the same unit he saw service in WW1.

8) Elizabeth Adelaide born 1884 Slough.

9) George Harold born 1890 Newport, IOW.

Martha Ann Hammett 1852 was named after her older namesake sibling, who had died an infant the previous year, and with her older siblings Elizabeth and Henry who died young, this Martha Ann would also join them as she died, aged just 15, and was buried in Tolpuddle on the 12th December 1867.

Sarah Hammett 1855 was the last child for John Hammett and Elizabeth Brown. Her birth year saw David Livingstone discovered Victoria Falls on his African exploration. Sarah had two baseborn children, the first one at aged 19 was Henry born in 1874 at Tolpuddle. He married Mary Norris in 1894 when he was 20 and, like his father-in-law Frederick, Henry was a bricklayer. In the 1901 census Henry and Mary are living at 21 Harvey's Buildings (now Harvey's Terrace) in Fordington, Dorchester. (This was the same address Mrs Freda Wade who was previously mentioned under James Hammett's son William's section lived as a child in the 1930's). By 1911 they had moved to Bournemouth and had lost one child Albert who was born in 1902, but still had John Henry born 1895 and Frederick Norris born 1902. Sarah Hammett's second baseborn child was Martha Louise born 1880 at Tolpuddle, who appears as a witness to brother Henry's marriage in 1894 at Tolpuddle. Aged 27 years Sarah married Alexander Richard McDonald in Tolpuddle in 1882. He was also 27 and born 1856 Newport, Monmouthshire, and with possible connections to the Scard family in Cerne. There is no indication to suggest Alexander was the father of Sarah's first two children, but they regarded him in that light for when Henry married he noted Alexander as his father. They lived most of their lives in Tolpuddle but later moved to the Poole area, with Alexander passing away in the Christchurch district in 1936. Sarah and Alexander had five children of their own:-

1) Robert John born 1883 was a carpenter who married Alice Eva Stroud in 1901. The couple lived in Tolpuddle and Bere Regis with their children.

2) Christopher Brown born 1887. A journeyman blacksmith, Christopher married Emily Isabel Payne in 1906. They lived in Tolpuddle and Poole with their children.

3) Alice Mabel born 1891-1891.

4) Ernest Harold born 1892. He signed up with the Navy at Portsmouth in 1910 and was discharged in 1921. He served on the Victory, Renown, Thetis and St Vincent vessels, was 5ft 5" tall with hazel eyes, brown hair and a scar on the side of his face (The National Archives ADM/188/1116/110125).

5) Alexander Scard born 1895. In 1911 he was a bricklayer labourer aged 15.

Elizabeth 1816-1907

Sister Elizabeth was born in the May of 1816, at Tolpuddle, and baptised there on the 6th April. That same year saw a huge economic depression as a result of the Napoleonic Wars accompanied by huge job losses and Jane Austin's *Emma* makes an appearance. Vicar Thomas Warren conducted her marriage by banns on the 19th November 1837 at Tolpuddle to Stephen Loveless, who was born in 1816 at Milborne St Andrew of parents John Loveless (1783-1857) and Elizabeth Gover (1794-1829). Their witnesses were John Mitchell (her brother-in-law who married her sister Sarah) and William Bullen.

They had many children, as listed below. Stephen died aged 83 on 13th March 1899 in Tolpuddle and Elizabeth died there too on the 21st November 1907 aged 90 of cardiac failure, with her daughter Anna Riglar present. Stephen's father had a brother William Loveless (1771-1832) who was married in 1796 to Jane Hoare. Their two daughters Elizabeth and Judith married two brothers, John and William Hammett, whose father Richard Hammett was younger half-brother to John Hammett, Elizabeth's father; thus linking back into the Hammett family. Stephen's father John Loveless was first cousin to siblings George, James and Diniah Loveless, two of the Tolpuddle Martyrs, and their sister Dinniah married Thomas Standfield, another Tolpuddle Martyr. Dinniah and Thomas Standfield had a son John, who was also a Tolpuddle Martyr, and a daughter Elizabeth who later married James Brine, another Tolpuddle Martyr.

As Stephen's wife Elizabeth's brother was James Hammett, one of the Tolpuddle Martyrs, the marriage of Stephen Loveless and Elizabeth Hammett connects all six Tolpuddle Martyrs together, although a couple of the marriages took place after the transportations. Therefore anyone descended from Elizabeth and Stephen is related to all six Tolpuddle Martyrs either by blood or marriage. Elizabeth and Stephen lived in Tolpuddle where they brought up their children:-

1) Elizabeth 1837
2) Ursula 1839
3) Stephen 1841-1841
4) Stephen 1842
5) Anna/Hannah 1844
6) Jane 1846
7) Maria 1847
8) Sarah 1849-1849
9) Samuel 1850
10) Sarah 1852
11) James 1854
12) William 1856
13) Emily 1858-1858
14) Mary Ann/Polly 1859

Elizabeth Hammett/Loveless 1837 was baseborn and baptised under the surname of Hammett on the 23rd October 1837, before her parents married, with her mother living at nearby Southover at the time. This same year a new monarch, the young Queen Victoria, ascended to the throne and in the third quarter (July onwards) the registration of births, marriage and deaths is introduced. The latter event was to become a much needed and required resource tool for future family historians. Elizabeth married Edward McGovern (born circa 1836 Lancashire of James McGovern and Mary Doley) at the Parish Church, Woolwich, Kent in 1863 with witnesses Ursula Loveless (her sister) and Charles Baugh. Bride and groom's address was 18 Artillery Place, Greenwich and they probably met back in Dorset, for in 1861 Edward was a gunner with the Royal Horse Artillery section of the army based in Fordington. Elizabeth was with child when she married as in the same quarter their firstborn Henry arrived.

After marrying, they remained for a few years in England. On the 13th July 1869 they set sail with their two young sons on The Young Australian bound for Australia, ironically, to the same part of the world where, some 35 years previously, her uncle along with his comrades from Tolpuddle (her other connected relatives) had been transported. No doubt since those days that country had grown and developed, after all she was going a free woman with her family. The difference in climate no doubt took some getting used to but here they settled and raised their growing family.

In Paddington, Brisbane Edward became a policeman, serving from 1870 until his dismissal on 20th September 1879. He started off well, being promoted on the 28th June 1870 to Constable, then to Senior Constable on 1st July 1875. But he was demoted to Constable again in 1878, before his dismissal. He then did labouring work.

Life did not get any easier for them, as on 26th September 1879 Edward was declared insolvent, due to losing his job, and needed support. Edward died first and was buried 24th October 1895 at Toowong Cemetery, Queensland, Grave No 1, Section 47, Portion 7A. Also in this grave is Elizabeth, who was buried on 14th September 1912, their grandson Thomas Edward McGovern buried 8th May 1897 an infant, and a stillborn McGovern child buried 20th September 1900, more than likely another grandchild. Elizabeth and Edward had children:-

1) Henry Edwin 1863, born Shoreditch, London, married Elizabeth Nelson circa 1884. They had six children who were Mary Elizabeth 1884, Henry 1886, Sarah 1889, Elizabeth 1891, Ivy 1894 and Violet 1896.

2) Samuel William 1868, born Woolwich, buried 1942 Toowong Cemetery with his sister Rose Ann Hayes.

3) Rose Ann 1870, born in Queensland. Married Thomas Martin Hayes circa 1894, and was buried in 1937 with her brother Samuel. She had two children who were Evelyn Maud 1895 and Maurice Edward 1896.

4) Arthur 1873, born in Queensland, unfortunately had a short life dying on the 28th November 1897 aged just 14. He was buried at Hemmant Cemetery, Queensland, Grave No 7, Section 5, Portion A. Arthur was sent to the Reformatory at Signal Hill in the late 1800's, for reasons research has not revealed. An inquest was held whereby it unfolded that a few days previous, on the 25th, Arthur had been put on duty to empty water from a water tank. This water tank sat on a low cart without sides and, whilst leaning over the tank with the bucket to fill, the tank slipped and ended up on top of Arthur. At first he seemed to be unhurt and was able to get up but over the next few days his condition deteriorated, ending with his death on the 28th November 1897. On the same day an autopsy was carried out on Arthur, which uncovered he had suffered fractures of the pelvis and a ruptured bladder. Death was recorded as accidental.

The mention of a reformatory institution would normally conjure up the idea of hardship, going without etc. But the one Arthur resided in, was not like that. It had facilities which were spacious and comfortable, had dormitories, classrooms and a workshop. The scene was more relaxed, given the thinking that treating these boys with kindness and respect would produce a workforce to be proud of. They did indeed work hard, producing a defence stockade surrounding Signal Hill; a good contribution for a boy to add to his working history but sadly not to be the case for Arthur.

5) James 1874, born in Queensland, no more information has been found for him.

6) Thomas Edward 1876, born in Queensland. He married Mary Burke in 1897. They had nine children who were Thomas Edward 1897, Olga Mary circa 1900, Arthur Cedrick, John circa 1902, Leo Ignatius circa 1906, Maurice Reginald Morton circa 1906, Kevin Stanisulaus circa 1908, Andra Mercia Nellie circa 1910, Leonard Patrick circa 1912 and Benedict Louis circa 1914.

7) Elizabeth 1878, born in Queensland, died aged 6 months old, buried Toowong Cemetery Grave No 6, Section 3 Portion 1.

8) Sarah Jane 1880, born in Brisbane. Sarah Jane married Edward James Crickmore in 1906. He was six years younger than her and served in WW1 in the 5/4 Pioneer Battalion. They had nine children who were Charles Edward 1902, Evelyn Maud 1906, Edna May 1908, Mary Elizabeth 1910-1915, Grace Mary 1913, Edward James 1915-1917, Edward Charles 1918, Frederick George 1920 and Walter Henry 1927.

Ursula Loveless 1839, possibly born in the Poole district in 1839, although noted in the census as Tolpuddle where she was baptised on the 19th January 1840. The year of her birth saw the invention of photography by William Fox Talbot and in Australia Edward John Eyre explores that country's interior. (Eyre was the master of James Hammett when he was transported to New South Wales and 1839 was the year James returned back to England from there).

Never marrying, Ursula died at Tolpuddle in the July of 1920 aged 80 from stomach cancer and exhaustion, with Ellen Parker of Tolpuddle by her side. Ursula was noted as a spinster and former domestic housekeeper. She had quite an eventful and interesting life moving around the country.

In 1861 both Ursula and her older sister Elizabeth were working as servants in Dorchester for two families in the same street, with her possibly accompanying Elizabeth to Greenwich where she was a witness at her wedding in 1863.

The 1881 census finds Ursula living and working at 11 Brunswick Villas, Kew Garden Road, Kew for a very well-known and connected family who were the Thiselton-Dyers. (Sir) William Turner Thiselton-Dyer (1842-1928, knighted in 1899) being her employer then and at the time still assistant director at the Royal Botanical Gardens in Kew. A few years later in 1885 he took over as director upon the retirement of his father-in-law Joseph Dalton Hooker who was one of the greatest British botanists and explorers of the 19th century, and close friend of Charles Darwin the famous naturalist. By all accounts Ursula's employer William Thiselton-Dyer had an authoritative nature, which demanded from his employees obedience and loyalty. He also regarded women as inferiors, as Beatrix Potter was to discover when he refused to see her botanical drawings. Perhaps Ursula also encountered this attitude and decided to leave. It is not known how long she worked for him in his household, nor if he was aware of her uncle James and her connection to the other Tolpuddle Martyrs. It is doubtful he would have approved.

The next census of 1891 finds Ursula living and working at The Royal George pub/inn at 1-5 Mackintosh Place, Roath, Cardiff, Wales, a business owned by her brother Samuel.

By 1901 she was on the move again living and working as a housekeeper for the Waterloo Hotel at 6 Waterhouse Parade, Newport, Wales. She was noted as being born in Torpeddle instead of Tolpuddle. This hotel was built in the 1870's and was a pub frequented by dockers. It could boast of having one of the longest bars, which was probably much needed when the dock workers clocked off work and headed for a drink. This hotel was owned by John Williams at that time. Presumably John Williams had sold it by 1911 when he is recorded as a retired hotelkeeper living in a smaller property with his wife. Ursula's work must have been appreciated by them. They appear to have taken her with them, as she is their housekeeper in 1911 at Sea Lawn, Weston-Super-Mare, Axbridge, Somerset.

Stephen Loveless 1842 was married twice, firstly to Hannah Atwell in 1874, who died aged 30 years in 1876. Then he married Elizabeth Thirza Crocker in 1877. Over the various censuses he was a labourer, bricklayer and journeyman builder, living in Tolpuddle, Moor Critchell and in Fordington at School Street, Cuckolds Row, Mill Street and Dukes Avenue. He died aged 80 in 1924. From his first marriage he had two children:-

1) Arthur William 1874, died young like his mother, albeit a year older than her aged 31 in Hampshire and was brought up by paternal grandparents in Tolpuddle and Fordington.

2) Annie Winifred 1876, brought up by maternal grandparents George and Letitia Atwell in Tarrant Hinton. The 1901 census shows her as a domestic kitchen maid living and working at Willesley House, Cranbrook, Ashford in Kent for Lord and Lady Arthur Butler. Lord James Arthur Wellington Foley Butler (1849-1943), although born Littlehampton, the family seat was Kilkenny Castle in Ireland. His wife was 17 years his junior, Ellen Stager whom he

90

married on 8th March 1887. She was born in America, the daughter of General Anson Stager. She had met her very wealthy future husband in London at a ball and then was proposed to at his family's castle in Kilkenny. With such a large household and many servants on the Willesley estate, Annie/Winifred probably never exchanged words with her influential employers, but would had an insight into their world. Annie Winifred married in the Chertsey, Surrey area in 1913 to Ernest G Topple, born Suffolk, who in 1911 was Royal Marine able seaman stationed on board the 1st Class Battleship *Russell* at Malta.

From his second marriage Stephen had three children:-

1) Elizabeth (Bessie) 1877 married Charles Henry Gregory, born 1876 Piddletown. They had eleven children who were Frederick William 1897, Walter John 1898, Nellie Edith 1899, Stephen Charles 1902, Henry Arthur 1903, Leonard 1905, Charles Henry 1906, William Vickers 1909, Edwin Pearsey 1911-1911, Leslie 1912-1913 and Linda May 1915.

2) Nellie 1880 who married Robert Vickers Gregory in 1904. He was brother of her sister Elizabeth's husband Charles. Nellie and Robert had a son Jack in 1904 and Nellie was remembered in her aunt Polly/Mary Ann Hammett's will in 1944 being left two pictures in carved frames and a small glass bell.

3) Hersella (Sella) 1886, married twice like her father, firstly to *William Loveless born Bolton in Lancashire, her first cousin, in 1908 at Fordington. Sadly William, like so many others, lost his life in WW1 and died on 6th June 1915. He was Private 7588, 1st Battalion, Border Regiment, and is remembered on the Helles Memorial in Turkey (Commonwealth War Graves Commission). They had three children who were Arthur William 1909-1909, Reginald William 1912 and Winfred Florence 1914, the latter who was also remembered by Polly/Mary Ann Hammett nee Loveless, her great aunt, in her will by way of being left a buff chest of drawers with pretty colours. Hersella then married Edward Bertie Coates in 1940 at Tolpuddle, a widowed blacksmith, before witnesses Mary Ann Hammett (her aunt) and C F Worth (her son-in-law). There were no children from this marriage. Hersella was noted as Ursula in her aunt Polly/Mary Ann's will of 1944, and was left her house and

91

garden in Tolpuddle (Hoad Cottage 27 Dorchester Road), with a mention that she especially did not want her to sell it, but it was sold not long afterwards. Hersella was also left a picture called *Salmon Fishing*, a small round table and a small glass bell.

Anna/Hannah Loveless 1844 aged just 17 was married to Charles Riggs on the 4th March 1862 at the parish church in Tolpuddle by Vicar George Nash with her father Stephen and her sister Jane as the witnesses. Charles was noted as a labourer of Affpuddle, full age, single and his father George Riggs a labourer. Charles was born and baptised in 1832 at Affpuddle of parents George Riggs and Jane Cake, his father noted as a labourer of Briantspuddle. His parents had married in Affpuddle in 1829 and had other children John 1829, Robert Cake 1833, Ann 1839, William Richard 1837, Elizabeth 1845 and Elias 1843. Charles therefore was some twelve years older than Anna and they appear to have had only one child Jane born 5th March 1862 in Tolpuddle. This was the day after her parents married.

By 1871 Charles does not appear with Anna, although her status was listed as married. On the 1870 birth certificate for her son the father's details are blank and by 1881 Anna stated she was a widow, but no death could be found for Charles. So it is assumed Charles was off the scene for whatever reasons by 1870, or possibly earlier. This conclusion is drawn by the fact that there were no other children for this couple since the year of their marriage and birth of their only assumed child in 1862. In addition Charles does not appear on any censuses with Anna. One could get the feeling that as Anna married Charles the day before their child was born, this marriage could have been one of convenience and for respectability's sake only. In Tolpuddle churchyard there is a headstone for a grave which reads:-

In loving memory of Charles Riggs who died 12th January 1899 aged 52 years. In the midst of life (we seeth?) death. Also of Elizabeth Riggs sister of the above who died 3rd October 1926.

Could this be Charles laid to rest with his sister? The only problem is that would mean Charles was born circa 1847 instead of 1832, and Elizabeth 1848 instead of 1845 (Elizabeth Riggs death noted Dec Q 1926 Dorchester aged 78). Another unsolved mystery.

In 1870 at Tolpuddle Ann gave birth to a baseborn son Samuel Riggs, no father was named on the birth certificate nor in the baptism details at Tolpuddle.

Anna married for a second time in 1906 to Isaac Riglar, a widower. In the 1880's at Tolpuddle he was the local spar maker (thatching). This marriage did not last a decade, as Isaac died in 1914 aged 71, and Anna died herself in 1925 aged 80, given their ages, obviously there were no children from this union.

Isaac already had had quite a few children, for in the 1891 census at Tolpuddle he was noted aged 48 born Powerstock an ag lab, with his wife Mary A 43 born Tolpuddle and their 10 children, Henry 21, Frederick 16, Martha 12, Frank 11, Ada 9, Tom 7, Margaret 6, Ethel 4, Frances 3 and George 2.

From the census entries for Anna, she was a dressmaker and in 1881 Tolpuddle with her two children she lists herself as a widow lodger with Mary Crocker. Also in the same household is Sarah Battrick aged 15 and her mother Harriett Hammett was Anna's first cousin. Anna also appears to have brought up a grandchild Ethel May Eason born in 1888 Mudford Sock (Yeovil), her mother being Jane Riggs, first born of Anna. This granddaughter was also remembered in the will of Polly/Mary Ann Hammett nee Loveless, by way of beds and bedding being left to her great niece. Granddaughters would come to stay with Anna, for whom she would make dresses with beads down the front. These memories made an impression on them, as did the huge bed she had.

When Jane, the only child of Anna and Charles Riggs, married at the Dorchester Registry Office in 1883 to George Easton (Eason) (born 1852 Mudford Sock of parents William Eason and Fanny nee Banfield) she named her father as Robert Riggs deceased. Perhaps this was the story she had been told, certainly a family history mystery which has been hard to unravel, and probably never will be! At the time both bride and groom were living in Holloway Road, Fordington with their witnesses being M Loveless and S Hammett; probably her aunt Mary Ann (Polly) Loveless and Samuel Hammett her mother's cousin (Mary Ann ((Polly)) and Samuel being first cousins who would later marry themselves). Earlier that year Jane

93

had given birth to a baseborn child in the workhouse at Pontypool in Monmouth, Wales, with no father's details given.

Perhaps as her uncle Samuel Loveless was already living in Monmouth, Jane could have been sent there to have her baby, or maybe she left Tolpuddle after the 1881 census was taken and went to work for him in his pub there, and subsequently became with child. Yet another mystery which will never be solved. Her child Kate adopted the name of Eason, went on to marry Thomas William Robinson and had four children. Jane Riggs and George Eason lived in the Yeovil area and had six children:-

1) Samuel Philip 1885, married Rosina Sams in 1909, had two children but only one survived. He died aged 28 serving his country in WW1 on 2nd November 1914 Private 6443 Somerset Light Infantry 1st Battalion (Commonwealth War Graves Commission), remembered in Yeovil on a memorial on the same panel as his distant cousin Conrad Hammett, also remembered on the Barwick and Stoford Memorial in Barwick Church and on panel 3 Ploegsteert Memorial in Belgium. His mother Jane never accepted his death and refused to have his name inscribed on the Yeovil WW1 memorial. This inscription only came about decades later, requested by his daughter and granddaughter.

2) Anna 1886, went to London to become a housekeeper for a doctor whom she became engaged to, but did not get to marry as he sadly died beforehand.

3) Ethel May 1888, was brought up in Tolpuddle by her grandmother Anna as mentioned above. She married Edward Charles Ballam in 1920 and had seven children, two died.

4) Walter 1889, in the 1911 census was a leather dresser for a glove manufacturer.

5) Edwin 1891, was witness at his sister Ethel's marriage in 1920.

6) Florence Georgina 1893. Married Charles Herbert William Arney, had five children, but one died of measles aged 13 months old. Two daughters would later recall visits to Aunt Polly/Mary Ann Hammett nee Loveless in Tolpuddle, with memories of her flagstone floor and rugs, and the well in the back yard where they were sent to draw water by the bucket. But above all, their visits across the road to have a tea of fresh bread and cakes with the baker Albert Miles

who was married to the daughter of their great uncle Samuel Riggs/Loveless who was the baker of Tolpuddle.

Just to confuse matters, Samuel Riggs, the baseborn son of Anna, also used the surname of Loveless. He married twice, first at the Union Chapel, Long Street, Sherborne in 1899 to Lizzie Margaret House (born 1874 Wareham, baptised 26th April 1874 Chaldon Herring, mother Mary Jane, father William), both were single. He was 30, a baker of Milborne St Andrew, Blandford, his father noted as Charles Riggs, a shepherd. Lizzie was 26 of Long Street, Sherborne, her father was William House, a farmer. Witnesses were Richard Rossieter and Mary House (possibly her mother).

Lizzie died in 1901 as Lizzie Margaret Loveless, but buried as Maggie on Saturday 12th October 1901 Chaldon Herring, aged 27. Lizzie or Maggie as she was known, was related to Samuel. They were second cousins once-removed. Lizzie's mother was Mary Jane Hammett born 1848 Tolpuddle, daughter of John Hammett who, along with his brother William Hammett the Methodist preacher, built the Methodist Chapel in Tolpuddle. Samuel and Lizzie/Maggie did not have any children.

Then Samuel married for a second time at the Wesleyan Chapel, Dorchester in 1903 aged 33, a widower, a baker (journeyman), of Milborne St Andrews, his father was given as Charles Riggs (deceased) a shepherd. His bride was Emily Way aged 23 a spinster of 12 Olga Road, Victoria Park, Dorchester, father George Way, a harness maker (journeyman), witnesses were Emma and Albert Way (the latter being her brother born 1885, her mother was Amelia nee David and she had another brother Herbert born 1878). Sadly Samuel was to be a widower again as Emily was buried on the 13th April 1938 in Tolpuddle parish churchyard. She was buried as Loveless, but the parish record said performed notice from Samuel Riggs, widower. How confusing. Samuel died on the 4th April 1945 and is buried with Emily in Tolpuddle. Their headstone reads:-

At rest In loving memory of Emily Loveless who died April 10th 1938 aged 58 years. Also of Samuel Loveless who died April 4th 1945 aged 75 years "Safe in the arms of Jesus".

The Tolpuddle Hammett family were a close intermingled lot, and in 1925 Samuel was listed as one of the sureties on Samuel

Hammett's probate details (son of James Hammett Tolpuddle Martyr, and who was also his mother Anna's first cousin). Samuel was noted on that document as a carrier. He would go into Dorchester with his horse and cart a couple of times a week taking provision orders from the villagers. This was quite remarkable really as he also had a wooden leg. It is not known how he lost it, but probably in an accident.

The other surety on Samuel Hammett's probate details was Albert Miles, the baker and son-in-law of Samuel Riggs/Loveless. He was also a lay preacher and played the cello. Samuel and Emily had two children Violet 1904 and Maggie 1905 who died aged 10. Violet married in 1924 to Albert George Miles, the baker in Tolpuddle and one of the sureties on Samuel Hammett's will in 1925. Violet and Albert had three children. Violet died young, and is buried in Tolpuddle with her younger sister, their headstone reads:-

In loving memory of Violet The beloved wife of Albert George Miles who passed away May 29th 1936 aged 32 years. Also of her sister Maggie who passed away July 1st 1915 aged 10 years.

Albert married again in 1947 to Beatrice M Cuss. They are buried together in Tolpuddle, just behind the grave of his first wife Violet and her sister Maggie and their headstone reads:-

In loving memory of a dear husband and father Albert George Miles died 19th February 1962 aged 61 years. So dearly loved So greatly missed. Also Beatrice Mabel Miles 6th March 1986 aged 80 years.

Jane Loveless 1846 like many other Dorset lasses moved counties in search of work and the 1871 census finds her working as a domestic servant in a household in Kingston-upon-Thames in Surrey. Seven years later in 1878 in the same district she married Arthur Rogers who was born in 1851 Smethcott, Shropshire. The next census, 1881, finds them living in Chiswick in Middlesex where he is a grocer and provisions merchant. Jane became a widow sometime between 1881 and 1891, but appears to have carried on living in the Chiswick area for a few decades. Jane and Arthur had four children:-

1) Arthur 1879, married in about 1901 to Winifred who was born circa 1881 in Bayswater, London. In 1911 they lived in Bognor,

West Sussex where he was a newsagent with their children Evelyn, Lionel and Dorothy.

2) Robert Flory 1880-1880

3) Stephen 1881-1881

4) William Samuel 1882. He made an early family tree, possibly with his mother and Aunt Polly (Mary Ann Hammett nee Loveless) for the 1934 Tolpuddle Martyr celebrations in Dorset. At that time he lived at 100 Commercial Street, Bitterne, Southampton. On the 16th October 1944 he proved his Aunt Polly's will. He was noted as still residing at the same abode and was an electrical engineer. He was the sole executor of that will and, after all expenses and people mentioned therein were honoured, the remainder was to become his property, along with a large glass bell, dining table, suite of arm chair and two small chairs and sofa. I am not sure if he married and had a family.

Maria Loveless 1847, like many Dorset folk, moved northward in search of employment, and was married there at St George's, Birmingham, Warwickshire in 1872 to Richard Hickman. He possibly was born in 1838 Wolverhampton of parents George and Maria. The 1881 census finds them residing at Back 14, House 2, Spencer Street, Birmingham, with Richard an assurance agent. With them is Maria's niece Elizabeth Loveless aged 1, and their daughter Sarah Jane who was born in 1872. She possibly went on to marry John Mosely in 1894 in the Birmingham area.

Samuel Loveless 1850 shared the same birth year as writer Robert Louis Stevenson. Unlike his other Dorset relatives, Samuel did not head northwards, but instead was drawn westwards in search of work to Wales. It was here he was to marry twice, firstly to Susan Moppett in 1879 within the Bristol area. She was born in 1853 in Rottingdean, Sussex of parents William and Sarah. In the 1881 census they were living at the Forge Hammer Inn, Commercial Street in Treventhin, Monmouth, Wales where he was the hotelkeeper (transcribed as Lovelass). This marriage produced three children:-

1) twin Daisy Adelaide E 1882. Married in 1912 to Christopher C Lewis in the Cardiff area, and was mentioned in the will of her Aunt Polly (Mary Ann Hammett nee Loveless) in 1944 when she was left

an old cup and teapot along with all the downstairs mantel pieces. At this time she was living in Llanduff.

2) twin Violet Louise E 1882. Married in the Cardiff area in 1906 to John Lister.

3) Leonard Samuel 1883 (married in the Cardiff area in 1936 to Dorothy M Johnson.

Samuel's first wife Susan died sometime between 1883 and 1890. Then he took a second wife with the same first name who was Susan Nott Burns in the December quarter of 1890 within the Cardiff area. She was born Susan Pugsley Nott in 1843 South Molton, Devon, but baptised in nearby Filleigh on the 30th July that year of parents William and Ann, the father's occupation noted as a valet. Samuel's second wife had been previously married too, to a Mr Burns, producing children from that union who were Beatrice Mary (born 1879), Edith Maria (born 1881, married Benjamin J Owen in 1913 in the Cardiff area) and Nellie Louise (born 1882, married in the Cardiff area in 1926 to Mr Hourahane).

The 1891 census entry finds Samuel and his family, including his sister Ursula and four servants, at The Royal George pub at 1-5 Mackintosh Place in Roath, Cardiff where he is the publican. Whilst this pub was built in 1878, it was only completed in 1891 with Samuel being the first publican there. On Monday 8th June 1891 he put an advertisement for builders to tender for alterations to the pub.

The 1901 and 1911 censuses also find Samuel still residing and working at The Royal George. Samuel's second marriage did not produce any offspring. Samuel died first in 1917 aged 67 and Susan followed in the year 1922 aged 76, both in the Cardiff district.

Sarah Loveless 1852 shared the same birth year as Alice Liddell who was the schoolgirl who inspired Charles Lutwidge Dodgson (otherwise Lewis Carroll) to create *Alice's Adventures in Wonderland*. Unfortunately Sarah was to have a short life as she died on the 11th April 1869 at Tolpuddle aged just 16. The cause of death was unknown, and not certified, with her mother Elizabeth being present at the time of death, giving some comfort to the poor child. Sarah was buried at Tolpuddle four days later on the 15th by the vicar George L Nash.

James Loveless 1854 had the same birth year as writer Oscar Wilde, the year which saw the departure of Florence Nightingale from English shores to care for those in the Crimean War (1854-56). Like his older brother Samuel, James would also marry twice. This was not uncommon in those times, for wives often were to die in either childbirth or from related health problems, and of course with the lack of the advance medication we all enjoy in modern times.

His first bride was Fanny Pearce in Tolpuddle on the 15th June 1876, James was noted as being a policeman from Bolton in Lancashire, and their witnesses were Stephen Loveless and Anna Riggs who were his father and sister. With the Industrial Revolution came boomtowns, of which Bolton was one at the time. Family rumour suggests that James and his younger brother William walked all the way from Tolpuddle in Dorset northwards, presumably being drawn there by the various employment avenues.

By the time of his marriage in 1876 James is stated as being from Bolton, and the following year his brother William married in Leigh, Lancashire. They both were in Tolpuddle in the 1871 census, presumably leaving for the North sometime between then and 1875. The latter date of 1875 was the year James joined the Police Force in the borough of Bolton, on 15th March, being recommended by his previous employer. He was 22, 5ft 8", blue eyes, brown hair, fresh complexion, a labourer/groom. He could read and write. His address given was 2 Tyler Street, Astley Bridge, Sharples, and his last employer Mr Thomas Hanesworth of Haulgh (Bolton). James was also noted as a member of the Oddfellows Friendly Society.

James remained with the Force for 25 years, retiring on the 8th June 1900. They also remained in the Bolton area and are listed in three censuses at the same address, a span of some twenty years or so. He died aged 72 on the 14th July 1926, and was buried on the 19th July 1926 at St Peter's, Halliwell near Bolton, grave 862K with his first wife Fanny (died aged 59 in 1914 her address was 11 Nith Street), his address given was 495 Tonge Moor Road.

Fanny was born in 1853 Briantspuddle, Wareham and knowing what an interwoven lot the Tolpuddle Hammetts were, it came as no surprise to discover Fanny's family would link back into them. Her parents were Thomas Harvey Pearce (1817) and Elizabeth Payne

(1821), who married in Puddletown on the 23rd October 1842. Thomas Harvey Pearce was baptised 30th November 1817 Affpuddle of Ann (nee Harvey) and Richard Pearce, whose older son William (1810-1861/71) was the second husband to Mary (nee Legg 1816-1890) Hammett, widow of William Hammett who was first cousin to James Hammett, Tolpuddle Martyr. Fanny had siblings Emma 1845, Sarah 1849, George 1851, Frederick 1855, Ellen 1858, Louisa 1861 and Alice 1864.

Also Fanny had a baseborn son called Alfred James L Pearce who was born in the March Quarter of 1874 at Briantspuddle. There is no evidence to suggest who the father was, but it probably was James and they took the baby with them to Lancashire. Alfred was in 1891 aged 16 working as a cotton mill piecer. Family rumour suggests he later became a gentleman of the road.

James and Fanny also took in and raised Stephen Loveless. He was the son of William, brother of James and therefore his nephew. This was due to Stephen's mother death. In 1881 the 3 month old baby is with them. After Fanny's death in 1914, James married his housekeeper Alice M Howell in 1923, which was a short marriage for he died three years later. Alice would follow him in 1928 aged 76. Children for James and Fanny were:-

1) Sarah Jane 1878-1880

2) *William (Bill) 1881, who married his first cousin Hersella (Sella) Loveless in 1908 Fordington. As mentioned under her section previously in this chapter, he sadly died in WW1 on the 6th June 1915, is remembered on the Helles Memorial in Turkey, Private 1st Bn Border Regiment. They had three children, see more under Hersella's previous section.

3) Henry (Harry) Hammett 1884, married 1909 to Lydia (Liddie) Whittle born in Parbold, Lancashire. He was an operative spinner in a cotton mill but sadly died young aged 38 in 1922 and was buried on the 24th August 1922 St Peter's, Halliwell, grave 861K with their son Henry who was born 1913 and died aged just one day old, he was buried on the 28th April.

4) Minnie Florence (Sissy) 1887. In the 1901 census was aged 13 and a mill worker. Married in 1909 to Harold Wood, who in 1911

was a wash-house man and Minnie a laundress, they had children Leonard 1913, Ronald 1916 and Phyllis 1919.

5) Elizabeth Maud 1889. In the 1901 census was living 13 Cottingley Springs, Beeston, Leeds with her Aunt Sarah Scott (nee Pearce) her mother's sister and husband Charles, also her cousin William Maidens - the son of her mother's other sister Emma Maidens (nee Pearce), aged 18 born Aldershot, Hampshire, a brickyard labourer. She married Thomas Corbridge in 1908. In 1911 he was a set weigher in the cotton spinning industry, and she a cop winder. They had two children who were Thomas 1909 and Jack 1914.

6) Leonard 1891 was a blacksmith who moved to Bradford working at the Manningham Mills, and in the 1911 census was a side piecer. Married Florence Hanson in 1914, and they had two children Leonard (Len) 1914 and James H D 1919.

7) Mary Ethel 1894. In the 1911 census she worked in a cotton mill as a jack frame tenter. Married 1914 to Thomas W Smethhurst, they had two children Annie F 1914 and Reginald G 1923.

William Loveless 1856 The first year of his life witnessed, in the United States of America, the anti-slavery Republican Party being formed. As mentioned above, William along with his elder brother James (who brought up his son Stephen from his first marriage), according to family rumour walked from Dorset to the North in search of work. He married twice, first to Ann Isherwood in 1877 Leigh Lancashire. Unfortunately she died aged 28 in the March quarter of 1881, which was the same quarter as the birth of their second child, which could have been a factor in her death. From this marriage, the children born were:-

1) Elizabeth 1879. After her mother's death she went to live with her father's sister Maria Hickman, and possibly died aged 3 in 1882.

2) Stephen 1881. Brought up by his father's brother James and his wife Fanny. Aged 20 years and 1 month Stephen signed up on the 11th February 1910 at Preston for service in the 2nd Boer War in South Africa as Private 7499 with the 2nd Volunteer Service Company, The Loyal North Lancashire Regiment. He was noted upon enlistment as a pricer, being 5ft 5½" tall, weight 123lbs, chest 33" when expanded 36", blue eyes, light brown hair with a fresh

complexion, religion Church of England. From 16th March until 15th August 1902 he was on active service in South Africa, being released on the 15th September 1902 (The National Archives WO/97) and awarded The Queen's South Africa medal, clasps Cape Colony (The National Archives WO/100/192). Shortly afterwards he married Edith Lavina Manuel and in the 1911 census is noted as a ring frame jobber in the cotton spinning industry. Stephen died in 1931 aged 50 and was buried on the 7th November in grave 613MG St Peter's Halliwell in Lancashire. Later his wife Edith would join him there on the 26th December 1939 aged 56. They had children Stephen 1904, Eleanor Ann 1907, James 1908 and William George 1910.

William married for a second time in 1882 in the Auckland area of Durham to Mary Morland, and they had children:-

1) Lily 1886, married 1907 to William Lamb. 1911 shows them living at Wheatley Hill, Thornley where he is a coal miner hewer. They went on to have children Robert 1907, Mary 1909, Jane 1911, possibly Elizabeth 1915 and James L 1920-1922.

2) William Ernest 1889, married 1909 to Florence Wilde who died aged 37 in 1923. In 1911 he was a newspaper packer. They went on to have children Edna 1909, Eva 1911, Dorothy 1913, George A 1914 and Tom 1917.

3) Frances Mary 1891-1892

4) Lena 1893, married 1913 to Joseph Martin, they had children Ella 1914 and Thomas W in 1924.

5) James 1895 who, like so many of his generation, was to have his life cut short by serving in WW1. James died aged 20 on the 31st May 1916, and is buried in grave No 637 Dalmeny & Queensferry Cemetery, West Lothian (Commonwealth War Graves Commission). He was Stocker 5900(s) Royal Naval Reserve on HMS Warspite, which was in the 5th Battle Squadron at the Action of Jutland in the North Sea near Denmark. This was the only major naval battle of WW1 and took place from the 31st May to the 1st June 1916. Beforehand, in the 1911 census, he worked at a coal mine.

Mary Ann/Polly Loveless 1859, known more commonly as Polly, was the last child born into the large family of Elizabeth Hammett and Stephen Loveless. Her entrance into the world was in 1859, with Vicar F L Nash baptising her in Tolpuddle on the 25th

December. The same year as her birth saw the death of engineer Isambard Kingdom Brunel and the publication of *The Origins of the Species* by Charles Darwin.

Mary Ann married late in life to her first cousin Samuel Hammett, son of her mother's brother James who was one of the Tolpuddle Martyrs. They married on the 2nd April 1919 at The Prebendal Church of St George, Fordington, Dorchester, with neither of them having been married before. Samuel was 64 years old, a mason and asylum attendant of Charminster, his father James Hammett deceased, a bricklayer. Mary Ann was 58 of 3 East Parade, Fordington, her father Stephen Loveless, a labourer. Their witnesses were Hannah White and Stephen Loveless (most probably her brother, as her father by the same name had died in 1899 which she failed to mention on her marriage certificate).

The marriage was only to last about six and a half years as Samuel died at home in Tolpuddle on the 21st December 1925, with his burial on Christmas Eve at the parish church of St John's in Tolpuddle. He had made a will with a gross value of estate being £460.5.9 (in 2012 equated to approximately £23,682.11), net personal being £240.5.9 (in 2012 equated to approximately £20,892.59) in favour of Mary Ann. They lived in the Church Hill area of Tolpuddle, just opposite the parish church. Church View was her given address in the 1930's.

From photographs of Mary Ann standing in her doorway, in modern times the house identified is the tiled roof property, "Hoad Cottage", 27 Dorchester Road. Next door is "Sweet William Cottage", 29 Dorchester Road, Tolpuddle. Number 29 was one of the thatched Church Hill Cottages, which used two shared wells for water at the back of the properties.

Certainly the house Mary Ann/Polly lived in had water fetched from a well out the back, as several of her great nieces would recall from their childhood visits to her. Mary Ann had once said her father-in-law lived at one time in the cottage next to hers (but not necessarily at the same time). He had also run a night school for the youngsters of Tolpuddle from his home. Perhaps this mentioned home of his was at No 29 next door to hers. Certainly there was a mention of a school in the Church Hill area of Tolpuddle. Perhaps Mary Ann with her teaching skills assisted.

In later years Mary Ann's mind was as sharp as ever, a fact confirmed by family members whose parents knew her well. She was quite strict too, and stood no nonsense, probably from her days as a local schoolmistress and teacher.

Polly certainly was an educated woman, and it was to her the various organisations interested in the Tolpuddle Martyrs would turn in the quest for knowledge about James Hammett, who was not only her father-in-law, but uncle too. She even assisted with the 1934 TUC book of The Martyrs of Tolpuddle. Although, from a local newspaper in 1934 (Bournemouth Times 21/08/1934 – Trade Union Congress Library), it would appear that she had been pestered so much by various folks that she resorted never to be photographed or interviewed again. That was the account one reporter in Tolpuddle gave, and came to be on the receiving end of Mary Anne's frustration. When he knocked on her door, from an upstairs window she said in her Dorset accent that she would not be interviewed, nor photographed, there was nothing on in Tolpuddle that day, but to return the following Friday for the ceremonies "and ketch me if you can".

The reporter also states he spoke to an older woman who was her sister and said that Mary was very deaf and it was no good trying to change her mind. Clearly Mary Ann must have got fed up with reporters and such like knocking on her door, and understandably too.

Mary Ann, it would appear, did not go far, geographically speaking, and seems to have remained in the Tolpuddle area for almost her entire life. She died aged 84 years on the 30th August 1944 at Damers House, Dorchester, which used to be the old workhouse. This is where some of her Hammett relatives had resided and even ended their days, including her uncle James who had been one of the Tolpuddle Martyrs. Mary Ann had suffered myocardial degeneration (I interpret from my medical dictionary this means heart problems), with A Jones, an occupier of Damers House being the informant, possibly a live-in nurse there. Mary Ann was buried in

Tolpuddle on the 4th September 1944. Earlier that year on 6th March, she made a will.

On 16th October 1944 that will was registered with the estate valued at a little over £418 (in 2012 equated to £15,697.12). The sole executor of the will was William Samuel Rogers of 100 Commercial Street, Bitterne, Southampton, Hampshire who was an electrical engineer and Mary Ann's nephew (his mother Jane Loveless born 1846 was her sister). William was listed as being left in the will, a large glass bell, dining table and suite of armchair and two small chairs and sofa. After paying for her funeral expenses and other items left to named persons in her will, anything else was his. Mary Ann was very generous and remembered several of her other relatives in her will.

Her house and garden in Tolpuddle (Hoad Cottage at 27 Dorchester Road) were to be left to her niece Mrs Ursula Coates (Hersella nee Loveless whose father Stephen Loveless 1842 was Mary Ann's brother) of Duke's Avenue, Dorchester, along with a picture Salmon Fishing, a small round table and a small glass bell. It was stipulated in the will by Mary Ann that she did not wish the house to be sold. Despite this it was sold shortly afterwards which caused some ripples within the family. Mary Ann's great niece Winnifred (daughter of Ursula/Hersella Coates mentioned previously) was left a buff chest of drawers with pretty coloured stripes. Left to another niece, Mrs Gregory (sister of the aforementioned Mrs Coates, who was Nellie Gregory nee Loveless whose father was Stephen Loveless 1842 and Mary Ann's brother), two pictures with carved frames and a small glass bell. Great niece Mrs Ballam (Ethel May nee Eason whose grandmother Anna Loveless 1844 was sister to Mary Ann) of 18 Pound Lane, Christchurch was left Mary Ann's beds and bedding. Another niece of Mary Ann's, Mrs Lewis of Llandaff (Adelaide E nee Loveless whose father Samuel Loveless 1850 was Mary Ann's brother), was left a looking glass (mirror), an old cup and teapot and all the downstairs mantel pieces.

Due to her long life and staying in Tolpuddle, Mary Ann seems to have been at the centre of the Hammett/Loveless families. She certainly remembered her sibling's descendants in her will and over the years had been a witness at family weddings. She attended the 1934 celebrations in Tolpuddle, with her name being mentioned in the various associated literature as niece to James Hammett, with photographs appearing too, one in the newspaper of the time. She would have been known to all in the village, and was even remembered in the 21st century by an elderly relative who still lived in Tolpuddle.

Mary Ann was the last link in some respects to those historical times and James Hammett. She would have known him very well, being his niece and later daughter-in-law. At the 1934 celebrations in Tolpuddle, along with James Hammett's only surviving child William, (who was not only her brother-in-law, but cousin), Mary Ann would have jointly been the closest family to James Hammett in attendance.

Later William and Mary Ann would kindly donate various items belonging to her husband and father-in-law to the Trades Union Congress; a bible belonging to Samuel, a framed original photograph of James, an inscribed silver pocket watch and an Illuminated Address awarded to him. Sadly the inscribed silver pocket watch was stolen from the museum in Tolpuddle in January 1989 and, despite a reward and appeals, has not been found. If we could talk to Mary Ann/Polly today, one can only speculate as to the stories and information she could enlighten the listener with.

Anna 1822-1886

Sister Anna was born in 1822 at Tolpuddle and baptised there on the 5th May 1822. That same year Thomas Young and Jean Francois Champollion decode hieroglyphs, using the Rosetta Stone (which the French had discovered in 1799), and the death penalty in Britain is removed for over one hundred crimes. Anna married John Hounsell in Tolpuddle on the 12th October 1840. He was a yeoman, with their respective fathers noted as John a mason for Anna, and Thomas a yeoman for John, witnesses being John Hammett (presumably her father) and William Bullen (who often appears as a witness in the Tolpuddle parish weddings, so possibly a clerk with the Church).

John was born in 1806 Axmouth, Devon and baptised there on 15th June 1806, his parents being Thomas Hounsell and Catherine

Long, who had married in Chardstock, Dorset on the 11th November 1799. John would have about 34 when he married Anna, who was 18, an age difference of some sixteen years between them, and some might say she married well, as he was a yeoman. It would appear Anna was with child when they married, as in the same quarter she gave birth to their son John.

From their census information, they moved around, starting off in Southover near Tolpuddle, Osmington, Puddletown, then Berrow in Worcestershire, finally settling in the Kingsclere area of Hampshire. It is possible there could have been more children for this couple, which I have missed out, as they did not appeared on the various census with the family. They both died aged 64, first John in 1871 Kingsclere, Hampshire, and then Anna in 1886 at the same locality. This couple had children John 1840, Elizabeth 1842, Jane Eleanor 1843, Thomas 1848 and Anna 1865.

John Hounsell 1840 married in 1867 in the Kingsclere area to Jane Rebecca B Hodge. The 'B' possibly stood for Buttress. Jane was rumoured to be his first cousin as her mother Eleanor Hounsell was the younger sister of his father who had married John Hodge. They then went to Canada, with their daughter Jane returning to England. After John died in 1882 Bromley, Kent aged 41, Jane possibly went back to Canada and took the children with her. From the census Jane was born in Colyton, Devon and they lived in Farnborough, Kent. Their children were Harold John 1868, Reginald Thomas 1869, Mabel Henrietta 1871, Edmund Percival 1873, Lionel Charlie 1875 and George Victor 1878.

Elizabeth Hounsell 1842 married 1866 in the Kingsclere area to George Ruddle, born in 1829 and baptised there on the 21st June 1829 at St Mary's of parents Rachel and Robert. This made George some thirteen years older than his wife. They lived on his farm called Harridens at Kingsclere where he employed a few labourers. This couple do not appear to have had any children of their own and George died before Elizabeth in 1905 aged 76, and was buried at St Mary's Kingsclere on the 6th July 1905. Elizabeth died in 1925 in the Romsey district aged 83.

Jane Eleanor Hounsell 1843 was baptised in Osmington, Dorset on the 27th August 1843, and married twenty years later in 1863 at

Kingsclere to Joseph Child who was born circa 1810 in Pangbourne, Berkshire. They only appear together in one census, 1871, where he is listed as a draper by trade and gives his age as 61 and hers as 28, a difference of some thirty-two years, which was quite a large gap in their ages. Moving from Hampshire, they ended up in the Islington area of London after their marriage. This is where the censuses find them with their family and who appear to have been born in that area too.

With such an age gap between this couple, it was a marriage which never was going to make many years, and Joseph died in 1874 in Islington aged 64. They had only been married about eleven years.

In the next census of 1881, I was not able to find Jane but her two sons Joseph and Arthur were both scholars and boarders at The Orphanage, Kingsbury House, Kingsbury in Middlesex. Although not orphans, perhaps after the loss of her husband Jane could not cope. The 1891 census finds her back in Hampshire with her sister Elizabeth Ruddle and 1901 living in the Southampton district on her own.

Rumour suggested she went to the America to be with her son Arthur. It is possible she left Southampton on the 22nd September 1906, sailing on the Philadelphia to New York, and entered at Ellis Island in 1906 aged 63, noted living in Southampton. She also possibly ended her days in 1921 in America.

I was not able to locate her in the 1911 census in England, which further suggests the Ellis Island information with abode having been in Southampton; all indicative of her starting a new life in America. Jane and Joseph Child had children all born in the Islington district who were Eleanor Mary A 1868-1876, Joseph Edward 1869 (possibly died 1884 in the Thanet district aged 14) and Arthur Richard born 1871 (possibly went to America before his mother, on the 21st October 1898 from Southampton to New York, sailing on the Kaiserin Auguste Victoria, with a wife and daughter).

Thomas Hounsell 1848 married 1880 in the Reading area to Eliza Palmer who was born circa 1848 at Beenham, near Reading, Berkshire. Thomas died in 1910, Portsmouth district aged 62, and in 1911 widow Eliza is living in North Southsea and her sister Matilda Purdue is with her. Although it is stated Eliza had had two children who were still alive, I have not been able to locate or confirm this. Eliza died in 1931 in the Portsmouth area aged 88.

Anna Catherine Hounsell 1865 married in 1896 Droxford, Hampshire to George Hooker who was born in 1872 and a fishmonger. They lived in the Southampton area and had children Clement T. E. A. H. 1898, William John 1900-1901, Dorothy circa 1903 and Frank circa 1907.

Part II Chapter 8

FAMILY TREE OF JAMES HAMMETT & SIBLINGS

John Hammett 1775-1823

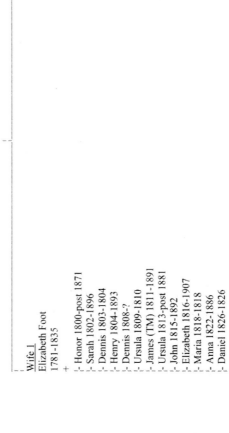

Wife 1
Elizabeth Foot
1781-1835
+

- Honor 1800-post 1871
- Sarah 1802-1896
- Dennis 1803-1804
- Henry 1804-1893
- Dennis 1808-?
- Ursula 1809-1810
- James (TM) 1811-1891
- Ursula 1813-post 1881
- John 1815-1892
- Elizabeth 1816-1907
- Maria 1818-1818
- Anna 1822-1886
- Daniel 1826-1826

Wife 2
Elizabeth Green
1796-1870
+
No issue

FAMILY TREE OF JAMES HAMMETT'S SISTER

Honour Hammett 1800-post 1871

baseborn Rebecca Lucas Hammett 1819-1820

baseborn Samuel Pope Hammett 1822-1884
wed Rebecca Bawcock 1823-1887
They had no issue but she had two baseborn-
George & Jane

wed William Daniels 1803-1875

George Daniels 1825	James Daniels 1829	William Daniels 1831	John Daniels 1833	Alfred Daniels 1835	Elizabeth Daniels 1839
M1: Hannah Gilbert			wed Emma Mary Muston		wed John Ball Roberts

- M1- William 1855

M2:
Elizabeth

John Daniels children:
- Isabella 1858
- William 1859
- John 1860
- Anna 1862-1862
- Frederick 1865-1865
- Alfred 1863
- Clara 1866
- Edwin 1872
- Ellen 1873
- Emma 1876

Elizabeth Daniels children:
- Mary 1865
- John 1867
- Sarah 1871
- James 1873

FAMILY TREE OF JAMES HAMMETT'S SISTER

Sarah Hammett 1802-1896
wed John Mitchell 1807-1841

Daniel 1829 wed Jane Legg
- Mary Jane 1853
- John 1855
- George 1858 wed Elizabeth
- James 1864 wed Marian Salter
  - Millicent 1892
  - George 1894
  - Arthur 1903-1903

Ann 1830

John 1833-1833

Dennis 1834 wed Jane Vincent

Elizabeth 1837 wed George Riggs
- Sarah Ann 1861-67
- Emma Jane 1862
- Mary Louise 1864
- John M 1866
- George Dennis 1868 wed Mary Ann Bennett
- Sarah Ann 1870-72
- Frank 1872 wed Annie Hibberd Wheeler
  - George 1892
  - Bertram 1893
  - Louisa 1894
  - Edwin 1896
  - Charles 1897
  - Edith 1900

John 1840 wed Ann Clark
- John Oliver 1868

FAMILY TREE OF JAMES HAMMETT'S SISTER

Ursula/Priscilla Hammett 1813-1896

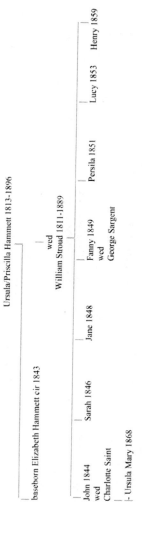

wed
William Stroud 1811-1889

baseborn Elizabeth Hammett cir 1843

John 1844
wed
Charlotte Saint

- Ursula Mary 1868

Sarah 1846

Jane 1848

Fanny 1849
wed
George Sargent

Persila 1851

Lucy 1853

Henry 1859

FAMILY TREE OF JAMES HAMMETT'S BROTHER

John Hammett 1815-1892
wed
Elizabeth Brown 1818-1886

Henry 1838	Daniel 1840	Elizabeth 1842	John 1845	Jane 1848	Martha	Martha	Sarah 1855
wed	wed		wed	wed	1850-1851	1852-1867	
Isabella Riggs	Ether Sansom		Jane Lane	George Pride Cox			

-Ada 1867-1868
-John (Jack) 1869 wed Christine Roberts
-Frederick 1869 wed 1 Amelia wed 2 Louisa Sabina Miles
-Amy 1871
-Beatrice 1873
-Edith 1874
-Agnes 1876
-Ellen 1877
-William George 1879 wed Louisa Maria Crumbleholme
-Gertrude Fanny 1881 wed James Arthur Loosemoore
-Alice Esther 1885 wed Alfred Enos Pike

-Annie Beatrice 1868
-John Henry 1870
-Joseph 1873
-Martha Florence 1875
-Frederick George 1877
-Frank 1880
-Catherine Barbara 1883 wed Arthur Norman Girling
-Elizabeth Adelaide 1884
-George Harold 1890

-baseborn Henry 1874 wed Mary Norris
-baseborn Martha Louise 1880

Alexander Richard McDonald   wed

-Robert John 1883
-Christopher 1887
-Alice 1891-1891
-Ernest 1892
-Alexander Scard 1895

FAMILY TREE OF JAMES HAMMETT'S SISTER

Elizabeth Hammett 1816-1907

wed

Stephen Loveless 1816-1899

- (baseborn) Elizabeth Hammett 1837 wed Edward McGovern
- Ursula Loveless 1839-1920
- Stephen Loveless 1841-1841
- Stephen Loveless 1842 wed 1: Hannah Atwell, wed 2: Elizabeth Thirza Crocker
- Anna/Hannah Loveless 1844 wed 1: Charles Riggs, wed 2: Isaac Riglar
- Jane Loveless 1846 wed Arthur Rogers
- Maria Loveless 1847 wed Richard Hickman
- Sarah Loveless 1849-1849
- Samuel Loveless 1850 wed 1: Susan Moppett, wed 2: Susan Nott Burns
- Sarah Loveless 1852-1869
- James Loveless 1854 wed 1: Fanny Pearce, wed 2: Alice M Howell
- William Loveless 1856 wed 1: Ann Isherwood, wed 2: Edith Lavina Manuel
- Emily Loveless 1858-1858
- Mary Ann (Polly) Loveless 1859 married Samuel Hammett

FAMILY TREE OF JAMES HAMMETT'S SISTER

Anna Hammett 1822-1886
wed
John Hounsell 1806-1871

John 1840 wed Jane Rebecca B Hodge	Elizabeth 1842 wed George Ruddle	Jane 1843 wed Joseph Child	Thomas 1848 wed Eliza Palmer	Anna 1865 wed George Hooker
-Harold 1868		-Eleanor 1868-1876		-Clement 1898
-Reginald 1869		-Joseph 1869-1884		-William 1900-1901
-Mabel 1871		-Arthur 1871		-Dorothy circa 1903
-Edmund 1873				-Frank circa 1907
-Lionel 1875				
-George 1878				

PART II

Chapter 9

JAMES HAMMETT'S PATERNAL GRANDFATHER AND EARLY ANCESTORS

James Hammett's paternal grandfather was William Hammett and head of the Tolpuddle Hammett family tree. He is the first Hammett I have been able to trace residing in Southover or Tolpuddle.

William was baptised on the 9th June 1751 at Bere Regis, the son of William Hammet and his entry into the world fell just within the Reformation and Restoration period (1500–1759). William's parents were married at Bere Regis on the 10th April 1748, with his mother's surname noted as Arnold. To go back any further within the ancestral lines of time for this family and James Hammett Tolpuddle Martyr, I have been unable to find that vital missing piece of the jigsaw. However, below are some pieces which could possibly help fill that void.

Listed in the Protestation returns of 1641-1642 (oath of loyalty to the King, the Civil War would follow in 1642) for the parish of Blandford in Dorset, there is a Daniell Hamatt. Noted in the Hearth Tax of 1664 a Dan Hammett is mentioned, most probably the same one as mentioned above. Perhaps he was an ancestor of ours.

Some research sources have suggested the earliest mention of the Hammett (and variants) surname in England was in Berkshire. Others have suggested the West Country, particularly Cornwall. The latter location is the one I would be in agreement with regarding the joint ancestral roots for both James and myself.

In Cornwall there was the Manor of Hammett at Quethiock, just east of Liskeard, which was owned by the Coryton family. The counties of Dorset and Cornwall were linked by the lawyer Sir John Tregonwell. He was a Cornishman who had served King Henry VIII in his divorce from Catherine of Aragon, and in the dissolution of the monasteries.

Sir John Tregonwell had bought the Abbey and associated lands at Milton/Middleton (Milton Abbey) in 1540 and later rented out the manors at Whitchurch and Whatcombe in Dorset. With his Cornish connections, perhaps Tregonwell was instrumental in the Cornish Hammetts moving to Dorset to work on his newly acquired estates there. This is one possible avenue I could concur with, but have no evidence to support it.

Over the years a village had grown up outside the Abbey gates at Milton/Middleton, but there was a change of ownership in 1752 and this settlement was demolished as it spoilt the vista from the new owner's abode and who wanted to make his estate more private.

The valley situated next to this village was deemed by Sir John Tregonwell to be the new location for this settlement which was a blot on his landscape. Work commenced to make this move and, when finished, it was named Milton Abbas. Nowadays it is a pretty village holding a biannual eighteenth-century street fair with the main road shut off to traffic.

But it was most probably within the old village itself that the ancestors I share with James Hammett married on the 26th June 1721. They were James Arnold and Honor Lovell. I have taken the leap to suggest it was their daughter Honor Arnold, baptised on the 29th May 1724, who at some point moved to Bere Regis. There she was married on the 10th April 1748 in the Church of St John The Baptist to William Hammett. This William could have originated from William Hammet of Blandford who made a will in 1727 (Dorset Archives MIC/R/197 DA6 1727) naming a son called William.

In 1727 William Hammet of Blandford made a will, mentioning his wife Margaret and children William, Rachel and Elizabeth, and also Daniel and Henry (not sure if these last two were his children or his son William's). I have taken the leap of suggesting that the son William mentioned therein could be the father of William Hammett who was baptised in 1751 at Bere Regis and married Honor Arnold there.

The James Arnold mentioned above could possibly have been baptised on the 25th February 1697 at Milton of parents James and

Mary. Now I am not suggesting for one moment that there is a connection (for I have not found one) to the Arnold family linked to Magistrate James Frampton and those of James Hammett Tolpuddle Martyr. But just imagine if there was one, what a story that would tell.

The William Hammett who had married in Bere Regis in 1748 had three children who were John 1749, William 1751 and Elizabeth 1754. William, born in 1751, is both an ancestor for James and myself, with James being descended from one of his sons, and myself from another.

The Arnold family of Bagbere (Bagbeare) in the parish of Milton/Middleton (Milton Abbas) had a manor and farm there from 1570, Richard Arnold being the Lord of the Manor. His roots lay in Monmouthshire with ancestors who were ancient Princes of Wales. Magistrate James Frampton who sealed the fate of the Tolpuddle Martyrs, more than likely had links to these Arnolds, his paternal grandmother was Judith Arnold. Her parents were Henry Arnold and Judith Squibb of Islington (Dorset). Magistrate James Frampton furthermore had likely links to the Tregonwell family mentioned above. His great grandfather William Frampton born 1607 had married Katherine daughter of John Tregonwell of Milton Abbas. Later the Framptons of Moreton would be noted as distant family cousins of T E (Thomas Edward) Lawrence (various internet sites). His father was Thomas Robert Tighe Chapman, 7th Baronet, and their ancestor Benjamin Chapman who had married Anne Tighe in Ireland. How they linked with the Frampton family is unclear. But of course the above can only be used as a suggestion. What is clear and documented, is that William Hammett and Honour Arnold had the following year after their marriage in Bere Regis their first child. John was his name and he was baptised on the 25th January 1749 in the same church his parents had married in. The family appear to have settled in Bere Regis for a few years, with the baptism of a daughter Betty on the 3rd June 1754.

The following year of 1755 would see burials for two members of this family. Firstly on the 20th May for William the father, and then on the 18th December for their daughter Elizabeth (Betty). I have not been able to trace what became of their mother Honor after these events.

It is possible William's elder brother John settled elsewhere in Dorset. He possibly married in Allington, Dorset on the 26th December 1769 to Elizabeth Musgrove. William at some stage would train as a mason (builder), perhaps as a result of William Frampton's Educational Foundation (The National Archives ED/37/39). This was formed in the will of William Frampton Esq in 1687, for the benefit of the poor deserving children resident in any one or more of the parishes of Affpuddle, Moreton and Tonerspuddle. They would be placed as apprentices and afterwards assisted with their trade or occupation.

William later settled in Southover not far from Tolpuddle, and so begun the Hammett of Tolpuddle clan. According to his age at death and burial in Tolpuddle in 1823, he was 73, so born circa 1750. He was buried by Vicar Thomas Warren on the 18th May 1823 and noted as a mason from nearby Southover (a settlement which although had a manor, came under the parish of Tolpuddle, and situated about one mile away in distance).

The earliest Hammett entry in the parish records for Tolpuddle was the baptism of William's son John in 1775, with the mention of William's wife Sarah as mother. I can find no marriage for Sarah and William, so have not been able to progress into Sarah's background. Therefore it is assumed William married Sarah before 1775 (their first born baptised that year) and she died sometime after 11th July 1785 but before 25th December 1786. This is because she was listed as the mother on the baptism details in 1785 for a son James but when he died in 1786, Mary was mentioned as the mother. Mary is also named in a couple of later baptism entries before his marriage to Caroline Riggs in 1800.

On the 14th August 1800 at Dewlish, William married Caroline Riggs. He was stated as being of Tolpuddle and William Vincent was the witness. Caroline was baptised at Dewlish on the 9th April 1775 to parents Robert and Cattern Riggs. Caroline had in later life been admitted to the Dorchester Union Workhouse, perhaps she found life hard after William's death in 1823. She never remarried and some eighteen years after his death she died there, but was buried in

Tolpuddle on the 23rd February 1841 aged 66 by Vicar Thomas Warren.

In 1815 William is living at Southover where he is legally settled according to a legal document concerning his son Richard (more of this document under Richard's life story). It is therefore concluded that William had married three times and had the following children:-

Marriage 1: Sarah

1) John baptised 1st March 1775 Tolpuddle, although the entry in the register stated "John, son of William and Sarah Hamet baptised by Mr Milbourne, as William Hamet declares Thursday October 21st 1794". His baptism was not entered until 1794. John died in 1857 aged 82. This John was the father of James Hammett.

2) Henry baptised 20th July 1777 Tolpuddle. No more information has been found for him.

3) William baptised 12th March 1780 Tolpuddle and possibly again in 1790. He died before 1851.

4) James baptised 3rd November 1781 buried 1782 Tolpuddle.

5) James baptised 11th July 1785, buried 25th December 1786 Tolpuddle.

Marriage 2: Mary

6) Richard born Southover 18th December 1788, baptised 23rd March 1788 Tolpuddle. He died in 1852.

7) John born 10th December 1789, baptised 21st December 1789 Tolpuddle. (Another son called John, not uncommon back in those days.) No more information has been located for him.

Marriage 3: Caroline Riggs

8) James born 7th April 1801, baptised 21st June 1801 at Tolpuddle.

FAMILY TREE OF JAMES HAMMETT'S PATERNAL GRANDFATHER AND EARLY ANCESTORS

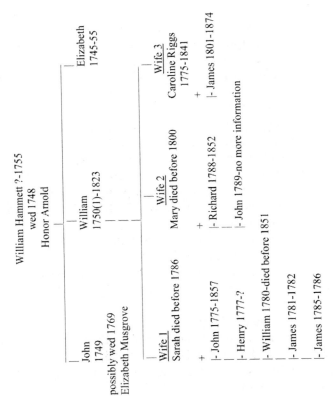

William Hammett ?-1755
wed 1748
Honor Arnold

John
1749
possibly wed 1769
Elizabeth Musgrove

William
1750(1)-1823

Elizabeth
1745-55

Wife 1
Sarah died before 1786

\+

- John 1775-1857
- Henry 1777-?
- William 1780-died before 1851
- James 1781-1782
- James 1785-1786

Wife 2
Mary died before 1800

\+

- Richard 1788-1852
- John 1789-no more information

Wife 3
Caroline Riggs
1775-1841

\+

- James 1801-1874

Front entrance to The National Archives (TNA) Kew

At times my second home
an establishment offering a wealth of historical information
for which I am eternally grateful

Photograph courtesy of Kevin McMahon

Badges commemorating the Tolpuddle Martyrs

Photographs courtesy of Kevin McMahon

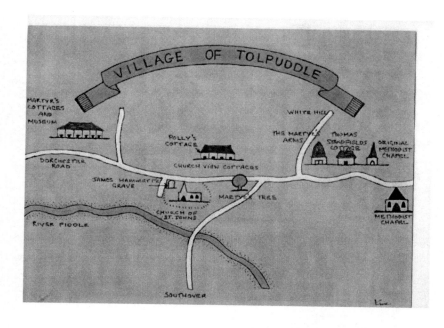

Photographs courtesy of Kevin McMahon

Tolpuddle

Church View Cottages, Martyrs Inn (previously The Crown Inn), Old School/Village Hall

Photographs courtesy of Kevin McMahon

Tolpuddle

Martyrs bench, tree and plaque
Manor House with church visible behind

Photographs courtesy of Kevin McMahon

**Tolpuddle Martyrs Museum
And Memorial Cottages**

Photographs courtesy of Kevin McMahon

Tolpuddle Martyrs Museum
And Memorial Cottages

Each of the six Memorial Cottages is numbered and named after one of the Tolpuddle
Martyrs. Number one is in honour of James Hammett and above one of the windows also has
his name plaque.

Photographs courtesy of Kevin McMahon

Tolpuddle Martyrs Museum
And Memorial Cottages

Martyrs sculpture made of Portland stone from Dorset by Thompson Dagnall at his Lancashire workshop, then transported back to Dorset. Central figure is that of George Loveless, leader of the Tolpuddle Martyrs. The six pillars representing each Tolpuddle Martyr, with the back being inscribed with their name along with a line from the poem *We Will Be Free* by George Loveless. Students from Weymouth College carved and engraved these pillars. Perhaps these pillars being symbolic of the pillar of truth

Photographs courtesy of Kevin McMahon

Tolpuddle Martyrs

Thomas Standfield's cottage where in the upper room members of the Friendly Society of agricultural labourers would meet

Photographs courtesy of Kevin McMahon

Dorchester Court House

First photograph taken from angle the relatives would have seen
Second photograph with three mock men is where the Tolpuddle Martyrs would have stood

Photographs courtesy of Kevin McMahon

Cell under Dorchester Court House

This was where the Tolpuddle Martyrs were held along with other prisoners

Photographs courtesy of Kevin McMahon

134

St Nicholas Churchyard, Studland
Headstone of Sergeant William Lawrence
(brother-in-law of Edward Legg – Tolpuddle Martyr informer)

To the honoured memory of Sergeant William Lawrence of the 40th Regiment Foot who after a long and eventful life in the service of his country peacefully ended his days at Studland November 11th 1869. He served with his distinguished Regiment in the war in South America 1805 and through the whole of the Peninsular War 1808-13. He received a silver medal and no less than ten clasps for the battles in which he was engaged ROLEIA – VIMIERA – TALAVERA – CIUDAD RODRIGO – BADAJOZ (in which desperate assault being one of the volunteers for the forlorn hope he was most severely wounded) –VITTORIA – PYRENEES – NIVELLES – ORTHES – TOULOUSE. He also fought in the glorious victory of WATERLOO June 18th 1815. While serving with his Regiment during the Occupation of Paris by the Allied Armies Sergeant Lawrence married Chlotilde Clairet at St Germain-en-Laye who died September 26th 1853 and was buried beneath this spot.

On the reverse of this headstone is the dedication to his wife with whom he is buried
Ci-git Clotilde Lawrence nee a St Germain-en-Laye France decedee a Studland 26 Septembre 1853

Photographs courtesy of Kevin McMahon

135

Historic waterfront Barbican area of Plymouth

The John Barry arrived here on Saturday 17th March 1838 (although the nearby plaque on the wall differs citing the 18th) bringing home from NSW (New South Wales, Australia) four of the Tolpuddle Martyrs; John and Thomas Standfield, James Brine and James Loveless. Close by is The Admiral MacBride public house, viewable to the four returning men, and an establishment possibly visited by them with John Putt being the licensee 1830-1864

Photographs courtesy of Kevin McMahon

St Andrew's Church, Greenstead, Essex
(the oldest wooden church in the world)

Reverend Philip W Ray was the parson here who made the Tolpuddle Martyrs unwelcome

This old church, in its simplicity and dignity, symbolises the primitive church of early Christian times and is the forerunner of the great cathedrals and churches of Norman and later epochs, which were not infrequently built on the sites of similar Saxon churches.

Photographs courtesy of Kevin McMahon

St Andrew's Church, Greenstead, Essex
(the oldest wooden church in the world)

Interior of the church both front and back
where on the 20th June 1839 James Brine, Tolpuddle Martyr married Elizabeth Standfield

Photographs courtesy of Kevin McMahon

138

New plaque is unveiled on the Clock Tower, Caledonian Park beside another and the family banner makes a first appearance in public

Photographs courtesy of Kevin McMahon

139

Tolpuddle KX event – 175th anniversary of the Grand Demonstration of 1834

Islington Mayor Stefan Kasprzyk with a descendant and relatives of the Tolpuddle Martyrs
in Edward Square and the Islington Trades Union Council banner

Photographs courtesy of Kevin McMahon

Islington Police Station, Tolpuddle Street

A few of the relatives could not resist this location on the weekend of Tolpuddle KX
Back in Tolpuldde at the Museum shop a framed collage and a list of contributors to the
family marching banner for the Tolpuddle Martyrs

BANNER CONTRIBUTORS

Glenda Alner
Clive Austin
Ian Austin
Len & Mary Austin
Edna Boniface
Kathy Claxton
Pam Collins
Vera Dunning
Barbara Dyer
Nari Fairbanks
Kath Gerault
Anthony Hammett
Wendy Lawrence
Wendy & Arthur Lepine
Enid McEvoy
Sally & Kevin McMahon
Margi Miller
Dawn Stewart
Olive Theobald
Marilyn Wass
Hazel Werner
Jed Werner
Russ Werner
Fred Worth

Photographs courtesy of Kevin McMahon

Edward Square, Kings Cross, London

Wall mural remembering the Grand Demonstration of 1834

Photographs courtesy of Kevin McMahon

Wall mural dedicated to the events of 1834 Copenhagen Fields

By Dave Bangs and opened in 1984

Lisa Pontecorvo is remembered in this mural by holding the sign – she led a campaign to clear the then derelict Edward Square and transform it. In 2008 she died aged 64 from an accident on the Holloway Road.

Photograph courtesy of Kevin McMahon

The Dorset Estate, Bethnal Green, London
Social Housing Estate

Robert Owen - Britain's first Socialist, of the Grand National Consolidated Trades Union
Arthur Wade clergyman headed up the Grand Demonstration with Robert Owen

Photographs courtesy of Kevin McMahon

The Dorset Estate, Bethnal Green, London
Social Housing Estate

Photographs courtesy of Kevin McMahon

<u>The Dorset Estate, Bethnal Green, London</u>
<u>Social Housing Estate</u>

James Hammett House

Photographs courtesy of Kevin McMahon

James Hammett TPM

Connected places of worship:-

St John the Baptist Church, Bere Regis — where his great grandparents Elizabeth Arnold and William Hammett were married in 1748 and where his grandfather William Hammett was baptised in 1751.

St John the Evangelist Church Tolpuddle — where James was baptised, married and buried, just as many of his relatives and neighbours were too.

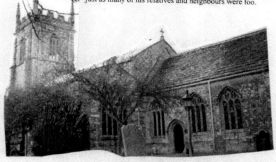

Photographs courtesy of Kevin McMahon

Original artwork by and courtesy of Kevin McMahon

James Hammett TPM

Sweet William, 29 Dorchester Road, Tolpuddle, thatched cottages known as Church View
according to his niece and daughter-in-law Mary Ann (Polly) Hammett
he once lived there, after his death she would live with his son Samuel next door at Hoad
Cottage No 27

Photographs courtesy of Kevin McMahon

149

James Hammett TPM

In the 1881 census he lived at White Hill
Signage in Tolpuddle churchyard to his grave

Photographs courtesy of Kevin McMahon

James Hammett TPM's descendants

Headstones of Sarah Trevett nee Battrick 1866-1898, granddaughter of James Hammett's
buried with her half-sister Alice Martha King nee Battrick born 1876
in the churchyard of Holy Trinity Church, Binscombe, Dorset
and that of
David Trevett 1826-1906, father-in-law of Sarah Battrick
buried St John's churchyard Tolpuddle

Photographs courtesy of Kevin McMahon

<u>**James Hammett TPM's niece and daughter-in-law**</u>

Mary Ann (Polly) Hammett nee Loveless lived with her husband/first cousin (son of James)
Samuel at Hoad Cottage 27 Dorchester Road, Tolpuddle
2009 blue door, 2010 green door and according to her next door (black door) was one time
home of James

Photographs courtesy of Kevin McMahon

James Hammett TPM sister Elizabeth's descendants

Headstones in St John the Evangelist churchyard, Tolpuddle

In loving memory of Charles Riggs who died 12th January 1899 aged 52 years. In the midst of life we seeth death. Also of Elizabeth Riggs sister of the above who died 3rd October 1926.
(Charles above was possibly the husband of Anna Loveless)
At rest in loving memory of Emily Loveless who died April 10th 1938 aged 58 years also of Samuel Loveless who died April 4th 1945 aged 75 years. "Safe in the arms of Jesus"
(Samuel was the baseborn child of Anna, who was buried here with second wife Emily.
Behind their headstone is that for James Hammett TPM, and to the top right that of Samuel's two daughters Violet Miles and Maggie Riggs)

Photographs courtesy of Kevin McMahon

153

James Hammett TPM sister Elizabeth's descendants

Headstones in St John the Evangelist churchyard, Tolpuddle

In loving memory of Violet The beloved wife of Albert George Miles who passed away May 29th 1936 aged 32 years also her sister Maggie who passed away July 1st 1915 aged 10 years (both daughters of Samuel Riggs/Loveless and behind their headstone is that of Violet's husband Albert George Miles and his second wife Beatrice Mabel Miles nee Cuss)
In loving memory of a dear husband and father Albert George Miles died February 19th 1962 aged 61 years so dearly loved so dearly missed also Beatrice Mabel Miles 6th March 1986 aged 80

Photographs courtesy of Kevin McMahon

154

James Hammett TPM brother John's descendants

Home to Henry Hammett in 1901
(home to Mrs Freda Wade in 1929 whose mother knew William Hammett, son of James TPM)

Photographs courtesy of Kevin McMahon

James Hammett TPM's uncle William's descendants

Sarah Fellowes nee Hammett born 1851, her daughter Sarah West nee Fellowes and later in life with her husband William, daughter Rita and granddaughter Sarah

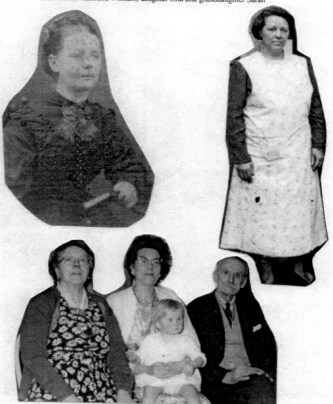

Photographs courtesy of West family collection

James Hammett TPM's uncle William's descendants

George (Gordon) Fellowes 1896-1962
seemingly had nine lives, here in this signed photograph
he aptly poses with a feline friend

Photograph courtesy of Angela McCormick

James Hammett TPM's sister Elizabeth and uncle William's descendants

S P Eason (Samuel Phillip Eason) – descendant of Elizabeth Loveless nee Hammett
and distant cousin
Conrad Hammett – descendant of William Hammett
Remembered on war memorial in Yeovil, Somerset

Photographs courtesy of Kevin McMahon

James Hammett TPM uncle Richard's descendants

Original Methodist Chapel
Second Methodist Chapel built by brothers William and John Hammett, with the former being a preacher within that circuit for 62 years

Photographs courtesy of Kevin McMahon

<u>**James Hammett TPM uncle Richard's descendants**</u>

Second Methodist Chapel built by brothers William and John Hammett, with panels either side of the entrance porch which were added later in 1912

Photographs courtesy of Kevin McMahon

James Hammett TPM uncle Richard's descendants

Entrance to second Methodist Chapel built by brothers William and John Hammett and internal wall scroll dedicated to William

Photographs courtesy of Kevin McMahon

James Hammett TPM uncle Richard's descendants

Headstones in front of second Methodist Chapel – William and Judith Hammett next to stone scroll for their daughters Sarah and Clara, and on opposite side is that for their daughter Jane Puckett beside her two daughters Margaret and Clara

Photographs courtesy of Kevin McMahon

162

James Hammett TPM's uncle Richard's descendants

Hammetts House, Main Road, Tolpuddle home of sisters Sarah and Clara Hammett
and later that of their nephew William Jabez Seth Puckett and his family

Photographs courtesy of Kevin McMahon

James Hammett TPM's uncle Richard's descendants

Jacob Gibbons (married to a descendant of Richard's)
Methodist Chapel, Studland (no longer a chapel as sold into private hands)
with plaque on side wall dedicated to Jacob Gibbons

Photographs courtesy of Kevin McMahon

New resting place for the plaque of Jacob Gibbons (married to a descendant of Richard's)
after the removal from the Methodist Chapel, Studland to St Nicholas Churchyard, Studland
which lays beside that of his son Arthur Gibbons and his wife Susan and reads
In loving memory of Arthur Gibbons 1916-2000
Susan Gibbons 1917-2006

Photographs courtesy of Kevin McMahon

James Hammett TPM's uncle Richard's descendants

Jacob Gibbons (married to a descendant of Richard's) sent a postcard from the Titanic to
Kate Payne of 26 The Green, Studland
second photograph shows this property on the far left behind the trees with attached
neighbouring cottages

Photographs courtesy of Kevin McMahon

James Hammett TPM uncle Richard's descendants

Buried in St John the Evangelist churchyard, Tolpuddle
To the memory of
Joseph
Son of John and Elizabeth Hammett
Who died November 29th 1855
Aged 8 months
He shall gather the lambs with his arm
Also carry them in his bosom

Photographs courtesy of Kevin McMahon

James Hammett TPM's uncle Richard's descendants

St Nicholas, East Chaldon, Dorset – Mary Jane House nee Hammett and husband William's upright headstone, and in front badly corroded one for their daughter Eva

Photographs courtesy of Kevin McMahon

James Hammett TPM uncle Richard's descendants

Buried in St John the Evangelist churchyard, Tolpuddle
*In memory of Francis Hammett who died April 4th 1849 aged 26 years.
Also Jane his wife who died July 24th 1868 aged 46 years.
This stone is erected by their only child.*

Photograph courtesy of Kevin McMahon

Tolpuddle Martyrs Festival

2007 descendants and relatives of James Hammett beside his grave
2009 descendants and relatives of James Hammett outside Dorchester Court House

Photographs courtesy of Kevin McMahon

Tolpuddle Martyrs Festival

2010 Tolpuddle Martyr relatives with family banner and Billy Bragg
also Unite the Union banner on the march

Photographs courtesy of Kevin McMahon

Tolpuddle Martyrs Festival

2013 Tony Benn waits to lay a wreath on James Hammett's grave, wreath from the relatives which reads *In memory of 6 courageous Martyrs from all the relatives* – 6 roses representing each man, relative to all these 6 men Fred waits behind Francis O'Grady TUC General Secretary to lay this wreath and the relatives on the march with the family banner and Canadian flag in memory of those Martyrs who went to Canada

Photographs courtesy of Kevin McMahon

Hammett/Loveless Family History Day 2010

Relatives with Mrs Freda Wade outside the 200 year old cottage William Hammett, son of James TPM called home in Fordington where in 1934 with her grandmother they spoke to William

Photographs courtesy of Kevin McMahon

Hammett/Loveless Family History Day 2010

Photographs courtesy of Kevin McMahon

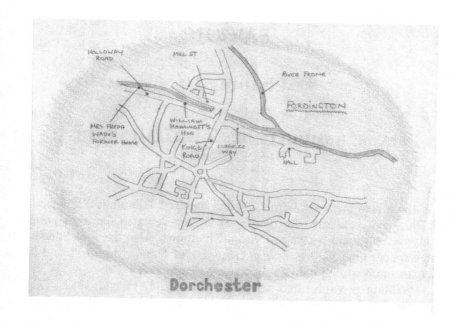

HOLLOWAY ROAD

MILL ST

RIVER FROME

FORDINGTON

MRS FREDA WADE'S FORMER HOME

WILLIAM HAMMETT'S HSE

KINGS ROAD

LUBBECKE WAY

HALL

Dorchester

PART II

Chapter 10

JAMES HAMMETT'S UNCLE WILLIAM AND HIS DESCENDANTS

William Hammett was born 1780 and baptised Tolpuddle 12th March 1780. That year saw the people of Britain react to the high taxes imposed on them by way of various petitions. Also the first Sunday newspaper arrived, *The British Gazette and Sunday Monitor*, and in Japan sumo wrestling in public made an entrance.

William possibly died sometime between 1841 and 1851. This conclusion has been drawn, as according to his son's marriage certificate in 1841 he was not noted as deceased, although this could of course have been an oversight. Also on the census for 1851 his wife Sarah was listed as a widow. But then again, it is possible he died before 1837 as I have not been able to find any children born to this couple after 1818. I have frustratingly not been able to find a death for him between the years either.

William married Sarah Pearce/Pearse in the parish church at Tolpuddle on the 14th August 1810, their witnesses being James Vye Roper and Samuel Bullen. William was a mason like his father William (whom he was more than likely named in honour of) and other Hammett relatives, and lived at Southover, just down the lane from Tolpuddle. He could have been the William Hammett listed as serving in the East Dorset Militia between the years 1808-1812 (The National Archives WO/13/3462). His father would have been too old then to serve and, from the information I have collected on other Dorset Hammett families, none have a William who could have been serving then.

His wife Sarah, or Sally as she sometimes was known, was born in 1782 (according to the 1851 census in Tolpuddle), baptised 24th February 1782 in the parish church in Tolpuddle, parents James and

Betty. Her father was a carpenter and the family lived at Southover, which is where she probably knew William from.

Both the Hammett and Pearce families were living at Southover in 1804. William's father William a bricklayer had three males and one female listed for his household there. Whilst Sarah's father James Pearse, a carpenter, had two males and nine females in his household. Unfortunately they are not listed by name.

Her father James Pearce was buried in Tolpuddle by Vicar Thomas Warren on the 8th February 1817 aged 63, and was noted as living at Southover. Her mother Elizabeth was also buried there by Vicar Thomas Warren on 16th May 1821 aged 65, and also noted as living at Southover.

Sarah died as Sarah Hammett in 1860 and but was buried as Sally Hammett in Tolpuddle on the 12th June that year aged 78 by Vicar George L Nash. She had died three days previously on the 9th in Tolpuddle of natural decay, which does not sound pleasant. The informant who was also present at death was Ann Loveless.

This lady could have been the same one, who a year later in the census at Tolpuddle is listed as a widow aged 78 born Wimborne and a former farm servant. Perhaps these two elderly widowed ladies being on their own with their husbands both dead, and various family members having taken their own paths in life, then decided to share an abode for joint company and to cut living costs.

In the 1851 census Sarah was noted as living at Brick Kilns, Hanger Hill, Binegar, East Stoke, Dorset aged 62, a widow born Tolpuddle, living with her son James and his family. William and Sarah had three known children, all born at Southover who were Sarah 1812, William 1815 and James 1818.

Sarah Hammett 1812-1883

Sarah, daughter of William 1780, was born in 1812 and baptised in Tolpuddle on the 22nd March that year. Her birth year was shared with Charles Dickens. The same year saw Britain at war with the United States, which would last until 1814, and the Elgin Marbles arrive in Britain from Athens. Sarah was more than likely named after her mother, and married on the 9th August 1835 at Tolpuddle to William Mayne (Maine) who was born circa 1807-1811

177

Hilton/Cranborne Dorset. Both put their marks of an X. William was noted as being from Toners Piddle (Turners Puddle), and their witnesses were Samuel Bullen and David Legg (*), the latter who also put his mark of an X.

William died (March Q 1864 Dorchester) on the 6th January 1864 at the Dorset County Hospital aged 56 from an infection from having his leg amputated, which was so often the case in those days. Sarah then seems to have gone North with her daughter Elizabeth and her family, just as so many other Dorset folk at the time did in search of work in the mills and such like, which the industrial revolution had opened up. Sarah died aged 70 in the first three months of 1883 in the Stockport district of Lancashire.

I have made mention of this man David Legg and the Legg/Pearse families as they tie in with this Tolpuddle Hammett descended family.

*David Legg was born 1791 Athelhampton and had a younger brother Charles 1796, who married a widower Elizabeth Paine 1831 Athelhampton, who already had a daughter also called Elizabeth Paine, who subsequently in 1842 at Puddletown married Thomas Harvey Pearce born 1817. His father was Richard Pearce (possibly related to Sarah Hammett's mother), who also had a son William in 1810.

Now these two sons connect to the Tolpuddle Hammetts. Firstly William married Mary Hammett nee Legg, the widow of William Hammett who was younger brother of Sarah Hammett 1812 in this chapter. Thomas Pearce had a daughter Fanny who married James Loveless, nephew of James Hammett Tolpuddle Martyr, and mentioned in a previous chapter. Mary Hammett nee Legg mentioned above was born 1816 Affpuddle and had a brother Richard Legg born 1813 Affpuddle. His son Herbert Legg, born 1843 married Elizabeth Maine who was the daughter of Sarah Hammett 1812.

I have tried to explain these various connections within a family tree diagram at the end of this chapter. This illustrates how close family ties were in some parts of Dorset in those days, before a time when people started to move around the country in search of work, or to shores further a field in the world at large.

In the 1841 census Sarah and her family lived in Piddletown, the next one of 1851 at Arne in the Wareham area, and the following on in 1861 at Turnerspuddle. I have not been able to locate them in the 1871 census, but in 1881 Sarah is living Heaton Norris in Lancashire. She is aged 69 born Topiela (which should read Tolpuddle), a widower with her daughter Jane Sexey (yes that really is her married name) and her family. Sarah Hammett and William Maine's marriage produced children, Mary 1837/38, James 1840, Elizabeth 1846 and Jane 1851.

Mary Maine 1837/38 The year of 1837 also saw the death of painter John Constable and the opening of London's first railway station at Euston. Mary married William George Lumber in 1862 who was born in 1841 to parents George and Rebecca. Through the census they lived in Dorset where he was a shepherd, and Mary died in 1913 aged 74 and William the next year aged 73. Their children were:-

1) Emily Jane Maine 1864, not baseborn but just given her mother's maiden name as an additional Christian name. She possibly married in either 1891 or 1893.

2) William Henry 1866, married 1890 to Lois Meaden. They had issue Sarah Louise 1890, Edith Emily 1891, William James 1894, Sidney Herbert 1897.

3) Edward George 1868, married 1890 Emily Elizabeth Gould nee Trim who already had children of her own. She then went on to have issue with Edward who were Alice, May and George. Edward was a sewer labourer, not a nice job but someone has to do it.

4) Sarah Elizabeth 1871, married 1893 Richard Massey born 1869 Congleton, Buiddulp, Staffordshire. From the mid to late 1890's they lived in Hanley, Staffordshire, where in 1850 Edward Smith, Captain of the Titanic, was born. In a later chapter of this book, Jacob Gibbons who married into the Hammett/Puckett family was a steward on the Titanic, and one of the fortunate ones, as he survived.

Richard Massey had a Botanical Brewery/mineral water factory at Forest Road, Hugglescote, but then subsequently moved this business to 36 Castle Street, Whitwick, Coalville, Leicestershire in

1916. Coalville was a mining town, and so named after the home of the owner of the Whitwick colliery which was Coalville House.

Sarah died aged 55 on 4th July 1926 at home 36 Castle Street, Whitwick, Leicestershire. She left effects at a gross value of £393 (in 2012 equated to £20,342.52), husband Richard Massey, mineral water manufacturer was given administration.

Richard died aged 65 on 15th November 1933 also at home at 36 Castle Street. His effects were predictably worth more than Sarah's, gross value being £1,047 1s 1d (in 2012 equated to £63,456.15). His probate was granted on the 30th December 1933 to executors Joseph Massey, mineral water manufacturer of 111 Loughborough Road, Whitwick, and Walter Massey, salesman, of The Compass Inn, Loughborough Road, Whitwick. These two individuals were Richard and Sarah's sons.

In his will Richard wished for his sons Richard and Harry James to receive £25 each (2012 equated to £1,515.18) and if any funds were left after expenses, then daughter Emily was to receive £100 (2012 equated to £6,060.75), which at time of will writing were invested in the premises at 36 Castle Street.

The Massey's Botanic Brewery was to be carried on in equal shares by children Joseph, Walter and Sarah Elizabeth. Daughter Emily was to be looked after until the age of 21 from funds from the business. Household items were to be equally divided between the four children. The exceptions being, the old china tea service to be given to Sarah Elizabeth, the unbreakable tea set to Edward, the blue service to Joseph, the large photo of their mother to Walter and the photo of himself to Emily. The two remaining burial graves at Whitwick Cemetery were to be used by the first two children who required them. Emily was also to receive a sewing machine and fittings.

The three children, Walter, Sarah and Edward ran Massey's Botanical Brewery until it was dissolved on the 31st December 1946 (The National Archives - The London Gazette 14/02/1947). Sarah and Richard had had eight children.

The first was William George 1896 who enlisted at Coalville on the 17th August 1914 to serve his county in WW1 as Private 2512 with the 1/5th Battalion Royal Leicestershire Regiment. He was noted as aged 18 years and 7 months, and a waggoner. His medical examination showed him to be 5ft 9½" tall, weighing 143lbs (10 stone 3lbs), chest 35½" with an expansion of 2½", brown eyes, black hair with a fresh complexion. His religion was Church of England. From enlistment until the 25th June 1915 he remained on home ground (The National Archives & Ancestry).

Then he sailed on the S.S. St. Petersburgh from Southampton, arriving at Rouen the next day. His parents Richard and Sarah E Massey were listed on the 30th May 1919 as living at 36 Castle Street, Whitwick, Leicestershire. He was one of the "Famous Fifty" which were a group of men originating from the Coalville area, who all joined up at the same time, and fought together. William was not one of the lucky ones. He died on the 9th August 1915 from a shot in the head whilst on sentry duty (Whitwick Community Information). William had served his country just 326 days. His father accepted in 1919 the receipt of his medals, the 1914-15 Star and Victory, along with the plaque and scroll. Any personal property of his was also forwarded on to Richard.

Other children for Richard and Sarah were Joseph 1897, Sarah Elizabeth 1899, Walter 1902, Richard 1903, Edward 1908, James Harry (Harry James) born circa 1910 and Emily 1918.

5) Walter James 1873, married twice. First in 1899 to Ellen Louisa Stevens who was born in 1869 at Wool of parents Joseph and Eliza. This marriage did not produce any children, and Ellen died in 1912 aged just 42. Walter then married for a second time in 1916 to Jane Attwood. They appear to have had two children called Walter and Eileen. Walter died in 1928 in the Wareham district aged 54.

Elizabeth Maine 1846 That year also saw the birth of the Irish political leader Stuart Parnell and the *Book of Nonsense* by Edward Lear. Elizabeth was married in 1864 to Herbert Legg, who was baptised 18th June 1843 Affpuddle of parents Richard John Legg and Anna Maria Sellaway. Herbert's father's sister, his aunt Mary Legg had married William Hammett, who was younger brother to Elizabeth's mother Sarah. Therefore Elizabeth married her uncle's nephew-in-law.

Their family name of Legg is sometimes spelt as Legge. Like many other Dorset born folk, they appear to have moved north, presumably in search of work in the various factories which the industrial revolution had produced. In this family's case, the move took them to Bosden near Stockport in Cheshire, sometime between the years of 1871 and 1875.

From the information gleaned on the family in the 1881 census the parents are still agricultural labourers, as no doubt they were in Dorset, with the three eldest children aged 16, 14 and 12 (Mary, Louisa and Elizabeth) are listed as cotton weavers. It was not uncommon for children to be employed in these industries, especially if they were of slight build, ideal for getting under the machines to clear up, or for any other reason. This was dangerous work. The immediate neighbours of the family in 1881 all appear to have been local, so no doubt the Dorset folk with their accents must have stood out.

The family then moved to America sometime after 1891, settling in the Rhode Island area. Some of their married children quite possibly went there before this time, but daughter Mary and her family sailed in 1895. What a change all this must have been to them, a move from Dorset to Cheshire, then sailing on a ship to America for a new life. Elizabeth Maine and Herbert Legg had five children who were:-

1) Mary Elizabeth 1863, married 1889 in the Manchester district to Edward Massey. Her first cousin Sarah Lumber had married Richard Massey in 1893 in Dorset, he was born in Staffordshire and they moved to Leicestershire and Nottingham. I have not been able to link these two Massey families, but do wonder if there was a connection. Mary and Edward with their two sons, sailed on the Gallia from Liverpool to Boston, USA on the 27th June 1895. Edward was listed as Edmond aged 28, English and listed as what looks like a machinist. Mary was 30, English and also seems to have been a machinist. With them are their children Arthur aged 5 and Harry aged 4 (The National Archives BT/27 & Ancestry). As the other passengers on their list seem to also be noted as spinners, machinists or labourers, I do wonder if the cotton industry played a part in their immigration to America, possibly helping towards payment of their passage.

2) Louisa Anne 1866, married 1888 in the Prestwick district of Lancashire to James Scanlon.

3) Elizabeth Maria 1869 married 1887 in the Prestwick district of Lancashire to Samuel Fletcher.

4) Frances Jane 1871.

5) Edwin George 1875.

Jane Maine 1851 The same year saw the death of writer Mary Shelley. Jane married 1872 to Charles Sexey (yes that really is his surname), who was born 1849 Bere Regis of parents Francis and Jane Sexey (nee Stroud).

Again, like so many Dorset folk, they were drawn to go northwards, and again most likely in search of work in the industries evolved from the industrial revolution. Sometime between the years of 1874 and 1877 they would have ventured north, putting roots down at Heaton Norris, near Stockport in Lancashire circa 1877.

They appear to have adopted a daughter Olive Sexey Brown/Olive Brown Sexey, but I have not been able to ascertain her parentage. Perhaps her parents were friends of Jane and Charles who died, one can only speculate.

Charles possibly died in 1921 aged 66 (aged not correct), and Jane died in 1928. From the census of 1891 Jane worked as a reeler in a cotton mill whilst Charles seems to have been a labourer of sorts throughout other census listings. It is also worth noting who else is with family members during the census transcripts. With Jane and her family in 1911 there is a lodger Florence Deaken (should be Dakin) 26 born Stockport, unwed, a bobbin winder in a cotton mill. This lodger later married Jane's son William. Jane Maine and Charles Sexey had children:-

1) Annie Mary 1874, married 1899 to William Hewitt, who was possibly born William Brown Hewitt in 1874 Stockport district. Perhaps he was related to the adopted daughter of his in-laws, Olive Brown. Both Annie and William worked in the cotton mill industry, with Annie being a cop winder and William a doubler. They had children Jessie 1900, Maud 1904 and Annie 1909.

2) Louisa Agnes born as Agnes Louisa 1877, married 1902 to John Thomas Higgins who was born 1870 Bakewell. Louisa like her older sister Annie was also a cop winder in a cotton mill, with

husband John a bricklayer. They had one child John Richard born in 1903.

3) William Harry 1879, married 1911 to Florence Dakin. She had in the 1911 census been noted as a lodger at his parent's home.

4) Adopted daughter Olive Brown Sexey born 1896 Stockport. I have not been able to find out her parentage, but she may have been related to William Hewitt who married her adopted parent's daughter Annie, as his middle name could have been Brown. But this is just pure guesswork. She possibly married as Olive Brown in 1917 to Albert Haycock, who was possibly born in 1886 in the Stockport district.

William Hammett 1815-1841

William, son of William 1780, was born in 1815 and baptised in Tolpuddle on the 2nd April that year. That same year also saw the birth of author Anthony Trollope and John Loudon McAdam upgraded the roadways with the use of crushed stones and tarmac. Probably named after his father and grandfather, William was a labourer for the duration of his short life (although on the only census he appeared on in 1841, he is listed what looks like a painter).

He died aged 26 years old from consumption (tuberculosis) on the 4th July 1841 at Tolpiddle (Tolpuddle), and buried there four days later by Vicar Thomas Warren on the 8th July. His wife Mary was present putting her mark of an X on the death certificate, which was indicative of her not being able to sign her name.

William had married at Moreton, which was a village not far from Tolpuddle, and the Frampton family seat for many centuries. This was in addition the home of local landlord and Magistrate James Frampton, who was the man behind the Tolpuddle Martyrs plight. This village also is the final resting place for T E Lawrence who was otherwise known as Lawrence of Arabia. His funeral there drew many V.I.P.s (very important persons) of the time in 1935, including Winston Churchill.

On the 10th April 1836 William Hammett married at this village of Moreton to Mary Legg. She had been born in 1816 at Pallington, baptised at Affpuddle in the same year as her parents, Thomas and Mary (nee Reason) Legg, had married there in 1800. This couple had eight other children, one of whom was Richard John Legg. He had in turn married Anna Maria Sellaway in 1835 at Moreton, her hometown. They had a family, and one son Herbert Legg born in 1843 went on to marry Elizabeth Maine (Mayne) in 1864 at Affpuddle. This bride was the daughter of Sarah Hammett, who was the sister of William Hammett 1815. Therefore William Hammett's niece Elizabeth married his wife Anna Maria's nephew Herbert. What interwoven family connections these Dorset folk produced.

William Hammett was more than likely the same named person referred to, and spelt as Hamet, in a letter sent by Elizabeth Loveless and the wives of the other Martyrs to a Mr Goode of Butts Lane, Coventry in 1834. The women described how their children along with themselves had known hard times since the departure of their husbands. Also that conditions in Tolpuddle had been for a long time despotic, and since the member's list (the list kept by George Loveless on the members of the union), had been taken (since the arrest), some names on that list had been suffering since. William Hamet (Hammett) was noted as being out of work, due to his refusing to work for four shillings a week for a whole year with the farmer. He was 21 years old. That would make his birth year 1813, and this William was born 1815. But I suspect these two were one and the same, with research pointing to the one born in 1815.

A William Hammett was noted in the member's book, and as a Unionist in correspondence from Mr Brine, Overseer of Tolpuddle, who was further described as a very idle young man who, if they can help it, nobody would want in their employ. Times must have been very difficult indeed for all connected to the Tolpuddle Martyrs or whose names appeared in the member's book.

Correspondence from the hand of Magistrate Frampton said instructions had been given to the Overseer not to allow parochial relief to anyone whose name appeared in the book which was evidence at the trial of the six Tolpuddle men. Funds in their support had come via union supporters, and it was considered that those who had had the funds to pay a shilling to join a union and thereafter pay a penny per week, could not be considered to be entitled to Parish support. None mentioned in the book had ever expressed regret or admitted they were wrong to have joined the union. Quite how all these folks managed to make a living afterwards is hard to imagine, and William was amongst them, already a marked man.

After William's death in 1841 Mary married in Tolpuddle less than three years later on the same day she had her baseborn daughter Emma Gentilla Hammett baptised. This child later died in 1847 under her new married name of Pearce; the father more than likely being her second husband William Pearce whom she married on the 31st March 1844. His father was noted as Richard Pearce, and from the census information William was between six and eight years older than Mary. They had one child, son Richard born 1848 Wareham.

Mary was to outlive another husband with William's death after the 1861 census. She married for a third and final time in 1865 to James Ingram who was baptised at Athelhampton in 1828 of Charles and Ann of Admiston. It would seem Mary had "bagged" herself a toy-boy, as James was at least twelve years her junior. This was also a third marriage for him. His previous wives being Rebecca (they had issue James circa 1852, Elizabeth circa 1855 and Edward 1859, she died 1860), and Ann (they had one child Martha Anne 1863 with the mother dying the same year). Little wonder James would marry an older woman to help bring up his children. They do not appear to have had any children themselves. Mary Ingram died aged 75 years in the Wareham district in 1890.

From the 1851 census, it would appear the two surviving children from her first marriage to William Hammett were put into the Dorchester Workhouse, with one very sadly spending the rest of her days there. Their children were Jane 1836, Harriett 1839 and Martha born 23rd April 1841, baptised 23rd May 1841 and buried aged 7 weeks old on 18th June 1841.

Jane Hammett 1836 That year saw the birth of cook Isabella Beeton and the Chartist Movement was formed demanding all male adults be allowed the vote, as up until then only male land/property owners had the right to vote. Jane was put in the workhouse at Fordington, Dorchester along with her sister Harriett, where they appear in the 1851 census. But unlike her sister, Jane is not there in subsequent censuses.

Jane must have kept in touch with her uncle, her father's brother James Hammett, for she moved to the Ringwood area where he lived. When she married a local lad there it was to Uncle James she turned to be one of the witnesses. I have not found her in any of the censuses connected with her mother, which is one of the reasons I traced her mother through time.

Perhaps after her mother's second marriage she no longer wanted the girls around and had them admitted into the workhouse with all links being severed, or perhaps this was the wish of her subsequent husbands. Jane does, however, seem to have had contact with her maternal grandmother, Mary Legg, whom she was visiting on the occasion of one census day.

Jane married in 1863 at St Thomas Chapel, Ringwood to William John Cox whose father was noted as John Cox, a bricklayer's labourer. Jane's own father William was noted as a farm labourer, but not as deceased, which he was. Jane and William appear to have spent their married life in Ringwood with him being a labourer and gardener. Jane died aged 69 years in 1905 and William possibly in 1910 aged 73. Their children were:-

1) Louisa Jane 1863, had a baseborn son Donald Ernest Snow Cox in 1883, perhaps the name of Snow is indicative of his paternal lineage. He married in 1905 to Edith Lester and had issue, Ivy, John and William. In the 1891 census Louisa is a patient at the Royal South Hampshire Infirmary, Fanshave Street in Southampton, which is the year she died aged 27. She married Robert Sutherland in 1884 and they had children Winifred Esther 1885, Herbert William 1887 (joined the Royal Navy on 1st May 1907, a bricklayer's labourer, 5ft 2½" tall, chest 36¼", brown hair, hazel eyes with a fresh complexion, three tattoos which were one of a lady's head on the right forearm, a female body and head on the left forearm and also on the left forearm what looked like four dots. He was stoker No: 104993 serving on many ships, including the period for WW1 until 1927 – The National Archives ADM/188/1110) and Albert Thomas 1889.

2) Albert Thomas 1865, died 1887.

3) Herbert William 1868, married 1891 Plymouth district to Kate Louise Griffin. They both were working in Devon then, with Herbert

stationed at Raglan Barracks St Aubyn, Stoke Dameral a private in the army. Kate meanwhile was a cook in a private household in Plymouth. Later they moved to Ringwood and Portsmouth, and had children Herbert John Griffin 1893, Charles William 1894 and Thomas George 1896.

4) Edna Cox 1870.

Harriett Hammett 1839, the same year also witnessed Westminster Abbey hosting the Coronation of Queen Victoria and Charles Darwin proposing marriage to Emma Wedgwood. I think, out of all the Tolpuddle Hammett family, Harriett is one of the ones who has always stuck in my mind. She spent most, if not all, of her entire life in the Dorchester Union Workhouse, Damer's Road, Fordington in Dorchester and has been described as an imbecile. What a sad life she must have had. There is no way of knowing the extent of her disability, and today with stimulation, who knows what positive goals she may have achieved with her life. From the various census information gleaned she would appear to have been able to sew shirts. Most likely this is how she spent her days.

A visit from the Commissioners in Lunacy on the 6th September 1895 to the workhouse, reported that there were four females of unsound mind residing there, but no males. Harriett was one of those mentioned, but on that day was out for the day. I like to think some relatives would from time to time come and visit her with the possibility of taking her out for the day. But I have no evidence to support this theory.

These four ladies were housed in the Infirmary on ground level, with a nurse (possibly Miss Frances Roberts) sleeping in the same room as them. This room served both as a day room and bedroom. There was some question as to whether they were fed enough. Two meat dinners and two bread and cheese dinners were not of the order for people of unsound mind. Instead they should receive more foods of subsidence than normal workhouse inmates (The National Archives MH/12/2790).

A previous report carried out earlier that year stated a female ward downstairs was very dirty, with invalids and old folks having to share this ward with imbeciles who were quarrelsome. This more than likely was where Harriett would have been housed. One can only imagine the horrors she had to endure in her lifetime.

This Harriett has sometimes been mistaken for James Hammett the Tolpuddle Martyr's daughter and granddaughter by the same name, the latter being born in the workhouse at Fordington. But sadly all census references referred to belong to this Harriett, who died there, but was buried back in her birth village of Tolpuddle on the 18th September 1908. During her time in the workhouse, Harriett would have resided there at the same time as her Tolpuddle Martyr relative James Hammett.

James Hammett 1818-1897

James, son of William 1780 was born in 1818, and baptised in Tolpuddle on the 28th June 1818 by the Rector of Moreton. That same year also bore witness to the birth of novelist Emily Bronte and Mary Shelley's *Frankenstein*. James was most probably named after his maternal grandfather James Pearse, the carpenter at Southover, and died aged 78 in 1897 at Netherhampton in Wiltshire of heart disease. His son Albert of North Street, Wilton was present at death, with James described as an agricultural labourer.

James would have been in the Tolpuddle area when his namesake first cousin was arrested and transported along with the other Tolpuddle Martyrs. He probably was also aware his older brother William was also a member of the society headed up by George Loveless. I have often wondered what James and the other Hammett family relatives thought and felt at that time. Did that event in history have a negative impact for James in his workplace as an agricultural labourer? Questions which will never be answered, but as James moved around from Dorset to Hampshire then finally Wiltshire, I do wonder. James married twice.

Firstly to Elizabeth Jane Gale at the parish church in Bere Regis in 1841; the very building which had also witnessed important events for his Hammett ancestors and relatives. James was noted as an agricultural labourer, with his father as William Hammett, a mason (there was no mention of him being deceased), and Elizabeth's father was John Gale, a labourer. Their witnesses were Henry Stroud and

Louisa Gale (Elizabeth's sister), with all four signing with an X for their mark.

Elizabeth was born in 1819, baptised the following year in the same church she would marry in. Her father John Gale (1791-1859) married twice, first to Elizabeth's mother Ann Selby/Sellers in 1814 at Morden before witnesses Sarah Selby/Sellers, Sarah Shave and William Cox. Ann then died in 1842, and John married in 1845 to Diannah (Dinah) Clark.

Aged just 47 in 1866 Elizabeth died at Ashley, Ringwood in Hampshire, due to being accidently killed by a railway train. She was a dairywoman at the time, and this was an accident which was so easily avoidable. Local papers of the time (Christchurch Times 09/03/1866 – Bournemouth Library Services and Salisbury & Winchester Journal 03/03/1866 – Christchurch Local History Society) reported her sad death at the Ashley level crossing of the Ringwood and Christchurch Railway. She was just about to step over this level crossing, when at seven fifty-three that Tuesday morning the train from Ringwood approached. She looked as though she was waiting for the train to pass, but perhaps momentarily forgot.

Elizabeth had that very morning received a letter and carte de visite (photograph) from her son (Charles) who was in the Navy (she perhaps could read a little since her marriage). By all accounts she was struck by the buffer and thrown into a ditch some thirty yards away. The train stopped and all was done to aid her, but she survived for just a short while.

An inquest into her death was held at The Fish Inn, Ashley, with the coroner Mr Moses Cull presiding. Apparently she had after the accident been taken to the nearest house where she was laid on a temporary bed on the floor and given some brandy. Then about an hour later she was moved to her own house, where a witness Maria Griffen was present for about quarter of an hour before Elizabeth died later that Tuesday at two o'clock in the afternoon. Maria Griffen had noted Elizabeth was not sensible at the time, and had bruises on her elbow and instep.

Another witness Mrs Churchill of Westover Farm had come to the house to assist Elizabeth earlier when she was making some sense, and her husband (James) had asked did she not see the train, she said not. Elizabeth appeared to have pain to her side (probably from internal injuries), and was under the impression the train was still on top of her killing her. Poor Elizabeth was more than likely in shock.

This witness said she died between one and two o'clock in the afternoon. Elizabeth must have been in a great deal of pain, since just before eight in the morning when this accident happened, until one or two in the afternoon when she died, was quite some time to have to endure pain. Dr Dyer who attended Elizabeth at both cottages, had said he had previously, on another day, attended to her about a pain in her side, but nothing was found then.

After her death this doctor carried out an examination and found no broken bones, and said Elizabeth had died of nervous shock from the accident. A post-mortem does not appear to have been carried out. The verdict of the court was that her death was accidental, with no one to blame. The level crossing at Ashley Gate was deemed a danger to the public and, with the Railway directors to look into it.

When you come across such a death, especially of one who is your direct ancestor, it can leave you with a feeling of such sadness. Sadness that she ended her short life that way and left a husband and children, and so many "what ifs" regarding her life. All who witnessed her accident that day, were wholly convinced she was waiting for the train to pass by, given her body language at the time. Perhaps she just misjudged the situation or just did not see the train.

A few years later in 1871 James is to be found in Wiltshire, a widow, not remarrying until over a decade later. He must have really loved and missed Elizabeth, as some men married again a lot quicker than he, especially if they had children as James did. I like to think so.

The second marriage for James and noted as Hammet, was in 1876 to Mary Durrington/Dorrington (1841-1930). She already had had a baseborn son George Vincent Dorrington (1873-1895). James had nine children with his first wife Elizabeth and two with his second wife Mary. They were Mary Ann 1842, James 1844, Charles 1848, Sarah 1851, John 1853, Eliza 1856, Louisa 1858, Daniel Albert 1860, Elizabeth Jane 1862-1862, Charles James 1877 and Fanny 1879.

Mary Ann Hammett 1842, the same year also saw Queen Victoria take her first train journey, which was from Slough railway station in Berkshire to Bishop's Bridge not far from Paddington, London. Also on the 30th March 1842 in America Dr Crawford Williamson Long was the first physician to use ether as anaesthetic when he removed a neck tumour from James Venable for the sum of $2. Mary Ann was most probably named in honour of one of her mother's sisters. I have not been able to locate Mary Ann after the 1861 census when she was aged 18 living in Ringwood and a servant to the baker Jane Burgess. It is possible she moved out of the area and married.

James Hammett 1844, was registered as Hamit on birth, baptised as William James Hammet in Affpuddle and probably named after his father and paternal grandfather. His birth year was a leap year and on the 8th August that year the new head of the Mormon Church was appointed as Brigham Young due to the death of Joseph Smith.

James signed up as Private 3342 with the 104th Foot Regiment, Bengal Fusiliers at Botley in Hampshire in 1864 aged 18. He was 5ft 7¼" tall, with blue eyes, brown hair and a fresh complexion and a labourer. His discharge in 1868 stated he was born in Ringwood, Hampshire and that is where he was going to return. Possibly his father James was still residing there as by 1871 he was in Wiltshire.

During his service, which was four years and one hundred and five days, James was awarded the good conduct badge. But in addition, his name also appeared in the defaulter's book with a court martial. Eventually he was invalided out unfit and unable to provide service any longer. On the muster lists for 1867 he was noted as absent due to being invalided proceeding to Calcutta. He left India for England the following year (The National Archives WO/12/9954, WO/12/9955, WO/12/9956 & WO/12/9957).

I have assumed this James is the same one who married in 1876 at the Parish Church of St Michaels in Stockwell, Surrey to Eliza Reeve/Reeves, both residing at 6 Halsted Street. James was aged 32, a labourer, and his father was noted as James a labourer. Eliza Reeve was aged 41 with her father noted as Henry Reeve, a labourer. Witnesses were Henry and Annie Jemima Reeve, Eliza's brother and his wife (Anne Jemima T Hughes) who had married in 1874.

Eliza was born in 1835 Saxstead, Suffolk of parents Henry Reeve and Amy Lay, and died aged 82 in 1917 Lambeth district. Before her marriage to James she had two baseborn children who were Alice Louise 1863-1914 and Harriet 1867.

James died in 1886 as William James Hammatt at the Brompton Hospital aged 41, a builder's labourer from phthisis bronchitis, with wife Eliza being present. Both were noted as living at 18 Burgoyne Road, Stockwell. Their marriage appears to have produced just one child:-

1) Mary Edith 1880, but baptised aged 8 at the North Brixton Church, Stockwell with father noted as William James Hammett deceased, mother Eliza and address as 3 Combermere Road, Stockwell. In the 1901 census Mary was noted as a daily domestic nurse and after this time no trace of her has been found, perhaps she moved abroad or married elsewhere.

Charles Hammett 1848, the same year artist George Cruikshank produced *The Drunkard's Children*. Also an ice jam upstream stopped the Niagara Falls flowing for hours, so much so that the river bed was exposed allowing people to walk on it and even find discarded or lost items. Lastly that year also saw the Boston University School of Medicine in America being the first in the world to teach women to become physicians. Charles was more than likely named after his mother's elder brother Charles Gale.

Charles was the son whose letter and carte de visite (photograph) were received by his mother Elizabeth, on the morning she was killed in the train accident at Ashley, Hampshire in 1866. Charles had entered into the service of The Royal Navy in 1863, signing up for ten year in 1866. He was 5 ft 7" tall, had dark brown hair, grey eyes and a pale complexion. His character was very good and excellent, along with being an able seaman and later other ratings (which I am unable to make out). His family must have been very proud of him and what wonders the world must have shown him since he sailed off the southern shores of England to the other corners of the globe (The National Archives ADM/188/253/9, ADM/188/22).

Charles was on HMS Lord Warden in 1873 (The National Archives ADM/53/10267) and stopped off at various ports in the

Mediterranean Sea, chiefly Malta, Athens, Corfu, Palermo, Taormina, Syracuse, Syra, Tenedos, Smyrna, Gibraltar, Cadiz, Cartagena, Alicante and Valencia. During those times visitors to the ship were the King and Queen of Greece, a Russian Admiral, the Archbishop of Corfu and Austrian, German, French and Italian Ministers.

Brief gleanings from this ship's log revealed midshipman Mr F M Martin drowned in Salamis Bay due to the shore boat capsizing, with his body never being found.

Thursday 1st May 1873 was a good day – the ship's company received their monthly pay.

Saturday 24th May 1873 in the morning, the ship was dressed with flags in honour of Her Majesty's birthday.

Friday 6th June 1873 in the evening William Scott was lost overboard, whilst manning the launching boats.

Late November there had been exchange of fire at Cartagena, and also annual prize firing.

From the Surgeon James N Dick's journal at the time Charles was on aboard and from the 6th December to the 8th 1873 he spent two days on the sick list with a wound. From the 27th March to the 1st April 1874 Charles spent five days on the sick list with a wound to the knee. The following extracts have been noted (The National Archives ADM/101/210, ADM/101/211).

Charles Boon 29 plumber suffered coughing and spitting blood with chest pains, discharged to Gibraltar Hospital.

John McGregor 32 Captain's Forecox suffered insanity (probably a nervous breakdown due to worrying about his duties), discharged on another vessel to a naval hospital at Malta.

George Hill 29 Captain's Coxswain suffered rheumatism, discharged to Gibraltar Hospital.

Dennis Bryan 23 sail maker's area suffered gonorrhoea, contracted at Malta. (These diseases could bring the Navy down and were taken very seriously, sometimes tracing the lady in question, arresting her and placing her in hospital until cured and so on, as not to further infect the crew.)

Robert Phillips 22 able seaman suffered from syphilis, again contracted in Malta.

Alexander Blunt 22 GMA (not sure what this rating was) suffered syphilis too, and contracted it in Malta.

Edward Lucks 19 ordinary seaman also suffered syphilis, contracted at Gibraltar.

William MacLaren 31 boatswain's mate suffered gonorrhoea, sent to Royal Naval Hospital Malta.

Ballentyne Cohier 26 gunner marine artillery suffered syphilis, received black wash and cold lotions and discharged to hospital, but not before he had identified the lady (as other cases had to do).

Richard Spraggs 19 ordinary seaman suffered gonorrhoea, the woman he caught it from in Malta was apprehended by the Police and put under surveillance in the Civil Hospital. He was sent to the Naval hospital at Malta.

Charles Biddel 29 leading stoker suffered gonorrhoea. The woman he contracted it from was arrested and put in hospital, but found to be free of disease. He was sent to the Naval hospital at Malta. (This hospital must have seen many cases such as these.)

From the ship's log - Friday 13th February 1874 at Malta the crew (along with Charles) left to board HMS Revenge (The National Archives ADM/53/10847) sailing from Malta to Gibraltar then Plymouth to Portsmouth, where men were discharged to HMS Duke of Wellington and the invalids to hospital.

Then from 4th March 1874 to 2nd March 1875 Charles was on board HMS Excellent (The National Archives ADM/53/10525), which appears to have been in Portsmouth.

Wednesday 3rd March 1875 saw the crew leave for HMS Undaunted, including Charles.

From 2nd March 1875 (although previous ship's log stated the 3rd) to 22nd October 1876 Charles was on board HMS Undaunted (The National Archives ADM/53/11002, ADM/53/11003).

On Tuesday 2nd March 1875 at Sheerness four o'clock in the afternoon a draft of one hundred and sixty-one seamen were received from the naval barracks.

From Friday 25th – Tuesday 30th March they were granted leave. Where did Charles go for that leave? One can only speculate, but afterwards he was never to return to those shores again.

On Sunday 11th April they were at sea towards Plymouth.

Wednesday 15th April 1875 they were docked at Plymouth and at nine-forty in the morning had quarterdeck prayers, presumably before leaving for Malta.

From thereupon the various destinations visited were Gibraltar, Port Said, Suez Canal, Aden, Seychelles, Zanzibar, Columbo, Bombay, Mauritius, Bournbon, Jamatase, Tamatave, Mozambique. All being a far cry from the roots Charles knew in Dorset and Hampshire. What Charles thought of, visiting and observing these new places, one can only guess.

Zanzibar had Arab rulers, and had enjoyed a thriving slave trade. African slaves made up a major part of the island, working on the various clove plantations and other industries. They were also exported to southwest Asia. Mozambique had been ruled by Portugal since 1787, and although Portugal had abolished the slavery in 1869, it still went on in Mozambique decades later. This would have been a world Charles encountered in these parts, with the British anti-slavery campaign at the very forefront. These crews would have been on the alert to slavery boats and dealt with them accordingly. The Sultan of Zanzibar, when Charles was there, was Sayyid Barghash bin Said Al-Busaid 1837-1888. He was the second Sultan of Zanzibar and helped abolish the slave trade in 1870.

Extracts from the ship's log during this period are as follows:-

Monday 17th May 1875 at Aden, the ship was dressed in flags in honour of His Majesty Sayyid Barghash Sultan of Zanzibar.

Tuesday 13th July 1875 Zanzibar at nine o'clock in the morning the Commander in Chief and staff visited His Highness the Regent of Zanzibar. The Fort saluted him on leaving with fifteen guns, with a returned salute of eight.

Wednesday 14th July 1875, the French Consul came on board, and on leaving saluted with seven guns.

The next day at nine-thirty in the morning at Zanzibar His Royal Highness the Regent of Zanzibar visited the Commander in Chief, and he was saluted leaving the shore and on leaving the ship with nineteen guns.

Monday 20th September 1875 at one o'clock in the afternoon the effects of the late Dr Clarke, Fleet Surgeon were sold.

Friday 1st October 1875 ship's company received monthly pay.

Monday 25th October 1875 Bombay at quarter past five in the evening the Governor of Bombay visited the ship, leaving at six-thirty in the evening.

Sunday 7th November 1875 at Bombay quarter past seven in the evening Mr Charles Feltham, surgeon put under arrest for insobriety (most likely drunk).

Monday 8th November 1875 at quarter past seven in the morning Bombay HMS Serapis was sighted with HRH Prince of Wales on board. Eight o'clock in the morning the ship was dressed with the royal standard at the main. Three-thirty in the afternoon HRH Prince of Wales left HMS Serapis.

Tuesday 9th November 1875 Bombay at eight o'clock in the morning the ship was dressed, noon fired a royal salute twenty-one guns in honour of HRH Prince of Wales birthday. Ten minutes past four in the afternoon saluted HRH Prince of Wales with twenty-one guns. Twelve minutes past five in the afternoon HRH Prince of Wales proceeded to HMS Marcissus, then Serapis.

Thursday 11th November 1875 Bombay two o'clock in the afternoon one hundred and fifty-eight seamen and twenty-two marines sent on shore for dinner given by the inhabitants of Bombay (wonder if Charles was amongst them?)

Wednesday 17th November 1875 Bombay four o'clock in the afternoon warrants were read for committing Walter Hallett R.M.L.I. for forty-two days hard labour. Also James Hutchins ordinary seaman 2nd class for forty-two days hard labour, and James Vickery Ordinary seaman 2nd class for twenty-one days hard labour in Byculla jail (does not say for what reasons).

Thursday 18th November 1875 Bombay nine o'clock in the morning warrant read for depriving Edward Mannicon (?) carpenter mater for fighting and quarrelling whilst on shore leave. Also Edward Richay for speaking improperly to Lt H W Hill, when spoken to by this officer regarding not paying attention to the steering of his boat (which was quite a serious matter). Fifty minutes past one in the afternoon HRH Prince of Wales came on board. Thirty-five minutes past three in the afternoon HRH Prince of Wales left ship (wonder if Charles got to catch a glimpse of him, and if so, what were his thoughts?).

Friday 19th November 1875 Bombay twenty-five minutes past one in the afternoon Court Martial – sentenced Mr Charles Feltham surgeon to lose eighteen months seniority (this was the doctor accused of being drunk, again not a good idea if you have to attend to the ship's crew).

Tuesday 30th November 1875 Bombay to Columbo eight o'clock in the evening lost overboard (oars?) by neglect of Henry Hayes ordinary seaman, and charged against his wages.

Wednesday 1st December 1875 Columbo forty-five minutes past eight in the morning dressed ship with masthead flags in honour of HRH Prince of Wales birthday.

Tuesday 21st December 1875 Columbo to Bombay nine-thirty in the morning investigating the case of drunkenness for which Mr George Haines, carpenter was placed under arrest at ten–thirty in the evening on the first watch of the 20th December 1875 (the night before, and for which the following would reveal was a mistake). He was brought before Fleet Surgeon Mason and Surgeon Connor, who said at eleven o'clock that same night he had spoken to him and found him sober. Presumably Commander Fanshave, Lieut Hill and myself (Captain) had been mistaken to his state. He was released.

Friday 31st December 1875 Bombay nine o'clock in the morning Frank Watson signalman was presented with the Human Society Medal. John Clodd (?) ship's steward, James Richards blacksmith and James Jones were presented with the Long Service and Good Service Medals. Herbert Churcher L.S., William Bunsell able seaman and Joseph Fluke ordinary seaman were all presented with the Ashantee Medal.

Saturday 8th January 1876 Bombay one o'clock in the afternoon Lieut P Hockin was discharged to hospital.

Saturday 15th January 1876 Bombay fifty minutes past twelve in the morning cries were heard of murder, which came from the English barque "Norwood". A boat with an officer was dispatched and found the First Mate had been assaulted and wounded. Fearing further harm if left, he was brought on board the Undaunted for the night.

Saturday 19th February 1876 Bombay four o'clock in the afternoon the warrant was read for committing George Lawrence crew's carpenter to prison for three months.

Sunday 12th March 1876 Bombay ten o'clock in the morning divine service. Nine o'clock in the evening HRH Prince of Wales came on board. Illuminated ship. Number of men on sick list was nineteen (The National Archives ADM/53/11003).

Monday 13th March 1876 twelve-thirty in the morning HRH Prince of Wales left ship (he had been on board some three and a half hours). Three-thirty in the afternoon HRH Prince of Wales on board Serapis ship, a royal salute fired in honour of him as they passed. Number of men on sick list is nineteen.

Tuesday 22nd August to 5th September 1876 ship at Mozambique.

Sunday 20th September Zanzibar seven-thirty in the morning Union Company Steamer Natal arrived.

Friday 22nd September 1876 Zanzibar eight o'clock in the morning foreman and black divers (were these ex slaves?) employed for five hours cleaning the ship's bottom. Discharged invalids to Union Natal for passage to England. The Number of men on sick list twenty-seven. Fifty minutes past two in the afternoon Union S J Natal sailed.

Charles was stated as serving on the Undaunted until 10th October 1876, then discharged dead in mail steamer Natal whilst on passage. His service terminated on 10th October 1876, which I have taken to mean his death date. It has been hard to establish exactly what happened, as under a register of accounts and wages and effects of deceased seamen received and disposed of, the only Hammett I could find was a Cornelius aged 21 of the Undaunted who died 24th May 1876 at sea by drowning. This was received on the 8th May 1877 at Cardiff. I was not able to find a service record for a Cornelius and therefore have assumed this was for Charles, with the error of a death date and name. These effects were sold 19th April 1879 (The National Archives BT/153/19).

Sarah Hammett 1851, the same year saw the birth of the American gambler and gunfighter Doc Holliday. Also a new city in the Oregon Territory, USA is determined by the flip of a coin, to be called either Boston or Portland with the latter winning. I have not been able to locate Sarah's birth being registered, but this was not uncommon at the time, as long as a baptism had taken place, which it had on the 25th May 1851 East Stoke, Dorset. The family were living that year at Brick Kilns, Hanger Hill, East Stoke, where she was probably born, and named in honour of her paternal grandmother.

After the death of her mother Elizabeth who had been run over by a train, and with her father James moving to Wiltshire sometime afterwards, it is quite possible Sarah went to a hiring fayre and ended up working in London.

She was not with the family for the 1871 census, but later that year she married at All Souls Church, St Marylebone, London to George Fellowes. She was 19, lived at 4B Margaret Street, St Marylebone, George was a widower aged 23½, a police officer of 13A Margaret Street, St Marylebone. Presumably as they both lived in the same street, this is how they met. Witnesses were George's sister Ellen and her husband Samuel Garfield. Family legend tells how Sarah was totally unaware that George had been married before until the banns were read out prior to the marriage, stating he was a widower. I have not found his first marriage, but it could only have been brief, with his first wife dying.

George Fellowes (originally spelt Fellows) was born in 1848 Stoke Doyle, Northamptonshire, was the fourth child of eight born to George Fellowes (1818-1883) and Alice Langford (1816-1911). He came from a long line of agricultural labourers in the Northamptonshire and surrounding areas, the earliest John (1688-1748) took his own life.

With the Enclosure Acts, people were forced into the cities in search of work. Presumably this was the case for George Fellowes, who came to London, and joined the Metropolitan Police in 1870 aged 22 at E Division (Bow Street, Holborn). He served for twenty-five years retiring in 1895, having worked his way up to a Detective in the Criminal Investigation Department Scotland Yard. His pension was £51 11s 9d per annum (in 2012 worth a little over £5,678). His retirement gift was (according to the family) a walking stick which held an inscribed sword inside (believed to have gone to his daughter Minnie's side of the family after his death). He also served in V division (West Hill, Wandsworth).

Family information passed down, told how he worked on the East End "Jack the Ripper" case. This is more than likely true, as police constables and sergeants were drafted in from other divisions to Whitechapel to help the detectives there in the search for "Jack".

The description the Police noted for George's service records were that he was 5ft 8", dark hair turning grey, grey eyes, fair complexion with a scar on the bridge of his nose (The National Archives MEPO/2/150, MEPO/4/340, MEPO/4/352).

On the occasion of Queen Victoria's Golden Jubilee in 1887, George was awarded a medal with his details on, serving in V division (in the possession of descendant of his daughter Sarah's). Police on duty during that time would have been on high alert and not had an easy time. The event was threatened by the disruption from a Fenian bombing campaign, which never happened.

Upon his retirement in 1895 the family moved first to Fotheringhay, near Oundle in Northamptonshire, (Mary Queen of Scots was convicted, tried and finally beheaded on 8th February 1587 at Fotheringhay Castle, now only a mound remains). Then George bought a small holding at Yarwell, near Peterborough, Cambridgeshire.

According to family gossip passed down, once in Yarwell, George tried to invent himself as somewhat the country squire. He had bought a smallholding with a cow and expected his wife, children and grandson to work it. He would meanwhile go off with the local vicar fishing. One day his youngest child, also called Sarah, complained of this arrangement and voiced her opinions in this regard. She was rewarded by being thrown out of the home and made her way to London around 1910. This left her mother Sarah and nephew Ted to look after things.

Sarah died aged 70 in 1921 at Yarwell from chronic Bright's Disease and uraemia (renal/kidney failure). She would have suffered greatly, experiencing back pain, vomiting, fever and oedema amongst other conditions, not a nice way to end one's days. She is buried at St Mary Magdalene Church in Yarwell with her daughter Edith Christian. Sarah's coffin was carried from home to the Church on a handcart with the mourners following behind.

After Sarah's death, George sold up and moved to the Brixton area of London where his daughter Minnie lived. He told her to find them a house, which she did and used the money from the sale in Yarwell to set this up. George was not to enjoy his new life for very long as he died there in 1922 aged 72 years old (two years out of his real age). Sarah and George's marriage produced eight children:-

1) George Walter 1872, that same year the London Metropolitan Police went on strike. Named after his father and grandfather, married in 1892 to the girl next door Ellen Spencer (she lived at No 3 May Villas, Herewood Road, Upper Tooting and he at No 4). In 1906 they set sail from Liverpool bound for Montreal in Canada on board S.S. Canada (The National Archives BT/27 & Ancestry) with their sons George, John and Albert, disembarking at Quebec, then travelled and settled in Winnipeg.

According to one of George's son's books, George was a railroad detective (I have found no evidence to support this, and in light of information I had released under the Freedom of Information Act regarding his son George who wrote these books mentioned, I have decided to take some of the information therein with a pinch of salt).

George died on the 1st February 1913 aged 41 from pneumonia, was a machinist at the time, buried on the 17th May 1913 (they had to wait for the ground to thaw to be able to bury him) at Elmwood Cemetery, Winnipeg, Grave No 447 Section 3. Ellen died in 1932 aged 60 from bronchial pneumonia and is also buried at Elmwood Cemetery, Grave No 469 Section 3. George and Ellen had children:-

*George (also known as Gordon) Walter 1896 - more on him below as there is quite a tale to tell for him.

Arthur Jack (known as John) 1899 served in WW1 with the Canadian Expeditionary Force as Private 701703, later Sergeant 700703 in the 101st and 21st battalions. He was 5ft 6" had black hair, brown eyes and weighed 115 lbs. He suffered a hand injury at Havre in 1917 (National Archives of Canada).

Finding love in WW1, he was granted permission to marry from the army in 1919 to Clara Mildred Saunders at Lambeth Registry Office. She was aged 23, a worker with Queen Mary's Army Auxiliary Corps and her father noted as William Saunders a labour exchange clerk. He took his new bride back to Canada but his happiness was to be short-lived. A daughter Elsie Ellen was born in June 1920 but the mother died the next month from septicaemia, with the child Elsie following, being buried aged one month and seven days old, cause of death bronchial pneumonia. They were buried together at Brookside Cemetery, Winnipeg.

John, as he was known, married again in 1922 to Emma Frances St Lawrence. He was 23, a widower, an accountant, she was 18, her father Percy a locomotive engineer. It is believed they later divorced. John Arthur died in 1957 and was buried at Brookside Cemetery, Winnipeg with his first wife Mildred and their child Elsie.

Albert Edward 1902 Not much is known about him, apart from that he too went to Canada with his parents and brothers in 1906, and possibly married as Edward Albert in 1925 to Lillian Wray.

Patrick (Pat) 1908 Not much is known about him either, other than he was born in the March of 1908 in Winnipeg, and appears with the family there for the 1911 census.

*George (also known as Gordon) Walter 1896 was born in Clapham Maternity, Lambeth, grew to be quite tall, 6ft 1", named after his father, grandfather and great grandfather and went to Canada with his family. He served in WW1 with the Canadian Overseas Expeditionary Force 1915-1916, but was sent home an invalid suffering conditions endocarditis, tuberculosis and shell shock. Then re-listed in March 1918 but was discharged in the August medically unfit (National Archives of Canada).

From his records he was listed as a mechanic, chauffer, electrician and engineer, had five vaccinations scars on left arm, shrapnel scar on the back of his left wrist, was 6ft tall (police records sated 6ft 1") with brown hair and eyes, and listed as Church of England (his parents had married in a Catholic Church, perhaps it was only his mother who was Catholic).

Upon his discharge in 1918 his address given was the British Recruiting Office, Chicago, Illinois. He completed a course on criminology at the University of California, and found a position as undercover man (secret service investigator) for the Californian State Insurance Fund.

In 1926 George investigated the Aimee Semple McPherson (1890-1944) kidnapping hoax scandal. She was an Evangelist who introduced popular slang and jazz into the Church. She was reportedly kidnapped and escaped, and many believed she had staged it herself. In 1927 the case was dropped. That same year George took the position of investigator for Associated Industries Insurance Company, a widespread business organization, to fight racketeering. Here George investigated numerous gangster activities for four years.

Working undercover he met Al Capone, who said one word to him, "scram". George had temporarily become a member of the Moran Gang, undercover of course, just before the St Valentine's Day Massacre on Thursday 14th February 1929 in Chicago, Illinois. The Moran Gang was headed up by George "Bugs" Moran, of Irish/Polish parents and from the North side of Chicago. Al Capone had his gang from the South side and did not like the fact that the Morans had been taking the *booze* trucks (lorries transporting illegal alcohol). Capone's gang dressed as police, giving the impression of intending to carry out a raid on the Morans at their headquarters. Instead they lined seven members of the Moran gang up against the wall and machine-gunned them down. What luck George was not still in that guise of undercover member then.

George also worked undercover as a rum-runner (illegal transportation and trading of alcohol) and escaped being sunk by a Customs vessel. He became the confidante of Vivian Gordon, who was otherwise known as Bonnie Franklin. She was the underworld queen whose body was found on the 26th February 1931, miles away from her home in a park in the Bronx, having been strangled. She was about to testify in the New York City's vice investigation and could bring down many well-known names of the time. George had known her since 1927. Whilst working on a case they had become friends, exchanging letters, and in one she told him how she expected to be murdered at any moment.

George's life was threatened, not only by criminals, but the corrupt police and people in power at the time. This all came to a head one night when the flat he shared with his second wife, an American, in St Louis, had a bullet pass through the window pane and lodge in the wall of their room. In his own written words he said, "If ever I return to the United States I shall risk death from a gun.

Gangland put the finger on me because I discovered too much, and I had to leave America in haste and in secret." This sounds like someone right off of Ian Fleming's James Bond pages. Their telephone lines had been cut, and the very next day they left for New York to catch a boat to Southampton.

Back in England they settled for a while and started a family. Here George wrote two books on his experiences mentioned above under the name of Gordon Fellowes, *They Took Me For A Ride* (1934) and *The Insurance Racketeers* (1935).

1934 press reviews of *They Took Me For A Ride* said how justice in America was turned into a farce, with the police, lawyers and officials getting rich with corruption running wild. George being a criminal investigator learned about gangsters of the likes of Dillinger, with his book having some gruesome photographs.

The Press reviews the next year for his other book *Insurance Racketeers* spoke of fraudulent claims, murder, suicide, conspiracies, shoplifting, fire-raising and how to get rid of a wife in order to collect on the insurance, all taking place in the United States.

Both of these books are now classified rare books. In the first book he mentions both his father and grandfather being in the Police.

George also gave lectures and speeches on these gangsters and criminals. One such event took place at the Regal, Marble Arch, just before the screening of James Cagney's G-Men film. On stage George had somehow managed to obtain and bring over from the States, a vehicle used in a shoot-out still bearing the bullet holes. In his book he said he had arranged for a vehicle to be brought over from the States to England, which was on exhibition. This car was the very one he was once picked up in by Al Capone's men and taken for a ride aboard, as they wanted to question his interest in a certain hotel and the Moran garage. At the time he had made a note of the number plate on this armoured vehicle and, when it was later captured by the police, George arranged for it to be shipped over.

It is more than likely that this screening was held on 24th June 1935, the same day George attended the Midnight Film Party in aid of the Cripples' Training College there (The National Archives - The Times 34/05/1935 made mention of the Midnight Party). Some of this information has been passed down in the family as sitting in the audience at The Regal that night was my uncle who was a first cousin of George's. The Times newspaper from 15th June until 9th July 1935 (The National Archives) advertised at The Regal, Marble Arch the G-Men film with James Cagney, and an appearance of Marcia Marsh, girlfriend of Dillinger (**see below).

My own grandmother, who was George's aunt, used to clean for a big house and one day saw a copy of one of George's books there on the table *They Took Me For A Ride*. She told her employer of her relationship with the author, and was allowed to borrow this book.

George also appeared on stage at the Astoria in Brighton at the showing of James Cagney's "G men" in 1935. He used the name Gordon Fellowes and was accompanied by Miss Marsh (see below paragraph).

On Saturday 19th May 1934 George appeared as a guest on the BBC radio broadcast *In Town Tonight* (Information & Archives BBC Written Archives Centre). An early type of radio chat-show which went on air every Saturday night at seven-thirty in the evening from Broadcasting House, Portland Place in London. The show first aired from this Art Deco building on the 18th November 1933, and thus would have still have been in its first year when George made a contribution.

George was billed as a journalist/crime investigator, with a mention of the gangsters in America, with part of the title of his book from that same year (mentioned above). His fellow guests that evening are listed below:-

Colonel F Bourne who had seen action in 1879 at Rorke's Drift, as a Colour Sergeant and been awarded the DCM (Distinguished Conduct Medal). He later would be the last known survivor of that battle. Aged 91 he died on a very historic day in British history the 8th May 1945, that date being VE Day (Victory in Europe).

Mark Hill who was a penny-farthing cyclist aged 90.

Albert Frisbee whose occupation had been a Hansom cab driver. A few years later he would be noted as only one of three left in London, as this type of transport had started to decline in the 1920's.

Lastly there was Captain G Drury Coleman, who was the Secretary for the Institute of Patentees.

What an interesting and varied group of guests London listened to that evening.

According to newspaper reports of 1935 (Paper Past National Library of New Zealand - Evening Post 10/08/1935), a (**)Miss Marcia Marsh was back in England, her birthplace. She had been working undercover in America, infiltrating the world of the gangsters, which was a career move she made after they had killed her FBI boyfriend, James Brennan. Gordon (George) Fellowes was referred to as one of America's foremost insurance detectives, who had employed her in his racketeering battle. Once secured within that world she was able to access information, such as when John Dillinger, America's Public Enemy Number One, was to attend a film showing in Chicago. The film was a crime melodrama called *Manhattan Melodrama*. Dillinger was shot dead on the 22nd July 1934 as he left. Although it has been stated he was betrayed by one of the two women he was with (Miss Marsh was not one of them, and Melvin Purvis stated it was Mrs Anna Sage), Miss Marsh said it was she who phoned Melvin Purvis, chief of the Chicago Department of Justice with the tip-off. Perhaps she was one of the sources who had previously informed his agents that Dillinger was in the Chicago area.

What I have gathered is that Miss Marsh obviously knew Gordon (George) Fellowes and most probably was the same lady who appeared with him at Brighton in 1935, the following year after Dillinger's death. From the description in the paper of her appearance, small and blonde, she is probably the same lady who appears in photographs on stage with George acting out gangster activity (from George's descendant's photographic collection which I was able to view).

George, it would seem, had the feline touch about him, meaning he had nine lives as the saying goes. Not only did he escape being killed in WW1, recovering from serious medical conditions received, but also escaped the numerous situations he was involved in during his undercover working career, and subsequent attempts on his life.

George first married Marguerite A (surname unknown) circa 1920/21 and they lived in Raymond, Illinois. She possibly died or they divorced, as he then married Grace in 1924 at St Louis, Missouri.

In England they lived in the Streatham, Lambeth and Tulse Hill areas, which were not far from Minnie his other aunt. He was also a journalist, tutor and made appearances at cinemas and theatres where the film subject was that of gangsters and crime. George would then be the source of the descriptive material.

Later in Canada, both George and his wife Grace were teachers. Grace and one of their daughters left Southampton bound for New York on the 7th April 1948 aboard the Queen Elizabeth (The National Archives BT/27/1627). Later that year they would go to Canada, where George and their other daughter were waiting, having previously travelled ahead in 1946 by aeroplane (Latter Day Saints – Immigration & Travel). George's wife Grace died in 1957, and George died on the 28th August 1962. Both are laid to rest at Mount Calvary Cemetery in Spanish, Ontario, Canada.

Researching George had been very difficult, as at first I was unaware he wrote under the name of Gordon and not George Fellowes. Also my family had initially told me he was an FBI man, a route I followed up, and which of course resulted in a negative outcome. Obtaining copies of his books were also virtually impossible, due to their rarity and being out of print. I was later lucky enough to purchase one and read the other in the British Library.

Some of the above information on George I gleaned from his books and the newspaper reports. However, the documents I gleaned from being released under the Freedom of Information Act painted a very different picture of him. I have to be honest and take the official facts as research evidence, so as not to mislead the reader.

A brief account of these findings via the official police records both in the UK and America via their correspondence with each other is thus (The National Archives MEPO/2/9183).

On the 23rd January 1923 in Los Angeles George was arrested on a charge of arson. He was again arrested at St Louis, Missouri on the 13th May 1930 for violating the Federal Radio Act 1928 (a huge case at the time, with him being the first to be tried under it.) He was found guilty, but as he was already awaiting deportation, was not sent to prison.

He was deported on the 24th May 1930 from New York to England. This is confirmed from the passenger list for the SS Leviathan, which left New York and arrived at Southampton on 30th May 1930. George was listed travelling third class, a deportee aged 34. His wife Grace was also there, aged 23, a housewife born in the USA. Two other deportees were also listed on the same vessel travelling third class, Frederick Crutch aged 36 and Edward Reynolds aged 25. What their crimes were, I do not know.

In America George appears to have been continually under suspicion by the police. He was receiving $30 a month disability pension from the war at this time. He presumably went to London first, but was in Nottingham in the July of 1931 as General Manager for the Colonial Mutual Assurance Company. He appeared before the City Petty Session on 16th March 1932 for assault and was given six months hard labour.

George then came back to London where it appears he was given some publicity by touring various cinemas, giving talks on well-known American criminals and even posed as a member of the FBI. About this time he wrote two books and appeared in newspapers and the radio.

Trouble was not far away, and George appears at Lambeth Magistrates Court on the 4th November 1937 for the possession of an unlicensed wireless transmitter, and had to pay £10 costs (in 2012 equated to £576.86). George appeared there again on 22nd July 1938 for the same offence. Once again he was fined and had to pay costs, but this time received three months imprisonment on the 25th January 1941 for two cases of posing as an intelligence officer.

George worked at the London County Hall in several positions, using both his real and pen name. He started in the November of 1940, but this came to an end with his imprisonment in 1941. He then applied again for work there under another name but that too ceased.

Not seeming to learn his lesson, George had also been severely cautioned by the police for causing public mischief. He had interfered in the Neville Heath case of 1946, which was a murder case. George even reached the heights of being mentioned in the parliamentary debates in the House of Commons.

With all this behind him, it looks as though George then decided to go back to Canada accompanied by one of his daughters, leaving his wife and other daughter to follow on joining them at a later date.

2) Ellen (Nellie) 1874, that same year Winston Churchill was born, author Thomas Hardy's *Far from the Madding Crowd* appeared, and in Eastern England agricultural workers went on strike. Named after her paternal aunt, she married as Nellie in 1897 to Henry James Berry. He was born in 1875 at Baker Street, London of parents James and Jane. Nellie and Henry lived in Streatham and had five children, all of whom were boys. Four of these boys were born as two sets of twins. With her parents living in Yarwell, Northamptonshire, Nellie certainly had her work cut out with no maternal support available.

One set of her twins died during the same quarter as she gave birth to her second set of twins. These were born in the Union Workhouse at Wandsworth on the 11th October 1901. Nellie's younger sister Minnie would also give birth in this establishment a few weeks later on the 25th October. Nellie died aged 31 in 1905, with her husband seemingly disappearing off the radar. Their sons were:-

James Henry 1899, possibly sent to the North Surrey District School Workhouse, North Surrey District in Croydon after his mother's death. He possibly died aged 19 in 1918.

Walter William 1900 twin, died aged one in 1901.

Harry Albert 1900 twin, possibly married as Henry A in 1919 to Amy Kilsby.

Edward George 1901 twin, also known as Ted. After his mother's death brought up by his maternal grandparents. He married and had a family, and was Church Warden of St Mary Magdalene in Yarwell, Northamptonshire where his grandmother and an aunt were buried.

Alfred George 1901 twin died the same quarter and year he was born in.

3) Elizabeth (born as Eliza) 1877 and probably named after her maternal grandmother, died between the years of 1891-1911.

4) Jane 1879, had a short life as she died age 2 in 1881 from a swing accident as family rumour passed down states.

5) Minnie 1881, the same year Spanish artist Pablo Picasso was born, and the army and navy abolished flogging. As a child she received elocution lessons as her mother felt this would aid her in her workplace, with her younger sister Sarah sometimes accompanying her. Minnie trained as a seamstress but it is not clear whether she accompanied the family back to Northamptonshire upon her father's retirement. She was still to be found living in the Wandsworth district and later Streatham and Brixton after the family left for Northamptonshire. Perhaps she had stayed in those areas with her brother before his departure to Canada or with her sister Nellie.

As mentioned above, Minnie gave birth to a child in the Union Workhouse, Wandsworth in the same month of 1901 as her sister Nellie. This child was baseborn and father unknown, as were the two that followed before her marriage to Reginald Farquharson in 1906, although Reggie was their named father.

Reggie, as he was known, was born Harry Reginald in 1874 Wiltshire of parents Archibald and Jessie. Reggie had signed up as a Private with the 4th Hussars at Colchester in 1892, previously he had been with the Royal Artillery. He saw overseas activity in India for just over six years, completing twenty-one years and three hundred and four days with the army when he left in 1914, but with one hundred and seventeen days fortified by desertion (The National Archives WO/364/1176/1788226).

The years 1903-1914 saw him as a reservist, which was when Minnie's third and fourth baseborn children were born and, after their marriage, a further child. Reggie did not live long after being discharged from the army, as he died aged 46 in 1915.

After this Minnie then appears to have lived with a man called Herbert Davies, known as Bert, believed to be a Welshman and boot maker, with whom she had two further baseborn children between 1916 and 1917.

Minnie's widowed father and nephew Ted came to live with them in about 1921, with George her father's death the following year, and then the nephew being asked to leave. Minnie then put the proceeds of his estate of which she was, according to her sister Sarah, the benefactor, to the purchase of a house, which she then ran as a gentlemen's boarding house. This was a business concern she still had in the 1930's when nieces came to stay with her during their school holidays.

One boarder was Chriss (Christian) George W Hood also known as Charlie, born in Norfolk to parents William Hood (born Norfolk) and Lina Apollonia Hennes (born Germany). Minnie married Charlie in 1924. He had served in WW1 as a Private with the Norfolk Regiment (The National Archives WO/373/10). Minnie died first in 1958 with Charlie following in 1962.

According to her sister Sarah, Minnie inherited amongst other items, their father's retirement present from his time served with the Police. This was an inscribed walking stick, which was also a sword. This item passed to Charlie and, as he died without leaving a will and not having children with Minnie, his sister Catherina put in a claim on his estate. It is presumed the walking stick became part of that estate and the whereabouts of it unknown now. This is so often the case with items of family history value. They can simply disappear forever from families denying their future generations the enjoyment of viewing them. Children for Minnie were:-

Frank Albert 1901 baseborn, father unknown, birth in the Union Workhouse in Wandsworth, died in 1903.

Elsie Minnie 1905 baseborn, given Reggie the father's surname.

Albert (Bert) 1905 baseborn, given Reggie the father's surname.

Rita E 1910 born within parents' Minnie and Reggie's marriage.

Winnifred Davies 1916 baseborn, and although born with Reggie's surname of Farqharson, he could not possibly have been her father as he died before she was conceived. Her middle name of Davies is indicative of her paternal line, although noted father was Bertram Farquharson, a bootmaker.

Alma Joan 1917 baseborn, known as Molly and born with the surname of Davies, father noted as Herbert Davies a bootmaker.

6) William 1885 twin, the same year saw the birth of author D H Lawrence and in New York the Statue of Liberty arrives from France as a gift. Most probably named after a paternal uncle, William was born a twin, and never married. He died aged 29 on Sunday 9th May 1915 serving his country in WW1.

His life expired at the Battle of Aubers Ridge, Rouges Bancs, Fromelles. This battle was collectively known as The Second Battle of Artois, the former being the British contribution. On that morning the British had launched an assault in the Fromelles area, to support the huge French attack against the hill of Notre Dame de Lorette. They did not stand a chance, being hit with German fire. The German Chief of Staff, General Ludendorff said of those men, "Those soldiers are fighting like lions but are led by donkeys". I like to think my great uncle William Fellowes was one of those lions (Regimental Museum The Royal Green Jackets, Winchester).

William was Rifleman 1088, 2nd Bn, Rifle Brigade, he is remembered on Panel 10, Ploegsteert Memorial, Comines-Warneton, Hainaut, Belgium, and also on the WW1 plaque in the church of St Mary Magdalene, Yarwell (Commonwealth War Graves Commission).

The newspapers covering the war at the time, reported William as missing (The Peterborough Advertiser 19/01/1918 and Peterborough & Huntingdonshire Standard 10/07/1915). One article talked of the war sorrow there (Yarwell) in June, as two of their lads were dead from wounds and two were missing. Those missing were Private Willie Andrews and Rifleman William Fellowes. Positive comments were made for their safe return. Obviously William's death had not been notified to his parents by then. The two lads who had died were Private Dickerson and Private Sharpe.

On 11th June 1915 St Barnabas day, a memorial service was held in the Church at Yarwell, and attended by a large congregation. The impact of those men, either missing or dead, must have sent huge shock waves through this little Northamptonshire rural community. William's death notification and death scroll, which did eventually arrive, were given first to his father, then to his sister Sarah upon their father's death, and then later passed on to one of her sons who was also William's nephew.

7)   Edith 1885 twin, in the same year the vacuum flask was invented by Sir James Dewar and the first modern bicycle called *The Rover Safety Bicycle* was invented by John Kemp Starley. Edith married in 1908 to William Christian born in Peterborough of parents William and Emily.

Edith possibly lived at Boston in Lincolnshire at some point. Like her twin William, Edith would not live to see old bones, for she died in 1910 aged 26 in the Oundle district of Northamptonshire. She was buried in the churchyard of St Mary Magdalen in Yarwell where her mother Sarah Fellowes nee Hammett would join her when she too was buried. After Edith's death, husband William appears to be living with his parents in Peterborough as a plumber and gas fitter. I have not been able to find issue for this marriage.

8) Sarah 1887, the same year as actor Boris Karloff was born and Buffalo Bill's Wild West Show came to London. She was born on the 28th January of that year at Wandle Road in Wimbledon, and her father George was then constable with "V" division which covered Wandsworth. Named after her mother and her paternal grandmother (Sarah Pearse), she was also known as Sally, just as her mother's paternal grandmother was.

Not only was she the youngest daughter, but also the youngest child, and it was expected that she would look after her parents in their old age, and remain a spinster. Just as well this was not the case, otherwise I would not have been born for she was my grandmother.

As stated previously, upon his retirement her father, who was then a DCI (Detective Constable Inspector) with the Police Force at Scotland Yard, moved the family back to his birth county of Northamptonshire. Sarah made that move with them, settling first in the village of Fotheringhay. The family then moved to Yarwell, where Sarah was once the May Queen. She was good looking with her dark hair, hazel eyes and petite frame accompanied by small feet and hands (the latter two being a female trait inherited by a few of her female descendants).

At some point in her younger years she had a row with her father on the subject matter of the time he spent fishing with the local vicar whilst the rest of the family were left to man the smallholding. Sarah dared to suggest he might assist them more than he did. For this she was thrown out of the family home.

Somehow she made her way back to London, possibly initially staying with her sister Minnie. Sarah managed to find a position as a scullery maid in a big house. It was whilst there she met and grew to know the local milkman who was William John Weeden West. This was one of the many addresses he made deliveries to with his horse and cart. The inevitable happened and they married in 1911 at The Registry Office, St George's, Hanover Square, London. Witnesses were her sister Minnie Farquharson and Emily Nellie Heath (possibly Sarah's friend). Sarah was 24, a spinster of 20 Hill Street, Knightsbridge, father George Fellowes, a police pensioner. William was 28, a milk carrier of 5 Montpelier Row, Knightsbridge, father deceased John West a coachman. Why they married in a registry office at Hanover Square is not clear, but perhaps as Sarah gave birth two months later to their first born, could be the indicator.

Although all their children were to be born and brought up as West, it was not until William was much older and all the children born, that he received a bombshell from his mother. This was in the form of his father not being the deceased John West a coachman as noted on his marriage certificate, but an Irishman called Walsh. He had disappeared when William was a baby, never to be seen again and she decided to change their name and the identity of his birth father. I have often wondered if she obtained the name John West off a tin of fish.

William served in WW1 as a rifleman with the King's Royal Rifle Regiment (K.R.R.). Whilst serving abroad in France, he was injured and taken as a P.O.W. (prisoner of war) (The National Archives WO/161/101 & WO/364/4579) to a camp in Germany, where he was put to work breaking stones in a quarry. This activity lost him part of a finger. Both when there and during time spent in the trenches, he sent Sarah letters home. He spoke of the terrible conditions in both.

For Sarah, with a small baby to look after and another on the way, this would have been a very worrying time for her. Eventually her husband William did come home safely, with their second born named after a town in France near to where he was captured. Sarah and William went on to have another three children.

During WW2 both their sons served in the army, and again this was a worrying time for Sarah, as one of them went missing presumed dead for six months. How relieved they must have been to learn eventually that he was in an Italian hospital receiving treatment for back wounds. Sarah and the girls, one of whom was married with a baby of her own at the time, were evacuated out of London, to Camborne in Cornwall. This then left William all alone in London.

In Camborne the girls and Sarah were all split up into different billets, with Sarah running the home of an elderly gentleman. There she was given free reign and she put to use the skills she had learned on her parent's smallholding in Yarwell, growing many vegetables and, together with her good cookery skills, they never went hungry there.

Sarah and William were never rich in finances but appear to have had a happy marriage. William died first aged 86 in 1967 at Lewisham Hospital, and was cremated at Mortlake, and Sarah died aged 83 at St Luke's Hospital, Chelsea in 1970 and was cremated at Mortlake with her ashes scattered in the Garden of Remembrance there. Sarah and William (Walsh) West had five children who were:-

William John Weeden 1911, named after his father, the Weeden name being his paternal grandmother's maiden name. Known as Bill, he served with the army in WW2 North Africa as a driver. Married and had two children.

Nancy Margaret West 1917, named after the place near to where her father was captured in WW1 France. Married and had two children.

Henry George West 1919, also known as Jock within the family due to once wearing a kilt as a youngster and so being called Jock by his brother William (Bill). He served with the army in WW2. Firstly with the Duke of Cornwall's Light Infantry whose headquarters were based at Bodmin in Cornwall. Whilst training at that location he was able to visit his mother and sisters at nearby Camborne. Later he was transferred to the Signals, seeing service in North Africa and Italy. He married but had no children.

Minnie Elizabeth West 1921, her names are both those of an aunt and maternal grandmother, the latter who was run over by a train at Ashley in Hampshire. She married but had no children.

Rita Lillian West 1926 named after her older cousin. She married and had one child.

John Hammett 1853, the same year artist Vincent van Gough was born, and David Livingston embarked on his great African exploration. Probably named after his maternal grandfather (John Gale), he married Helen Ruth Wilton in 1884 at Netherhampton, Wiltshire. She was born in Beverly, Yorkshire (a location where other Tolpuddle Hammett relatives would be drawn to) in 1859 of parents James and Matilda.

Helen's mother was born in Compton Basset, Wiltshire, whilst her father was Scottish, being born in Leven, Fife. From the various censuses Helen's family moved around the county with her father being a huntsman. They are in Yorkshire for 1861, in Suffolk for 1871, and in 1881 Helen is in Andover, Hampshire. Meanwhile her parents are in the same village of Netherhampton as John's father James and family. This is probably how the two met and married there.

In 1881 John was working at nearby Wilton House in Wilton as a whip to the hounds, living in rooms above the stables. His employer was George Herbert, 13th Earl of Pembroke and also 10th Earl of Montgomery. Residing in Wiltshire for a few years, John and his family then moved to Worcestershire where he worked as kennel huntsman for Mr Greswold-Williams (family seat Malvern Hall, Warwick which was sold the same year as John's death). It was whilst in the employment of Greswolde-Williams that John would die in 1896 aged 42 from injuries sustained from falling off his horse at Banner's Brook, Doddenham Road, Leigh, Martley in Worcestershire.

An inquest was held two days later at the Royal Oak Inn, Broadwas (Worcestershire County Council – Berrows Worcester Journal 14/03/1896). Harry Cooper, butler to Mr Greswolde-Williams recalled their employer had given instructions to John Hammett. These were for him to go around to various locations informing of a hunt the next day. John was sober and in good health, riding a grey pony belonging to Mr Greswolde-Williams, and was seen by a farmer who said the same of his appearance.

Later John was found badly hurt having been thrown by the horse at a corner leading out of Hopton Court Road into Leigh Road. John was quite insensible with a large bleeding wound on the left side of his forehead, losing consciousness to never awaken again. The findings were that the horse had slipped on stones going down the hill and around the corner.

A witness had seen the horse without a rider galloping away with dirt on the shoulders and hindquarters, evidence dove-tailing with a fall. One stirrup leather was missing which was found close to John's side.

A surgeon had tried to save John, whom he said was suffering from concussion of the brain. He had a bruise on the left hip but no bones were broken. The surgical operation of trephining (whereby a small circular section of his skull was removed to relieve the pressure) was carried out on John. But really his injuries were too far gone for treatment, with his death resulting from a fracture of the skull and laceration of the brain.

The inquest jury gave the verdict of his death from injuries caused by accidently falling from his horse. What a sad end for John and no doubt he had rode a horse many times without anything untoward happening.

He then left his widow Helen to bring up their three children alone. It would appear she moved on to a more developed area where factories and industries would have been, becoming a shirt maker living in St John's, Worcester. At least she had her mother to help her, as she lived with them before her death in 1901.

Some time before 1931 Helen moved to Winterborne Monkton, just outside Dorchester in Dorset, where she was the local school teacher, and died there at the School House aged 91 in 1950 of pneumonia, daughter Ethel being present. John and Ruth's marriage produced four children who were:-

1) Elsie 1884, buried at Netherhampton on the 24th September 1884.

2) Mabel 1885 Wilton, last noted as living at home in 1911 Worcester an assistant teacher at an elementary school for the County Council.

3) Frederick (Fred) James 1889, married May Brown in 1923 at The Parish Church (St Mary Magdalene), The Tything, Worcester, the same place where May was baptised in 1888 of parents Thomas Joseph Brown and Ellen Burrows.

4) Ethel 1894, travelled first class from Liverpool in 1931 bound for Penang, Malaysia, where she was going to live in Siam, was noted aged 37 from Monkton, Dorchester, a nursing sister (The National Archives BT/27 & Ancestry). Ethel returned back to Dorset, married in 1934 to Leslie R Willis, who was possibly born in 1900 Exeter as Leslie Radcliffe Willis.

Eliza Hammett 1856, the same year Bramwell Booth General of the Salvation Army was born, in the September The Royal British Bank collapses with debts of more than £500,000, and The Treaty of Paris is signed, thus ending the Crimean War.

In the May of 1875 Eliza gave birth to a baseborn daughter in the Union Workhouse, South Newton, Wilton, Wiltshire, with no indication as to who the father was. This event occurred just a few months after her younger sister Louisa had also given birth to a daughter out of wedlock, in that very same institution. I have not been able to locate Eliza after this event in 1875. Her daughter was:-

1) Mary Louise 1875, probably brought up by her maternal grandfather James Hammett and his second wife. She married George John Thomas in 1894 (1866-1934), lived in the Amesbury area of Wiltshire and had children: Frederick John 1899, Victoria Louise 1901, Doris Hilda 1903, Conrad James 1906 (probably named after mother's cousin Conrad Hammett, and mother's grandfather James Hammett), and Arthur Francis 1910.

Louisa Hammett 1858, the same year as prison hulks were abolished by the British, the British Empire took over the British East India Company and the transatlantic telegraph cable began business when US President James Buchanan and Queen Victoria exchanged pleasantries. Louisa, most probably named after her mother's sister (Louisa Gale), had at least ten children. Her first was a child out of wedlock (Elizabeth) a few months before her older sister Eliza experienced the same event. Both were in the South Newton Union Workhouse, Wilton. Neither father was noted. Perhaps these two sisters were servant girls who had been taken advantage of, not uncommon in those times.

Louisa married the following year in 1876 to George Muspratt (1848-1928). With the Industrial Revolution taking place northwards, Louise like so many of her other Dorset relatives, gyrated in that direction with her daughter and new husband soon afterwards, settling in Burton-upon-Trent, Staffordshire. George's married sister Emma Jane Kilford also went up with them, possibly at the same time. The two families in 1881 shared a house there with the occupations of the husbands noted as brewer's labourers.

Burton-upon-Trent was the epicentre for the brewing industry, which had about thirty-two breweries in 1881 employing eight thousand people. George Muspratt worked for Bass & Co, the main brewery there in their Middle Yard from 6th October 1876, and left on the 1st June 1877. He was re-employed on the 21st July 1877 and on the gratuity list 7th April 1917.

His three sons, Albert, Arthur and William were all employed there too (Coors Brewers Ltd – BBM.87.0067.00 Register of Men Employed in Middle Yard by Bass & Co). Burton-Upon-Trent offered employment, railway connections and all that comes with a busy and prosperous town, which was a very different place from where they had all come from in Wiltshire. But with coal being the main source of fuel in the industries there, it would have been very smoky and dirty, unlike the clean fresh air of the Wiltshire countryside. Most breweries did however have annual outings to the coast or other places by train, so some sort of light relief was to be had.

The December quarter of 1889 was a very sad time for Louisa and George with two of their baby daughters dying. Perhaps the local environment played a part. Louisa died in 1910 aged just 53, her children were:-

1) Elizabeth 1875, baseborn, probably named after her maternal grandmother who was run over by the train in Hampshire. She appears to have moved around in the censuses, Burton-upon- Trent, Leicester and Carnarvonshire in Conway. She possibly never married and died as Elizabeth Muspratt in 1945 aged 70.

2) Albert 1879, was a brewer's labourer, married in 1909 to Florence Annie Parker/Parkes. This marriage would not last long with Albert dying within a three month period aged 30. Florence would marry again in 1914 to Albert Gray.

3) Arthur 1881, like his father George, worked for Bass & Co, starting on the 5th April 1894 and leaving on the 28th July 1900. He

married Harriett Sanders in 1906. They had three children, but sadly they all died.

4) Annie Louise 1882 was married in 1903 to William John Griffin (born Bombay, India). They had a daughter Edith Annie in 1903.

5) William 1885, worked for Bass & Co as his father and brothers did, starting on the 25th October 1898 and left on 16th February 1900, noted as a boy. In 1911 was a boiler maker. He married in 1907 to Edith Rosaline/Rosalie Weston (1888-1967). William died in 1943 aged 58, with his children being Beatrice Louise, Dora May, Albert H, William A, James H, John, Gladys E, Walter V, Edith W and Shirley J.

6) Mary Edna 1887, died in 1889.

7) Alice 1889, died in 1889.

8) Edith 1891, died in 1911 aged 19.

9) May 1893, married Charles T Jones in 1912. They had children Ivy N M, Lawrence C, George H, Phyllis A, and Gordon C.

10) John 1898, died the same year.

Daniel Albert Hammett 1860, but known as Albert. His birth year also saw the birth of author J M Barrie, Florence Nightingale's *Notes on Nursing*, and in the United States the Pony Express embarked on the mail delivery express. Daniel married as Albert Daniel in 1889 to Mary Ann Seabourn (should be Leabourn, born 1856 of parents George Thomas Leabourn and Ann Brazier), although his military record states it was a year later. He possibly died as Albert Hammett in 1941 Pontypridd aged 80 years, and Mary in 1947 Yeovil aged 90 years.

Albert signed up with the army on 16th/18th August 1880 at Norwich with the 6th (Inniskillings) Dragoon Guards who were based there at the time. He was noted as Private 2104, aged 19 years 11 months, born Ringwood, Hampshire and a groom. His physical description was that of being 5ft 7¾" tall (a later examination stated 6ft 7¾" which I think is an error), 34" chest, a fresh complexion, grey eyes, dark brown hair, had brown marks between shoulders and had been vaccinated as a child. His religion was that of Church of England and next of kin noted as his father James of Netherhampton,

Salisbury. Albert acquired fourth class certificate on the 31st December 1880 and had a good character. He served:-

One hundred and forty-eight days 16/08/1880 - 10/01/1881 at home

Seven years and one hundred and forty-four days 11/01/1881 - 02/06/1888 South Africa

Forty-eight days 03/06/1888 – 18/-7/1888 South Africa

Four years and twenty-eight days 19/09/1888 – 15/08/1892 Home

Four years 24/08/1892 – 23/08/1896 army reservist

In total Albert served fourteen years with the 6th (Inniskillings) Dragoons and was discharged at Canterbury, appointed Corporal on the 6th April 1884 – 22nd December 1884, then back to Private.

He was stationed at Bennitt's Drift, Natal, South Africa on 3rd April 1881, and was in hospital there for two days on the 18th to the 19th November 1881 with febricula (fever). Then taken to Best Hospital, Newcastle, Natal the next day 20th – 26th for 7 days with the same condition. It must have been more than a simple fever as he stayed here for a further ninety-seven days until 1st March 1882.

Albert is stationed at Pinetown, Natal on the 22nd April where he appears for medical attention on the 8th until the 14th June 1883 for contusion (bruise) of side. Here he spends seven days in hospital. At the same location on the 17th September 1883 to 29th January 1884 Albert has an operation for an abscess of the buttock and spends one hundred and thirty-five days in hospital. This condition most probably brought on from riding. Again at the same location on the 25th until the 29th April 1884 Albert suffers fever and diarrhoea, spending five days in hospital.

June 1884 Albert is stationed at Zululand. He then is stationed at Pinetown on the 23rd October 1885, where from the 2nd until the 11th January 1886 Albert spends ten days in hospital for contusion (bruising) of the leg at the ball of the foot.

On the 19th May 1886 Albert is stationed at Fort Napier, Pietermaritzburg, Natal where he probably remained until leaving Natal for England in mid 1888. This fort was the base camp for his regiment 1881-1890 (The National Archives WO/97/2968).

South Africa must have seemed very different to the countryside Albert knew back in Dorset, Hampshire and Wiltshire. In South Africa there would have been the different languages, people and climate, not to mention the dangerous wild animals and reptiles. Also the threat from the native population and the Boers, although with the latter, a peace treaty had been established on the 23rd March 1881, just prior to Albert's arrival.

Albert had also missed the Zulu War of the 22nd January 1879 at Rorke's Drift on the borders of Natal/Zululand. No doubt these battles were still fresh in the minds of many. His Regiment was stationed at Norwich in 1880, arrived in Durban, South Africa in February 1881, in Transvaal 1881, and in Bechuanaland, Natal and Zululand in 1884-1890. The Regiment spent a total of nine years in South Africa, then returned in 1890 to be stationed in Brighton.

In 1901 Albert was a patient in a nursing home at Clifton, Bristol, perhaps as a result of his army service. The next census sees him as a porter of carriage, and they are living in Yeovil, Somerset with their only child who was:-

1) Conrad 1892, who had been a pupil at The Wilton Free School from the years 1902 to 1903. This was where twenty Foundation Boys were educated for free, with an interview after the application. Here they were deemed to receive a better education than that to be received at the National School. Conrad also attended school in Yetminster and Sherborne.

He signed up at Cheltenham in November 1913 as Sapper 25585 with the Royal Engineers. With them he saw much action in WW1 France and Flanders, at Armentieres, Ypres, Albert, Festubert and Cambrai. Unfortunately Conrad suffered injuries on the 25th March 1918 near Courcelette where he was shot in the thigh, and died on Monday 15th April 1918 aged 25 in the General Hospital at Etaples. Conrad had a record of three years unbroken service in France and had just returned from a fortnight's leave on the 2nd March 1918.

Before the war Conrad had served an apprenticeship with Messrs Jesty & Co of Middle Street, Wilton, Wiltshire, where he was a cabinet maker. This establishment was a furniture shop. Conrad was buried at Grave XXIX.B.21 Etaples Military Cemetery, Pas de Calais, France, and is also remembered on the Yeovil War Memorial, which was unveiled on the 15th July 1921 with two hundred and twenty-six names on it. He was awarded three medals, the Victory, British and Star (The National Archives WO/97/6338, WO/372/8, De Ruvigny's Roll of Honour 1914-1924, Commonwealth War Graves Commission and The Western Gazette 26/04/1916).

Charles James Hammett 1877, the first born of his father's second marriage, the same year saw the publication of Anna Sewell's *Black Beauty*, The Ambulance Association founded (later to become the St John Ambulance Brigade), and the record-player invented by American Thomas Edison. Charles was probably named after an elder half-brother, who died in 1876, with the middle name in honour of their father.

Charles signed up with the 6th Dragoon Guards (Carabiniers) as Private 3897 at Aldershot, Hampshire on 28th March 1898. He was noted as a groom aged 20 years and 11 months. Three days earlier at Dalston, on the 25th March 1898, he had a medical examination, where his description was that of being 5ft 7" (and five eighths) tall, weighed 126 lbs, chest minimum 33", maximum 35", fresh complexion, grey eyes, dark brown hair and a scar on right heel. His religion was that of Church of England. His twelve year service record with them was thus:-

Home	25/03/1898 - 02/11/1899
South Africa	03/11/1899 - 15/08/1902
India	16/08/1902 - 31/01/1906
Home	01/02/1906 - 24/03/1906
Army Reservist	25/03/1906 - 24/03/1910.

Medal award was for The Queen's South Africa Medal with clasps:-
Cape Colony
Paardebert
Dreifontein
Johannesburg
Belfast
Diamond Hill.
(The National Archives WO/97/6338).

Charles married in 1913 to Alice Annie Padden (1881-1969, parents Charles and Selina), with whom he had six children, three of whom were triplets. Before their marriage in 1911, Alice was a cook in Salisbury for Major Reginald Seaburne May. He later became a General commanding the 49th West Riding Division, serving the British Army from 1898-1939. He was in the Second Boer War and World War 1. His awards listed:-

Knight Commander of the Order of the Bath
Knight Commander of the Order of the British Empire
Companion of the Order of St Michael and St George
Distinguished Service Order.

Meanwhile that year in 1911 Charles was a groom in nearby Wilton. Charles died in 1952 at Salisbury aged 75. Charles and Annie's six children were:-

1) Marjory 1913 Wilton, married 1937 to Leslie G Scott and had two children.

2) Mary S (Selina) 1916 Wilton, named presumably in honour of both her grandmothers. Married 1941 to James Heuston, had two children.

3) Triplet John (Jack) Charles 1921, married twice, 1951 to Catherine Mary Shearmon, and 1962 to Hilda Elizabeth Stainer.

4) Triplet Eva Kate 1921, never married.

5) Triplet Alice E 1921, died 1922.

6) Dorothy V 1924, married 1948 to Arthur Ernest Unwin, had two children.

Fanny Hammett 1879 was the second and last child born of her father's second marriage. Her birth year also saw the Natural History Museum in London designed by Alfred Waterhouse, Gilbert and Sullivan's opera *Pirates of Penzance* premiered in New York City's Fifth Avenue Theatre, and in Utica New York Frank Winfield Woolworth's first *five-and-dime* store opened, only to fail within weeks.

Fanny married in 1909 to William Alexander Standhaft (1881-1962), who in WW1 was possibly Private 202676 with the Hampshire Regiment, and awarded the medals of Victory and British (The National Archives WO/372 & Ancestry).

In the 1901 census Fanny was a cook for the Hubbert family in the Branksome area of Bournemouth, but in 1911 she was married and found living with husband William, a house decorator in Hereford. They returned eastwards again and settled in William's birth area of Christchurch where their children were born. Fanny died aged 81 in 1960 in the Christchurch area. Fanny and William had three children who were:-

1) Constance M 1910.
2) Alec 1913, possibly died in 1931 aged 17.
3) Stanley 1915.

FAMILY TREE OF JAMES HAMMETT'S UNCLE WILLIAM 1780 -1841/1851

William Hammett wed Sarah Pearce

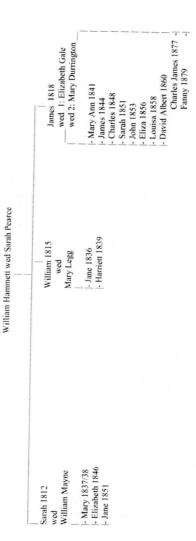

Sarah 1812
wed
William Mayne

|- Mary 1837/38
|- Elizabeth 1846
|- Jane 1851

William 1815
wed
Mary Legg

|- Jane 1836
|- Harriett 1839

James 1818
wed 1: Elizabeth Gale
wed 2: Mary Durrington

|- Mary Ann 1841
|- James 1844
|- Charles 1848
|- Sarah 1851
|- John 1853
|- Eliza 1856
|- Louisa 1858
|- David Albert 1860
    |- Charles James 1877 -
    |- Fanny 1879

FAMILY TREE OF JAMES HAMMETT'S COUSIN SARAH HAMMETT 1812

Sarah Hammett wed William Mayne

Mary 1837	Elizabeth 1846	Jane 1851
wed	wed	wed
William George Lumber	Herbert Legg	Charles Sexey

Mary 1837
wed
William George Lumber

- Emily Jane Maine 1864
- William Henry 1866 wed Lois Meaden
- Edward George 1868 wed Emily Elizabeth Gould
- Sarah Elizabeth 1871 wed Richard Massey
- Walter James 1873 wed 1: Ellen Louise Stevens
  wed 2: Jane Attwood

Elizabeth 1846
wed
Herbert Legg

- Mary Elizabeth 1863 wed Edward Massey
- Louisa Anne 1866 wed James Scanlon
- Elizabeth Maria 1869 wed Samuel Fletcher
- Frances Jane 1871
- Edwin George 1875

Jane 1851
wed
Charles Sexey

- Annie Mary 1874
  wed William Hewitt
- Louisa Agnes 1877
  wed John Thomas Higgins
- William Harry 1879
  wed Florence Dakin
- adopted Olive Brown 1896
  possibly wed Albert Haycock

FAMILY TREE OF JAMES HAMMETT'S COUSIN WILLIAM HAMMETT 1815

William Hammett wed Mary Legg

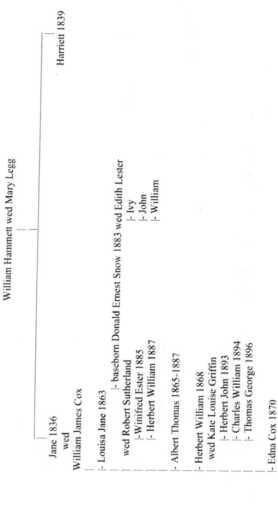

Jane 1836
wed
William James Cox

Harriett 1839

|- Louisa Jane 1863

    |- baseborn Donald Ernest Snow 1883 wed Edith Lester

        |- Ivy
        |- John
        |- William

    wed Robert Sutherland
      |- Winifred Ester 1885
      |- Herbert William 1887

|- Albert Thomas 1865-1887

|- Herbert William 1868
    wed Kate Louise Griffin
      |- Herbert John 1893
      |- Charles William 1894
      |- Thomas George 1896

|- Edna Cox 1870

FAMILY TREE OF JAMES HAMMETT'S COUSIN JAMES HAMMETT 1818

James Hammett wed 1: Elizabeth Gale

- Mary Ann 1842

- James 1844 wed Eliza Reeves – issue Mary Edith 1880

- Charles 1848-1876

- Sarah 1851 wed George Fellowes – issue George Walter 1872, Ellen 1874, Elizabeth 1877, Jane 1879, Minnie 1881, twins 1885 William & Edith, Sarah 1887

- John 1853 wed Helen Ruth Wilson – issue Elsie 1884, Mabel 1885, Frederick James 1889, Ethel 1894

- Eliza 1856 had baseborn Mary Louise 1875 who wed George John Thomas

- Louisa 1858 had baseborn Elizabeth 1875, then wed George Muspratt – issue Albert 1879, Arthur 1881, Annie Louise 1882. William 1885, Mary Edna 1887, Alice 1889, Edith 1891, May 1893, John 1898

- Daniel Albert 1860 wed Mary Ann Seabourn/Leaburn – issue Conrad 1892

- Elizabeth Jane 1862-1862

wed 2: Mary Durrington

- Charles James 1877 wed Alice Annie Padden – issue Marjory 1913, Mary Selina 1916, triplets John Charles, Eva Kate, Alice 1921, Dorothy 1924

- Fanny 1879 wed William Alexander Standhaft – issue Constance 1910, Alec 1913, Stanley 1915

PART II

Chapter 11

JAMES HAMMETT'S UNCLE RICHARD AND HIS DESCENDANTS

Richard Hammett was born 1788 to his father's second wife Mary at Southover and baptised in nearby Tolpuddle on the 18th December of that year. The same year saw the birth of (Sir) Robert Peel, a future Prime Minister, Botany Bay in Australia received the first ship carrying English convicts and King George III's mental state declined that year only to recover later.

According to his Settlement Examination in the county of Southampton (Hampshire) in 1815 (Hampshire Record Office – 22M84/PO113a/19), Richard was confined in Winchester Bridewell prison. It also noted he had been born in Southover, Dorset, where his father resided legally. Further information stated he had married his wife Eliza (not Elizabeth) in Ringwood in 1814 by banns and that they had a daughter Sarah aged 6 weeks old, with Richard being able to sign his name to this document. Richard, under the surname of Hammitt, had married Elizabeth Welch on the 26th November 1814 at Ringwood (although later she stated her father's surname was Springer). Elizabeth was born either in 1781 (as per her age at death), 1790 or 1791 (from census information).

Richard returned to Tolpuddle sometime between the latter part of 1826 and mid 1833, bringing his family with him. He was linked by birth to the Tolpuddle Martyrs as he was the half-uncle to James Hammett Tolpuddle Martyr and his sister Elizabeth who married Stephen Loveless whose father John* was first cousin to Tolpuddle Martyrs George and James Loveless and their sister Diniah who married Thomas Standfield another Tolpuddle Martyr. Richard later would connect further to the Tolpuddle Martyrs, when two of his sons married two Loveless sisters. Their father William Loveless was brother to John* mentioned above.

A mason (bricklayer) by trade, Richard was buried aged 65 in Tolpuddle during the August of 1852 with the notation of being from Puddletown (Piddletown). Elizabeth then married again in 1855 at Tolpuddle to labourer Benjamin Spicer who also had lost his spouse. His father had also been a labourer by the same name. Both bride and groom resided at Tolpuddle, and Elizabeth revealed her father as Thomas Springer, a labourer.

Elizabeth died in 1865 and was buried at Tolpuddle aged 74 on the 10th June by Vicar George L Nash. Benjamin died in 1867 aged 73 and is also buried in Tolpuddle.

During her time married to Richard Hammett, Elizabeth had had their six children in Ringwood where they had settled. These children were Sarah 1815 (possibly buried as an infant on the 31st December 1815 Ringwood, no other information has been gleaned for her), Samuel (possibly born 1817 and buried as an infant at Ringwood on the 11th June 1817), William 1819, John 1822/23, Francis 1823 and Richard 1826.

William Hammett 1819-1898

William, son of Richard 1788, was born 1819 Ringwood, Hampshire and baptised there on the 30th May that year as Hammitt. The same year Queen Victoria was born and the Factory Act was passed. Noted as a mason, William married at Tolpuddle in 1840 to Judith Loveless before witnesses Charles Orman and Elizabeth Loveless (the latter was probably Judith's sister who would later marry William's brother John).

Judith was born at Tolpuddle in 1809, and baptised there on the 9th April that year of parents William and Jane (nee Hoare) Loveless. Her father, William Loveless, was first cousin to George and James Loveless (two of the six Tolpuddle Martyrs) and their sister Diniah (who married another Tolpuddle Martyr Thomas Standfield). William Loveless also had a brother John who was father to Stephen who married Elizabeth Hammett, a sister of James Hammett (Tolpuddle Martyr), both these Hammett siblings were in turn first half-cousins to William Hammett, son-in-law to William Loveless himself. What a tangled lot these Tolpuddle Hammett and Loveless families were, many of whom were Methodists.

William Hammett himself would join his Methodist relatives by converting and became a staunch Methodist lay preacher serving for over 60 years. This was a duty which would have involved travelling around to the various Methodist Chapels in other towns and villages. He would also find the time to build the second Methodist Chapel in Tolpuddle. The first had been the nearby barn on the opposite side of the road. This building project was aided by his brother John who was also a Methodist, along with other local people assisting, including their half-cousin, Tolpuddle Martyr James Hammett.

The two brothers had entered into a mortgage on the 17th October 1849 (Dorset History Centre – NM2/S/19/TS/3/1). They also had their own building business partnership and traded under the name of W & J Hammett. This arrangement came to a mutual end on the 13th June 1861 (The National Archives – The London Gazette 28/06/1861).

By the time of construction of the Chapel, William was noted as being in occupation at Church Close, where a piece of land measuring 63ft in depth by 28ft in width was part of it. This land was to be where the Methodist Chapel would be built. Therefore, not only did William own the chapel, but the land too.

The first service was held on the 1st January 1863 by Rev Mr Richards. The chapel had taken about two years to complete. The Memorial Arch in memory and honour of the Tolpuddle Martyrs was erected in 1912 just to the front of this chapel on the pavement side. The unveiling was carried out by Arthur Henderson, a Labour MP and Methodist, on the 27th May 1912. Inside the Methodist Chapel William built with his brother John is a scroll on the wall dedicated to him. This reads:-

In memory of William Hammett who died August 9th 1898 aged 79 years. For sixty-two years a local preacher in this circuit. This tablet is erected by the local preachers in grateful remembrance of his work.

According to his grandson, William Jabez Seth Puckett (1878-1969), Tolpuddle had not always been so kind to him (Pamela Kitchener of ((Swindon?)) Evening Advertiser 19/07/1961). He was turned out of his ancestral village because of his Methodist beliefs and family connections to the Tolpuddle Martyrs. For forty years he suffered this and only returned with the aid of a friend who helped him, and presumably his brother John, buy land, which did not belong to the local influential people or the Church of England. Although William appears in Tolpuddle on all the censuses, his time of banishment could have been before 1841.

There had been local confrontation associated with Methodism years before the deportation of the Tolpuddle Martyrs in 1834. As early as 13th October 1818 in Tolpuddle, the opening of the first Methodist Chapel (barn) saw a mob of one hundred strong await the Ministers and congregation who were pelted with missiles. One unfortunate lady was pushed into a ditch whilst others were hurt and carriages damaged with the horses startled.

Folks who entered the Wesleyan Chapel in Tolpuddle were denied work, banished and persecuted, as George Loveless (Tolpuddle Martyr) would later recall. His father Thomas, in 1810, had his home in Tolpuddle licensed as a place of worship. With both son and father George and Thomas Loveless being related to Judith Loveless, William's wife, and therefore relatives of William Jabez and Seth Pucket, perhaps his statement of ancestral banishment also referred to them.

William died in 1898, leaving a will with effects valued at £830 16s 10d (in 2012 roughly equates to £91,356). William Richard Snook, postmaster, and Gideon Denner Wight, provision merchant, were both named as the executors. William's wife Judith had died just over three years earlier than him in 1895 aged 86. In between this (second) Methodist Chapel and the Memorial Arch, is a small area where there are some graves with headstones. William and Judith are buried together in one, whilst their two daughters Sarah and Clare are buried nearby in another together. Their headstones read as follows:-

"In loving memory of Judith the beloved wife of William Hammett who died March 29th 1895 aged 86 years. The memory of the just is blessed. Also of the above William Hammett who died August 9th 1898 aged 79 years. "So he bringth them unto their desired haven".

The headstone for their daughters is next to them, and reads:-

In loving memory of Sarah and Clara Hammett.

On the opposite side of this little area are another two graves, which hold William and Judith's daughter Jane and in the other her daughters, who were their grandchildren. These read:-

In loving memory of our dear little mother Jane Puckett at rest.
And

In loving memory of Margaret Clara the beloved daughter of Seth and Jane Puckett born August 27th 1871 died January 27th 1892. "The maid is not dead but sleepeth." Also Edith sister of the above born March 22nd 1870 died March 20th 1882. "He called a little child unto him."

Over the years there has been mention of a photograph of an elderly couple with the man standing beside the woman who is sitting on a chair. The photograph was by W Pouncy with Dorchester and Swanage noted, and apparently on the reverse bore the words of Mr and Mrs Hammett, Tolpuddle. Some have jumped to conclusions and suggested this was of James Hammett the Tolpuddle Martyr and his wife.

But this is not the case, for the photograph is in fact of William Hammett and his wife Judith in their twilight years. W Pouncy was Walter Pouncy (born 1845 Fordington - 1918), who took over from his father John, a pioneer in photography in 1872. Therefore this photograph can be dated after that period.

William and Judith had children Jane 1844, Sarah Ann 1845, William 1847 and Clara 1852.

Jane 1844, the same year saw the first workers' Co-operative Society opened called the *Pioneers of Rochdale*, the safety match invented by a Swedish man called Gustaf Erik Pasch, and the United States of America elected James K Polk as the 11th president. Jane married Seth Puckett in 1867 by licence at Tolpuddle Parish Church with Vicar George Nash conducting. Their witnesses that day were William and Sarah Ann Hammett (Jane's father or brother and sister). Seth was recorded as a widowed gamekeeper of Harewood, Yorkshire and Jane a dressmaker of Tolpuddle.

Seth was born in 1839 at Tincleton in Dorset of parents James Puckett and Tabitha Wellstead who had themselves married in

235

Tincleton in 1834. Seth was first married in the Dorchester area of 1862 to Emma Rawles, but she died in 1864.

There is a Yorkshire connection to this section of Hammetts, as Jane's uncle Richard moved to the region circa 1871-1881. Seth Puckett was working and living at Harewood in 1867 at the time of his marriage in Tolpuddle, and then they moved back up there until the 1871 census which sees them residing in Tolpuddle (their first two children were born in Yorkshire).

The question arises what drew them up to Yorkshire in the first place? Was it family connections, work or could it have been associated with the Methodist Church. Whatever the reasons were, they returned to Dorset.

Seth would die before Jane, aged 80 in 1919 within the Poole district, and Jane in the same area aged 81 in 1925. Jane was buried in the little graveyard at the front of the Methodist Chapel in Tolpuddle, next to her two daughters, with her parents and two sisters in two graves on the opposite side. Children for Jane and Seth were:-

1) Mary Judith Loveless born 1868, the same year as the last public hanging at Newgate Prison (Michael Barrett, a Fenian bomber) and the first Trade Union Congress is held in Manchester. Mary wed Thomas Job Fox (1868-1938) in 1891. They had children Leonard Douglas 1894 (possibly married Amy D Summerfield), Clifford William 1897 (possibly married Margaret Lind), Margaret Hilda 1900 and Aubrey Harry 1906 (married Oive M Sleeman).

2) Edith Annie Sarah born 1870 Yorkshire, died 1882 aged 11, buried Tolpuddle Methodist Church with sister Margaret.

3) Margaret Clara born 1871, died 1892 aged 20, buried Tolpuddle Methodist Church with sister Edith. In her short life, was a dressmaker.

4) Harry William Hammett born 1873, the same year David Livingstone the explorer died in Zambia Africa, in London Alexandra Palace is opened only to be destroyed by fire 16 days later, and in New York Central Park is created. Harry married in 1897 to Martha Elizabeth Shave born in 1878 of parents George Gill Shave and Ellen. Harry was not to have a long life as he died aged 35

on Friday 27th November 1908 at ten minutes to eight in the morning in the Christchurch district aged 34.

He was accidently shot by Mr E Caudwell and died from those injuries. An inquest to his death was held at Palmer's Ford Farm, Fernwood the next day, with coroner Robert Druitt attending (Christchurch Times 1908 – Christchurch Local History Society).

Harry had been a gamekeeper employed by George Parrott of Princes Street, Cavendish Square, London, and Harry's Martha identified his body. She stated her husband was 34 (not 35) and that Harry had said little since the accident, apart from telling her he was dying.

Hensley John Dear of St Leonard's was under-gamekeeper to George Parrott. He recalled that he was at a shooting party with Harry at Burnt Common on the Thursday before Harry had died. Others there were Charles Button a coach proprietor of Sopley, Mr William Henry Turner a corn and coal merchant of 127 Holdenhurst Road, Bournemouth and Mr E Caudwell. They all spread out in search of rabbits. One was sighted and when they all turned in that direction Mr Caudwell's gun went off hitting Harry.

Doctors Cressey and Gott were called for. They did what they could for him but he was badly hurt with wounds in the front just above the groin and at the back above the right buttock between the hip and spine. It was not a pretty sight and I spare the reader more of the details, sufficed to say the doctors probably knew there was no hope for him.

He was put on a stretcher and taken home where they tried to perform an operation, but Harry's injuries were too great and he died the following morning. Shock from being shot was given as cause of death. It would appear it was an accident with either Mr Caudwell's finger or coat button hitting the trigger upon turning.

Harry had managed to say to Mr Caudwell that, whether he died or not, he was not to blame for the accident. Charles Button said he was with Harry from when he was shot until eleven o'clock that evening. Harry had told him it was an accident with no one to blame and that Mr Caudwell was one of the most careful shots he had had with him that season. People who knew both the deceased and Mr Caudwell had said they had the best of relations between them.

The jury gave the verdict that Harry had died from shock consequent on a gunshot wound. The newspaper report further went on to say Harry was buried he following Wednesday afternoon at Verwood.

Martha possibly died in 1947 in the Dorchester district aged 69. Harry and Martha's children were Margaret Annie 1902 (married William Herbert Loader), and (Ena) Harryena W M 1909 obviously named after her father (married Evan Willoughby C Smith).

5) Lottie Jane born 1875, the same year saw John Buchan the writer and politician born, and Captain Matthew Webb become the first person to swim the English Channel, which took him twenty-one hours and forty-five minutes. Additionally in Venezuela and Columbia an earthquake took sixteen thousand lives.

Lottie married 1898 to Jacob William Gibbons born 1875 of parents Jacob Gibbons and Keziah Gibbs Record. His father Jacob was once employed and lived at the Dorset County Lunatic Asylum in Charminster as an attendant. This establishment had also employed other individuals in the Tolpuddle Hammett family tree, and presumably was a main source of work in the area during those times.

Some may jump to the conclusion that there is a link between this family of Gibbons and that of Harriett, James Hammett Tolpuddle Martyr's first wife. From my research, this does not appear to be the case.

Jacob was head gardener employed by Sir Eustace Edward Twistlton-Wykeham-Fiennes (1864-1943, 1st Baronet, soldier, Liberal Politian and Colonial Administrator, grandfather of explorer Sir Ranulph Fiennes, and great grandfather of actors Ralph and Joseph Fiennes).

The Fiennes family had a house called Kya-Lami (now Studland Bay House) at Studland. *Kyalami* is a Zulu word which means my home, and presumably a word Sir Fiennes picked up previously whilst serving in the military campaigns in South Africa, or possibly named by his wife, who was born in South Africa. He had previously in Canada run out of funds then tried his luck in Cape Town where he met his wife in 1894.

This wife was called Florence Agnes Rathfelder, a wealthy widow of Prussian descent. Her first husband had been Arthur Fletcher, a native of Scotland, who had died when thrown from a horse.

Sir Fiennes would die himself in 1943. Sir Ranulph Fiennes, mentioned above, made a brief mention of the Tolpuddle Martyrs in his book *Mad Dogs and Englishmen an Expedition round my family*. By all accounts Sir Eustace Fiennes was a generous employer and appears to have paid for Jacob's peritonitis operation. This operation was a success and part of the healing process saw Jacob signing up as a steward on board the Titanic. The taking of sea air was beneficial to recovery and presumably with lighter duties than to those of a gardener.

Aged 36 and married with five children Jacob was to find himself signing up for work on board RMS Titanic of the White Star Line on the 4th April 1912 at Southampton, in the capacity of a second-class steward.

Jacob's monthly wage was £3 15s (equated in 2012 to roughly £290.17), and his home address given was that of Harbour View, Studland Bay. He was to be on board by six o'clock in the morning of Wednesday 10th April 1912. This was the day Titanic would sail out of Southampton at quarter past twelve in the afternoon bound for New York via Cherbourg, France where it arrived at six thirty that evening and left again at ten past eight that night. Sailing off to Queenstown/Cobh in Ireland where it would arrive on Thursday 11th April at eleven thirty that morning, only to leave again at one thirty that afternoon.

For both Jacob and the Titanic, this would be their maiden voyage, as neither had sailed before. What luxury this liner and the distinguished guests aboard must have appeared to Jacob. He even mailed a postcard he bought on board to Miss K Payne who resided at The Green, Studland Bay, Dorset from Queenstown on the 11th April 1912. The message on that postcard read:-

Nearing Queenstown. Good voyage up to now. Kind regards to all. J. W. Gibbons.

This postcard sold at auction in 2002 for £7,750.00 (2012 equated to £10,676.73). Another newspaper stated £8,912.00 (2012 equated to £13,655.19), perhaps including the buyer's premium, to a British collector. Sadly the price went over the £3,000.00 (2012 equates to £4,132.93), which the Gibbons family had set aside to purchase it to add to the family collection.

Kate Payne lived at 26 The Green, Studland with her sisters. All were Methodists and presumably this was the connection to Jacob. 1911 living at The Green, Studland is Walter Payne 67 widower carpenter, with his three unmarried daughters who were Kate 35 a laundress, Blanche 31 a laundress and Ida 27 assisting laundress, all born at Studland. 1901 at the same address Walter Payne is 57 an assistant overseer of the poor, his wife is Elizabeth 57 a laundress born Studland, with daughters Mabel K (Kate) 26 a laundress and Ida 17 a domestic housemaid (Blanche is not there). Now this address is a seventeenth century white-washed cob cottage and, when I visited, it is a holiday let.

On Sunday 14th April 1912 just before midnight, at about eleven forty on a clear star-filled sky in the calm seas of the North Atlantic Ocean the Titanic was struck by an iceberg. In fact the Titanic had been receiving iceberg warnings in the sea but chose to ignore them. She sent out a distress message at a quarter past eleven that night giving the position of latitude 41.46N longitude 50.14W, along with the text:-

We have struck iceberg sinking fast come to our assistance.

This message was picked up by SS Birma, a Russian ship, whose position was south west one hundred miles away, and who would arrive at six thirty the next morning, which would be too late to pick up survivors. At one forty in the morning, SS Birma also picked up another message from Titanic which read:-

SOS SOS CQD – MGY We are sinking fast. Passengers being put into boats.

SOS stood for save our souls and was the newly introduced international code. CQD meant come quick danger and MGY was Titanic's call code. Titanic sank some two hours and forty minutes after hitting the iceberg on Monday 14th April 1912 at twenty past two in the morning.

Out of the two thousand and two hundred and twenty-seven passengers and crew on board, only seven hundred and five were rescued, with three of those dying later. The passenger numbers for this ship are not exact and are based on the records available at the time.

By all accounts approximately one thousand five hundred and seventeen people had lost their lives. Jacob was one of the lucky ones to survive. The timing of the iceberg collision and Jacob's shift finishing were said to be about the same time. Therefore, unlike his crewmates whom he had tried to stir, and who did not believe him, Jacob was alert to the situation.

Jacob's lifesaver was lifeboat No. 11 which launched at one thirty-five in the morning starboard side, the twelfth lifeboat to be lowered into the icy ocean.

A sailor on Titanic shouted down to them to row fast otherwise the suction from the sinking ship would take them down too. It was overloaded with over seventy (another source said sixty) people on board it, including Jacob and some passengers and two little children whom he would later talk of helping into it. He had looked for more people to assist getting into the boat but he could see none. Apparently many wanted to stay on board the main ship, some even going back into their cabins for treasured possessions.

Lifeboat No. 11 was about half a mile away when the Titanic sank. Jacob recalled the terrible cries of those left on board and said the memory would never leave him. He further went on to say the band was playing at the time the tune *Nearer my God to Thee*.

Jacob, along with the other Titanic survivors, was finally rescued by SS Carpathia of the Cunard Line, which arrived at four o'clock that Monday morning. This ship had been fifty-eight miles away when it learned of Titanic's situation and upon arrival at the last known position of Titanic no ship was to be found. Turning off her engines to listen, a green flare was sighted which came from one of the lifeboats.

As dawn broke the vista would reveal a dreadful sight, a sea full of wreckage including the dead and lifeboats full of frozen people.

First-class passenger Elizabeth Walton-Allen was the first to set foot on SS Carpathia at ten past four that morning, and informed them that the Titanic had indeed sunk. Eventually all the lifeboats came to the sides of the ship to be rescued, the last being number twelve at half past eight that morning, overloaded with people. At nine o'clock that morning the last survivor from Titanic to be rescued boarded SS Carpathia.

The night of Thursday 18th April 1912 saw SS Carpathia's arrival in New York, where at Pier 54, Little West 12th Street the survivors of the Titanic disembarked. Thousands of people, including the media and press waited to greet them.

Meanwhile back in Studland, Dorset, Jacob's family must have thought the worst, as they had received condolences, including a telegram from the House of Commons. So, how relieved they must have been a few days later to receive one dated the 20th April 1912 directly from Jacob himself, simply saying:-

Saved well. Daddy.

But the family would not set eyes on Jacob for at least another ten days as, once in New York, Jacob, along with one hundred and sixty-six crew members from the Titanic, was transferred to the Red Star Line SS Lapland.

Having spent little time in America, they set sail for Plymouth arriving at eight o'clock on the morning of Sunday 28th April 1912 at Cawsand Bay. The Great Western Railway tender Sir Richard Grenville would ferry them to the Millbay Docks in Plymouth just after noon that day, where modified accommodation had been set up for them.

This is where a hot meal awaited them and, once they had signed their statements for the Board of Trade Inquiry, they were free to leave the dock, provided they returned to sleep the night there. The women, however, were to spend the night in a nearby hotel. A special train would transport them the next day back to Southampton.

Two officials from the British Seafarers Union, namely Mr T Lewis who was the President, and Mr A Cannon who was the Secretary, had arrived to ensure that the rights and liberties of the crew were respected. They had encountered problems trying to get word to the crew whilst on board SS Lapland, but did manage this act whilst they were transported on the tender. As a result, the crew flatly refused to sign any statements unless these Union officials were present.

How Jacob must have longed to just get on the train homeward bound, and this would explain the delay, for he did not arrive at Swanage Station until half past seven on the evening of Tuesday 30th April 1912.

As it was the weekly practice night of the local bell ringers in Swanage, this was the sound which greeted him and his fellow Titanic crew-member, Charles Burgess. Charles was younger than Jacob, being born in 1893, a baker who had worked at sea before. His last address was in Southampton, so I wonder if perhaps Jacob was taking him to his home at Harbour View. Accounts told how tired and fatigued Jacob looked when he returned, but one of his first ports of call was to visit his mother. The worry of it all had reduced her to her sick bed.

Another Titanic survivor in lifeboat No. 11 with Jacob was the "Titanic Baby". This was 10 month old Frank Phillip Aks (1911-1991). Whilst still on board Titanic during the confusion of the forthcoming tragedy he had been taken from his mother's arms by someone who had panicked and put him into that lifeboat.

Frank's mother Leah was a young married woman from Warsaw, who was travelling in third-class. She had been unable to board the same lifeboat as Frank and instead managed to get into lifeboat No 13, which was not unlucky for her. It is amazing that she even managed to get out of third-class, as many from that area had not been able to escape. So to find herself just beforehand standing on Titanic's deck beside Lady Astor must have seemed unreal. Furthermore Lady Astor gave her a white silk scarf to wrap baby Frank in. Once on board lifeboat No. 11 Frank was further wrapped in a woollen lap blanket.

Later, on the Carpathia, Leah spotted Frank in the arms of an Italian woman and asked Captain Rostron to assist her with his rightful return to her. Leah identified her son by his strawberry birthmark and this proof was enough to reunite mother and baby. This pair would later go on to collect one of the largest individual collections of Titanic memorabilia, later known as the Frank Aks collection.

Some have said Jacob worked on the Canadian Pacific Railway, possibly in the capacity of cook, for about a year. As the employee records do not seem to be available, I have not been able to clarify this theory. However, I did come across a J Gibbons, aged 37, a waiter born England, who was noted on the passenger list, third-class for the Grampian steamship of the Allan Line. This vessel departed from Liverpool in March 1913 bound for Saint John in Canada. No other information was available for verification.

Jacob certainly was a man of many talents donning various hats, that of head gardener, beekeeper, saloon steward. He ran a boarding house and was a good cook. The latter occupation apparently took him to France in WW1 where his employer, the Hon Florence Fiennes, had a hospital for the troops. She in fact had had two convalescent homes for the war-wounded, one in Dunkirk, France, and one in her Studland home where Jacob had worked as head gardener. But sadly the one at Dunkirk had to be closed after the German army fired shells on it, with Florence escaping.

The Hon Florence Fiennes would later be awarded the French medal and the OBE. Jacob had worked as a cook at this Dunkirk convalescent home, presumably until it was shut down. He then joined the British Red Cross Society and the Order of St John of Jerusalem as a chauffeur for the ambulances. Jacob already possessed culinary skills but would also have been trained in first aid. His awards were for the 1914 Star, Victory and British medals.

Once the war was over Jacob returned home to Studland and ran the boarding house with wife Lotti and their family. Lotti died in 1955 aged 79 and her ashes were scattered over her mother's grave situated at the frontage of the Methodist Chapel in Tolpuddle.

(Bournemouth Echo 02/05/1912 – Bournemouth Library Services, Bournemouth Echo 29/03/2002, 30/04/2002, 16/04/2007 – Bournemouth Echo Archives, Warwick & Warwick Collectable Auctioneers, Encyclopedia Titanica, Mad Dogs and Englishmen an Expedition round my family – Sir Ranulph Fiennes, Who Sailed on Titanic – Debbie Beavis, private correspondence with the Gibbons family, The National Archives BT/100/259, BT/27, WO/372/7/244/278, WO/372/244611.)

Jacob died in 1965 at the General Hospital in Swanage aged 89. His death certificate noted he was a retired hotelier and blind pensioner of 19 Woodside, Studland Bay. His ashes were scattered in the graveyard of the Methodist Church in Studland, of which he was a founding member. Here a stone on the chapel wall was erected which read:-

In memory of Jacob Gibbons lifelong Methodist Survivor of the Titanic disaster 1912, 10.10.1875 – 25.2.1965.

This chapel closed on Sunday 26th June 2011 and the following day the stone was removed to nearby St Nicholas Church to be close to other relatives. Jacob had lived a long and very eventful life, with history demonstrating just how lucky he had been to escape disaster and death. The following census and dates reveal the noted information for Lottie and Jacob along with his employers the Fiennes family:-

<u>1911</u> Living in 8 rooms at Harbour View, Studland. Jacob is 37 born Charminster and a lodging house proprietor. Wife Lottie is 37 born Tolpuddle and assists in the business of the lodging house. They had been married for twelve years with five children all of whom were alive and with them. These were Annie 10, Edith 8, William 6, Freda 3 and baby (Jeanie) 3 days old.

<u>1911</u> Florence Fiennes (wife of Sir Eustace Edward Twistlton-Wykeham-Fiennes who was not there, these being the employers of Jacob) is living at 8 Buckingham Palace Gardens, London. She is aged 44, married and born Wynberg (Cape Town), South Africa. With her are Ethel Fletcher 22, single and born Cape Town (most probably Florence's daughter), Ranulph Fiennes 5½ and born Cromwell Place, London. Also a German lady unwed, 40 and whose surname looks like von Jonte. Lastly there were five servants who were: Elizabeth Abbott 34 born Lambeth the cook, Emily Charlotte Cullen 22 born Clapham the kitchen maid, Albert (cannot read his surname or place of birth) 28 the butler, Lucy Guest 20 born Notting Hill the housemaid, and Mabel Bloomfield 27 born Reading the maid.

Florence Agnes Rathfelder, otherwise Florence Fiennes was born circa 1868 at Wynberg near Cape Town. Her father was John of Constantia which was also near Cape Town. There had been noted a Johan (John) George Rathfelder who was a Quarter Master in the cavalry at Wynberg and Simon's Town during the years 1857-1861. Perhaps this was Florence's father. Florence had first married Arthur

Woodward Fletcher, then married Lt Col Eustace Edward Twisleton-Wykeham-Fiennes 1st Baronet at Pretoria in South Africa on 6th November 1894. She died on the 31st October 1950.

1915 Jacob William Gibbons is listed in Kelly's Directory at Harbour View, Studland – apartments, home comforts, board if required.

1915 Hon Eustace Edward Twisleton-Wykeham-Fiennes M.P., J.P. is listed in Kelly's Directory at Kya-Lami, Studland.

Children for Lottie Jane Puckett and Jacob William Gibbons were:-

1) **Annie Clara Constance 1900**, married William J Strong.

2) **Kezia Edith Gibbs 1903**, named as Kezia Gibbs after her paternal grandmother. Married as Edith K G Gibbons to William A Grant.

3) **William Henry Robert 1905**, married Joan E M Smith.

4) **Freda Mabel Elizabeth 1908**, married Henry A Sales whose brother Edward A Sales married Freda's sister Jeanie.

5) **Jeanie Lottie Record 1911**, named Lottie after her mother, and Record after her paternal grandmother. She married Edward A Sales whose brother Henry A Sales married Jeanie's sister Freda).

6) **Arthur George Jacob 1916**, married Susan Taylor.

6) Arthur James born 1877, baptised Tolpuddle 7th July 1877, died the same year.

7) William Jabez Seth born 1878. The same year witnessed the death of Anne Sewell who was the author of *Black Beauty*, Thomas Hardy's *Return of the Native* was introduced and David Edward Hughes invented the microphone. William married 1915 in the Fulham, London district to Cissie Agnes Ball (1894-1992).

Not long after this event, he signed up on the 10th April 1915 for WW1 service. He served in the Army Service Corps as driver T/35172, Royal Horse Artillery and Royal Field Artillery as No. 246230. William was awarded medals Victory, British and Star (The National Archives WO/372/16/103365).

William and Cissie later came to Tolpuddle to look after William's maiden aunts who were Sarah and Clara Puckett. They resided at Hammetts House, Main Road, Tolpuddle, a house which is still there today.

Upon the deaths of these aunts, sometime after 1922, William managed to purchase this property of Hammetts House. Here he lived with his wife and family. In 1933 and 1934 both William and Cissie were noted on the voting lists for Tolpuddle with residence and occupation qualifications. Cissie ran the village shop until about 1962.

During the 126th anniversary celebrations of the Tolpuddle Martyrs in Tolpuddle, both William and his sister Mabel spoke to a newspaper reporter (Pamela Kitchener of ((Swindon?)) Evening Advertiser 19/07/1961). At that time two hundred people were stated as living there and enjoying electricity and a mains water supply. I have put Mabel's account under her section.

William's account then was that the local influential people did not partake in the Tolpuddle Martyr celebrations and that his namesake grandfather was a Methodist preacher who had been turned out of his village because of his religion and connection to James Hammett Tolpuddle Martyr. He suffered this for forty years, only coming back to Tolpuddle (although his grandfather William appears in Tolpuddle on all censuses) with the help of a friend. This then enabled him to buy the only bit of land that did not belong to "Them" (presumably he means the local influential people and Church of England). On this land he built his house and Chapel, and is now buried in the graveyard there.

William further stated things seemed better on the surface, but with the Tories and Anglicans on one side and Chapel folk (Methodists) and working men on the other, one with the influence and one without. In Tolpuddle he said they had no time for the Martyrs or anything to do with them. He also spoke of the many visitors who came to the open house his sister and himself kept regarding the Martyrs and family collection, (as they were both well aware their ancestors were related not only to Hammett but to the Loveless family too).

These visitors included (David) Lloyd George, Citrine (Sir Walter McLennan Citrine, 1st Baron), Arthur Henderson, (James) Ramsay MacDonald and (Baron) Beaverbrook (Sir William Maxwell Aitken, a Canadian). William recalled how once Lloyd George said he would rather be descended from his grandfather than from William the

Conqueror. (I also noted Lloyd George was reported as making the same statement to William Hammett, son of James Hammett the Tolpuddle Martyr, but said from your father instead of grandfather.)

William died in 1969 and Cissie 1992, and they had three children, one boy and two girls.

<u>1911</u> Living in seven rooms at Keepers House, Wassell, Burnt Yates, Via Leeds, North Yorkshire (this area is north/west of Harrogate). William is aged 32 born Tolpuddle, unwed, a gamekeeper.

<u>1911</u> Cissie Agnes Ball is 18 born Chelsea, London, unwed, a domestic kitchen maid living in at Elsenham Hall, Elsenham, Essex. This property has forty-seven rooms with thirteen persons residing there. These were Edward Foucher 22 born France is private secretary (presumably to Sir Walter Gilbey). The others are domestic housemaids, a cook, a scullery maid, footmen, a hall boy and a retired butler. Cissie was the only kitchen maid.

Elsenham Hall was the property of Sir Walter Gilbey (1831-1914) a wine merchant and philanthropist. Previously on this site is said to be an ancient manor hall. Nowadays the hall has been converted into flats. In Cissie's time this was the location of *the most expensive jam in the world*, which was the marketing slogan for The Elsenham Jam Company which was based here. The company was started in 1893 by Sir Walter Gilbey. The fruits were grown in his orchards and made in the kitchens at Elsenham Hall. No doubt Cissie would have been involved somewhere in this procedure.

8) Miriam Lillian born 1881, the same year the Labour politician Ernest Bevin was born and work commenced on the Channel Tunnel but ceased after eight hundred and seventy-nine yards. Miriam married in 1905 to Charles Edmund Hunt (born 1871), a widower. Charles had previously married Emily Gertrude Thatcher in 1897, but she died aged 32 in 1900. This first marriage of Charles Hunt's produced a son Charles Stanbrook Hunt in 1898. Children for Miriam and Charles were Edmund John (1907) and Dorcas M (1911).

9) Mabel Edith M born 1883, the same year the Boy's Brigade was founded in Glasgow by Sir William Smith, the parcel post was born and the Orient Express embarked on her first trip. Mabel

married in 1910 to Ernest Aubrey Roberts (born 1882 Ulverston Cumbria/Lancs).

Ernest's father was the Reverend Arthur Roberts, a Wesleyan Minister who married his mother Hannah Ellen Bunkall in 1869 Downham, Norfolk. This family moved around all over the country, from Norfolk, Kent, Shetland and Yorkshire. Arthur Roberts was listed as a Wesleyan Minister serving in the Shetland Isles 1873-1875.

His son Ernest would also move around the country and the 1911 census finds Mabel and Ernest in Hertfordshire with their residence named *Studland*, presumably after Mabel's connection to that part of the country. Ernest in the latter census was listed as a junior reporter, and then a journalist/editor. Mabel possibly once lived in Cardiff, but in later life at Tolpuddle.

In the July of 1961 it was the 126th anniversary in Tolpuddle for the Martyrs and Mabel, along with her brother William, spoke to one of the reporters there. Mabel's input was to state that nothing had really changed since those times as the farmers still fought the agricultural labourer on rises in their wages. The reporter further added that Mrs Roberts and her brother William Puckett kept an open house for all to see the various documents and photographs in their possession and to hear their stories. How I wish I had been there then. William's input is noted above and is within his section. Mabel died in 1967 aged 84, having had no children.

10) Bertie Augustus Frank born 1886. The same year saw Dr John Stith Pemberton make Coca-Cola, Geronimo the Apache chief gave himself up to the military in the USA, and *The Mayor of Casterbridge* by Thomas Hardy was published (Casterbridge really being Dorchester in Dorset). Bertie married 1916 to Ann (Annie) Yeatman, (born 1884). He was possibly the same person named in the Kelly's directory for 1935 Shaftsbury as residing at Holyrood farm. Annie died 1954 aged 70, and Bertie 1967 aged 81, both in the Salisbury district of Wiltshire.

On the 1911 census Bertie was working at Broughton in Hampshire on the farm of his sister Miriam's husband Charles Hunt, whilst his future bride was a district nurse in the same area. Children for Bertie and Ann were Mary Margaret 1917, Harry 1919, and Margaret J 1921.

Sarah Ann 1845. The same year self-raising flour was patented by Henry Jones, the world's largest telescope was made by the Earl of Rosse which for the first time enabled the viewer to look at galaxies beyond our own, and in South Africa Zulu reserves are built introducing the first act of segregation there. Sarah never married and once their parents had died, lived with sister Clara, also a spinster at Hammetts House, Main Road, Tolpuddle. In their latter years their nephew William Puckett and his wife would join them there. Sarah died aged 72 in 1919, and is buried with her sister Clara in the little graveyard which fronts the Methodist Chapel which their father helped build and preached in. Their headstone simply reads

In loving memory of Sarah and Clara Hammett.

William 1847. The same year witnessed the completion of The British Museum by Sir Robert Smirke, in Merseyside the world's first civic public park *Birkenhead Park* opened, and the actor and comic writer George Grossmith died. William was more than likely named after his father whom he followed into the building trade as a carpenter/joiner.

William married in 1872 to Annie Hopkins (born 1843/1844, father Timothy Hopkins a shoemaker, listed in 1859 as a boot & shoemaker in Christchurch parish). As I could not find William and Annie in any of the English censuses after their marriage, I wondered if perhaps they were part of the Yeovil Colonists, who went out to Minnesota, America in a couple of groups in 1873.

The first group left Liverpool dock on 25th March, and the second in the last week of April that year. The Reverend George Ro(d)gers had in 1872 and 1873 been holding meetings for the public in Yeovil, Somerset in his quest to establish a town by the same name in Minnesota, America. He had made arrangements for pieces of land to be purchased from the Northern Pacific Railway Company, on the boundaries of their tract land in Minnesota, these being twelve townships in Clay County Minnesota. Many of those who left England for this new life came from Somerset and Devonshire (would have included Dorset). The Reverend's wife Emily nee Chant was born and baptised herself in Dorset (1837 Haydon, daughter of

George & Harriet of Wincanton, Somerset, father a joiner), although they had married in 1866 Barton, Lancashire.

The seventy-six English folks who arrived at New York in April 1873 aboard the steamer *City of Bristol* and who possibly had left Liverpool on the 25th March, then took the Erie Railroad for Chicago heading to Western Minnesota. Their destination was that of Hawley in Clay County. This place had briefly been named New Yeovil before reverting back to the original name of Hawley, as this settlement had failed.

Bad weather initially greeted them. Good land had already been given to settlers there with the lots available being smaller than anticipated. The Northern Pacific Railroad went into receivership and was therefore unable to help the colony and so some English settlers moved to Dakota Territory (The New York Times 10/04/1873, Western Gazette 01/09/2011, on-line Minnesota Encyclopedia – Kathryn R Goath).

I did indeed find William and Annie in Clay County, Minnesota, but this was a few years after the Yeovil Colonists. Maybe William and Annie already had contacts amongst them out there.

It would appear that William and Annie, after their marriage, had lived in the Dorchester area and possibly even Tolpuddle. They had their two sons born within the Dorchester district which covered Tolpuddle. Then some time later they all embarked from Bristol on board the S. S. Gloucester, arriving at Castle Garden (New York) on the 25th August 1880. William was aged 33 a carpenter, Annie is noted as Anne aged 37, with sons August 4 and W George 6 (The National Archives BT/27, & Ancestry).

The family are later picked up on the American census living in Clay County, Minnesota (Latter Day Saints – FamilySearch.Org site). The family first lived at Hawley village. Then two years later (possibly when William initiated his Citizenship) a farm was bought at Cromwell. Here William resided until retirement and then returned to Hawley Village.

William and Annie appear to have had five children, one of whom had died. William's first step to becoming an American citizen was in June 188(2) when he appeared before District Court 11 Judicial District for the State of Minnesota Declaration of Intent

(First Paper). He would then have had to return five years later with a witness to receive his citizenship certificate (Final Paper). From the First Paper it was noted he was born in England but in 1857 (not 1847), arrived at New York in August 1880 (Historical and Cultural Society of Clay County). Perhaps after giving it a go for a couple of years out in America, William had then decided to make his life permanent there.

William died first on the 5th December 1923 at Hawley, Clay, Minnesota aged 76, stated as born 1847, parents noted as William Hammett and Judith Loveless. Newspapers of the time reported he was one of the pioneers of eastern Clay county had died at home on a Tuesday evening from an illness which had resided with him for a few months.

To be exact William was 76 years 5 months and 14 days old at the time of death. His funeral was held in the afternoon of Friday 7th December 1923 at the Hawley Union (United Methodist) Church, with the Reverend S G Hauge instructing, and the choir singing. Prior to this a service was held at his home. Burial was at the Hawley cemetery. William was noted as being of a sterling upright character, with no complaints and a cheery fellow. He was of a strong religious belief and an active contributor to the Union Church, a devoted husband and loving father. His surviving wife children and sister Jane Puckett were also mentioned (Clay County Herald 07/12/1923 & 14/12/1923 – Historical & Cultural Society of Clay County).

Annie would die a few years later on the 19th February 1926 at Moorhead, Clay, Minnesota aged 82, stated as born in 1844, parents Timothy Hopkins and Judith (Du.... unable to read further – Latter Day Saints FamilySearch.org site).

1895 Living Cromwell, Clay, Minnesota, the family have resided in that state for fourteen years and nine months, and in that district for twelve years nine months. William is aged 47 born England a farmer. Anne is 52 a housewife born England, with their children George 21, Augustus 18, Lillie C 12 and Edith 9.

1900 Living Hawley Village, Clay, Minnesota, William is aged 57 (although said 62 mixed up with Annie's and also a few years out) born England June 1847 a carpenter. Annie is 62 born England May 1843. They have been married twenty-eight years and have five children, four of whom are still alive. With them are their daughters Lilly C aged 17 born May 1883 Minnesota, and Edith J aged 15 born November 1885 Minnesota.

1905 Living Hawley Village, Clay, Minnesota, William is aged 57 born England a farmer and had lived in both the state and district for 24 years and 9 months. Annie is aged 61 born England and has lived the same amount of time in state and district as William. With them is daughter Lilly C aged 22 born Minnesota who has lived in the state and district all her life.

1910 Living Hawley, Clay, Minnesota, William is aged 62 born England, immigrated in 1880. Annie is 66 and daughter Lilly is with them aged 25.

1920 Living Clay, Minnesota, William is aged 72 born 1848 England. Annie is 76 and daughter Lillian C is with them aged 36.

Children for William Hammett and Annie Hopkins were :-

1) Possibly Annie Louise 1873 Christchurch, died aged 1 in 1874 Christchurch.

2) William George 1874 Dorchester district, married Florence M (surname unknown, but born Ohio circa 1874) circa 1901-1905. He was, at the time of his father's death in 1923, the County Attorney at Moorhead, Clay County. In 1895 was a teacher and in 1905 a lawyer. They had a child William R circa 1919 in North Dakota.

3) Augustus Timothy 1876 Dorchester district, died aged 27 on 24th May 1902 at Cromwell, Clay County, Minnesota, buried at Hawley. He left an estate worth £62 11s 5d, and died intestate, with his brother William George's lawyer Henry Osmond Lock overseeing this. This lawyer's office was in Dorchester, Dorset and was no relative of John Lock, who was one of the informers of the Tolpuddle Martyrs, so far as I have been able to research. However, this will was not sorted out until the 18th September 1925 with the death year of Augustus being noted as 1903.

In 1902 £62 would have been worth in 2012 about £6,453.38, and for 1925 in 2012 about £3,191.99. In 1900 Augustus was living Price & Neva Towns, Langlade, Wisconsin as August, a boarder in the household of Edward Legg and his family. This being another Dorset surname and one shared by another of the informers on the

Tolpuddle Martyrs. Augustus was noted as a telephone operator and had been so for two years.

4) Lillie/Lilly/Lillian C 1883 Minnesota. She appears not to have married and lived most if not all of her life with her parents until their deaths. When her father died in 1923 she was residing at Moorhead.

5) Edith D J 1885 Minnesota. She married Rolland Ebright Shuck born 21st June 1883 Iowa (parents Thomas Daniel Shuck 1858-1894 and Mary Decker 1860-1949 - who married again to Uris Daniel Runkle 1855-1925). In 1930 Rolland's mother Mary, whose parents were born in Germany, is with them. This couple appear to have just had the one child Gladys born circa 1911/12 in Minnesota. From the newspaper reports of William's death a daughter called Mrs R E Shuck of Livingstone, Montana attended. This was Edith and the initials her husband Rolland's.

Clara 1852. The same year the Earl of Derby's Conservatives won the general election the new Lord Lieutenant of Ireland was Lord Eglinton and the Second Burmese War commenced when Britain blockaded the port of Rangoon. Clara, like her sister Sarah, never married and they appear to have spent their entire lives together. Clara died 1922 aged 70 and was buried on the 22nd November 1922 at Tolpuddle with her sister Sarah in the little graveyard which fronts the Methodist Chapel that their father helped build, and preached in. Their headstone simply reads:-

In loving memory of Sarah and Clara Hammett.

John Hammett 1822/23-1901

John, son of Richard 1788, was born 1822/23 Ringwood, Hampshire and baptised there as Hammitt on the 24th August 1823. The year 1823 saw artist John Constable paint Salisbury Cathedral a waterproof material was invented by Charles Mackintosh and in Brighton the Chain Pier was opened. This John has sometimes been mistaken for his namesake half-cousin, who was brother to James Hammett the Tolpuddle Martyr. Further confusion fuelled by the fact they both had wives called Elizabeth.

He married Elizabeth Loveless (1813-1896) at Tolpuddle in 1843 before witnesses William Hammett (probably his brother) and

Martha Loveless (her sister). As mentioned before, John and brother William had married two sisters, Elizabeth and Judith. Martha was their younger sister. These girls were also the great-aunts to William Hammett who was the son of James the Martyr, who was a half-cousin to their husbands, John and William Hammett.

John's wife Elizabeth Loveless was older than him as she was born in 1813 at Tolpuddle died aged 83 in 1896 Christchurch and was buried at St Clements Bournemouth on the 17th March 1896, previously of Wyndham Road.

As stated earlier, John Hammett along with brother William played a part in building the Methodist Chapel in Tolpuddle. They both were masons and at some point John may have owned land with William, due to the fact a mortgage had been taken out in both their names. What is factual, is that they had their own building company trading as W and J Hammett. This arrangement ceased mutually on 13th June 1861.

John died aged 79 on the 28th March 1901, and was buried at St Laurence's Church, Affpuddle (his headstone was not visible in 2010). All their children were born in Tolpuddle and were William Lewis 1845, Mary Jane 1848, Francis (Frank) 1851, John Sidney 1853 and lastly Joseph 1855 Dorchester, died 1855, buried Tolpuddle 5th December 1855 aged 8 months old. His headstone in Tolpuddle churchyard reads:-

To the memory of Joseph son of John & Elizabeth Hammett who died 29th November 1855 aged 8 months. He shall gather the lambs with his arm and carry them in his bosom.

William Lewis 1845. The same year saw SS Great Britain sail to New York on her maiden voyage and in Saint Petersburg Russia the Russian Geographical Society was born. Meanwhile in Quebec Canada that year two fires within a month of each other destroyed many buildings with fatalities. Firstly on the 25th May one thousand and seven hundred buildings were destroyed resulting in thirty people being burnt to death and fifty missing. Secondly the month of June witnessed one thousand and three hundred houses being destroyed. William married Elizabeth Ann Lord (born 1847 Halifax - Sowerby Bridge, West Yorks) sometime between the years 1871-1872 (I have not been able to find a marriage for this couple).

Although William started out as a carpenter he became an Inland Revenue Officer then Supervisor and travelled around England and even Scotland. On 1st February 1907 at Norwich he was a Supervisor on a wage of £266.13 4 (in 2012 roughly equated to £27,955.89) (The National Archives CUST/39/157).

Elizabeth died aged 47 in 1895 at Plomesgate, Aldesburgh, Suffolk and, according to William's later will, she was buried at Saxmundham churchyard, Suffolk. This is where he wished to be laid to rest, with her, and most probably was.

William died aged 74 on the 8th February 1919 at 23 Granville Road, Watford, Hertfordshire. This was the home of his son Harry who was present at his death. William's previous address noted was 67 Newmarket Road, Norwich.

In his will, both of his sons were the Executors. Harry was a schoolmaster and Percy lived 18 Clifton Avenue, Church End, Finchley, Middx. The gross value of his estate was £2,407.15.8 (in 2012 equated to roughly £105,248.54) and the net £2,330.13.6 (in 2012 equated to roughly £101,881.63) in favour to his sons Percy and Harry.

William's job of Inland Revenue (Excise) took him all over the country with the various census years finding him residing in:-

1871 at Market Bosworth, Sparkenhoe in Leicestershire

1881 at Campbeltown, Argyll in Scotland

1891 at Saxmundham in Suffolk

1901 at Heighham, Norwich in Norfolk.

When William retired in 1911 he was living at Norwich. William and Elizabeth had children:-

1) Harry born 1872 Market Bosworth, married 1898 Hannah Elizabeth Turton (born 1876 Walsall) and went into teaching, moving around the country.

1891-1904 Assistant Master at the High School in Shipley, Yorkshire.

1905-1909 Master in Charge Pupil of Teachers' Section at the Grammar School in Macclesfield.

1909 Chief English Master at the Grammar School in Watford, Hertfordshire where he still was in 1917 when he registered with the

Teachers' Registration Council for a fee of £1:1:0, with his qualification of B.A. London being noted (Findmypast).

In 1942 aged 70 Harry died in Kettering, Northamptonshire leaving a will worth £2,843:13:6 (in 2012 equated to roughly £113,435.69), net £2,049.2.11 (in 2012 equated to roughly £81,755.09). His wife Hannah and son-in-law Graeme Hopkins were the executors of the will and were looked on favourably in it, as were his children Marjorie and Lewis.

Aged 72 Hannah died in 1948 in the Bournemouth area. Their children were Lewis Reginald 1899, and Marjorie Elizabeth H 1904 (who married Graeme Hopkins, a schoolmaster in 1925 Watford area).

2) Percy born circa 1883, Campbeltown, Argyle, Scotland, married 1908 Hampstead to Daisy Ashdown (born 1887 Hampstead, daughter of music publisher Edwin Ashdown (1826/7-1912) and his second wife Hannah Bryan whom he married in 1880 after his first wife Elizabeth Sarah Arnsby died, whom he had married in 1846 St Giles area and who died 1879 Hendon aged 51 years.)

In 1911 Percy is noted as a secretary to a music publisher, and wife Daisy noted as a music publisher. Daisy possibly died in 1921 St Albans aged 31 (age a couple of years out), with Percy possibly marrying in 1924 to Lillian Winnifred Bond (born 1900 West Ham), and having two daughters.

Mary Jane 1848. The same year as authoress Emily Bronte died, in London the Waterloo Station opened and in Prussia the Jews were given equal rights. Mary married in 1872 Christchurch to William House (born 1849 East Knighton of John and Elizabeth). Mary died in 1908, and was buried in the churchyard at St Nicholas, East Chaldon. Her headstone inscription reads:-

In loving memory of Mary House The beloved wife of William House who died February 19th 1908 aged 60 years.

This headstone is upright with a cross on top. Directly in front of it and positioned horizontally (quite hard to read) is the headstone for William. This reads:-

In loving memory of William House who died April 1934 aged 85 And of his daughter Eva Loving wife of the late John Woods who died 28th August 1958 aged 75 years.

I note that the surname of Tipper is missed out on the headstone as that was the surname of Eva's husband John, Woods being his middle name. This could be due to the difficulty I had in reading this weathered headstone.

The various censuses noted Mary and William living in 1881 at Carpenter's Shop House, Chaldon Herring, Dorset where he was a carpenter. In 1891 they lived at Dairy House, Affpuddle where he was a dairy farmer. For 1901 home was Fossil Farm House, Chaldon Herring where he was a farmer and the same for the census of 1911.

Children for Mary Jane and William were:-

1) Lizzie Margaret (known as Maggie) born 1874 East Chaldon, baptised there on the 26th April that year. She married Samuel Riggs (he also went by the name of Loveless, and was the great-nephew of James Hammett Tolpuddle Martyr) on the 2nd October 1899 at the Sherborne Union Chapel. This was before witnesses Richard Rossieter and Mary House, the latter being possibly Lizzie's mother. Samuel was aged 30 and a baker residing at Milborne St Andrew, his father noted as Charles Riggs a shepherd.

This was not to be a long marriage, as Lizzie died aged 27 in 1901, but was buried as Maggie Loveless on Saturday 12th October that year at Chaldon Herring. Samuel and Lizzie were related, as they were second cousins once-removed. This marriage did not produce any children.

2) Lillian born 1881 East Chaldon, married 1909 John Woods Tipper (1885-1956, parents John Tipper born 1852 Uxbridge Middlesex, and Miriam Woods born 1854 Stamford, Lincolnshire). Lillian died aged 38 in 1919. Widow John went on to marry his sister-in-law Eva House who was Lillian's sister. John died aged 71 in the Bournemouth area in 1956. Children for Lillian and John were Evelyn Miriam 1910 and Elsa M 1914.

3) Eva born 1883, married her widowed brother-in-law John Woods Tipper in 1924 in the Wimborne district. I did not locate any children for them. Eva died on the 28th August 1958 aged 75 and is buried with her father William in the churchyard at East Chaldon, with an inscription included on their shared headstone, previously mentioned.

4) William Arthur born 1885, married Daisy Martha Westmacott (born 1885 East Knighton of parents Henry and Lucy Jane) in 1909. They had children Violet M 1912, and Arthur R 1917.

5) Herbert John born 1889 Briantspuddle, married in 1912 to Jessie P Bowditch (born Jessie Emily P Bowditch 1893). Possible children for them were William 1913, Albert A 1916, Gerald 1918, Sylvia 1919, Gwendoline 1923 and Poppy C 1925.

Francis 1851. The same year witnessed Isaac Singer patenting the sewing machine, in Hawaii they issued their first postage stamps, and in Boston Massachusetts the first American YMCA was opened. Francis married in 1873 Bridport area to Elizabeth Hussey (born 1851 Chideock of parents Robert and Catherine). Francis died aged 83 in 1934 and Elizabeth aged 91 in 1942, both in the Dorchester district.

During his life, Francis possessed skills of both carpentry and building, which he may have used on the building projects of shopping arcades in Bournemouth by Henry Joy. Later his son Joseph would marry Henry Joy's granddaughter. Francis and Elizabeth had a large family of ten children, not all of whom survived into adulthood. They were :-

1) Arthur William born 1874, died aged 5 in 1879, buried St Clements, Bournemouth as William Arthur on 8th April that year.

2) Joseph Charles (Charlie) Hussey born 1876. He married Isabel Maud Joy in 1902. She was born in 1875 to parents Joseph and Emmeline Joy. Isabel's paternal grandfather Henry Joy was a property developer whose projects in Bournemouth included two shopping arcades. The first built at 26-28 Old Christchurch Road saw a blue plaque unveiled in 1986. This reads:-

Bournemouth Arcade 1866 built by Henry Joy originally as two rows of shops the glazed arcade roof was added in 1872.

The other at Westbourne has two entrances, one into Poole Road and one into Seamoor Road. In the brickwork above these entrances is inscribed:-

Westbourne – Henry Joy's Arcade 1884.

Henry Joy died on the 14th April 1906 and resided at "Duncairn", Manor Road, Bournemouth. His probate was dated 30th May that year to Leslie Sweet and John Joy (possibly his son). First figure given was £46319 10s 5d (in 2012 roughly equated to £4,769,362.82), later re-sworn to £47154 3s 3d (in 2012 roughly equated to £4,855,340.89). Not bad for someone who in 1861 was a carpenter living in Holdenhurst with his wife and children.

Joseph died aged 86 in 1962, and Isabel aged 88 in 1963. In the 1911 census Joseph was a life assurance agent living with Isabel and their family at 41 Victoria Road in Bournemouth. Their children were Gladys Hilda L 1903, Arthur Jack 1908 (married 1937 to Frances R Sims), Kathleen 1910 (married 1933 to Frank R Harwood), Irene 1911 and Joseph C 1915 (married as Charles J Hammett 1939 to Joyce J Mervish, died as Charles Joseph aged 73 in 1989).

3)   Sidney John (Jack) born 1878. He married twice, first to Mary Bessie Sims in 1906 in the Alverstoke area of Southampton. She was born in 1870 and died in 1917 aged 47. His second marriage was to Ivy Beatrice Masterman in 1928 in the Alverstoke area. She was born in 1890 and died in 1976. Sidney died in 1971. In 1911 Sidney and first wife Mary lived in Gosport with him noted as a hosier manager. They had a daughter Mary C 1911.

4) Elizabeth Kate (Lizzy) born 1880. She never married, in 1911 was a dairy worker living near Dorchester in Dorset, and died aged 79 in 1959.

5) Alice born 1882, died aged 3 months and was buried on the 1st November that year at St Clements, Bournemouth.

6)   Ernest William born 1884 was also was known as William Ernest which is how he was noted when he died aged 83 in 1968. Married as Ernest William to Jeanette Crocker in 1906. She was born in 1885 of parents Walter Crocker (1849-1927) and Anna Eliza (1857-1918). Jeannette died in 1965 aged 80. In 1911 they were living with their family at Stratton near Dorchester where he was noted as working on a farm. In 1915 Jeanette was listed as sub-postmistress for Grimstone, and in 1918 she and William Ernest appear on the voting lists for Stratton. Their children were Percy Hugh 1907, Cecil William 1909, Bernard George 1914, Sylvia Alice 1917, Pamela Jeanette 1921, Marie Anna Louise 1924 and Anthony Walter Frank 1927.

7) Alice born 1886 and probably named after an older sibling who died an infant. She followed in the footsteps of her elder sister Lizzy by never getting married, and died in 1987 aged 100. In 1911 she was a dairy worker living near Dorchester.

8) George Frank born 1889, died aged 3 and was buried on the 26th September 1892 at St Clements, Bournemouth, noted of Springbourne.

9) Ethel born 1891, died aged 22 days old and was buried on the 16th December 1891 at St Clements, Bournemouth, noted of Springbourne.

10) Henry Frank born 1893, died aged 8 months old and was buried on the 18th June 1894, noted of 116 Wyndham Road.

John Sidney 1853. The same year the politician and businessman Cecil Rhodes was born, the potato chip was invented in New York by George Crum, and in Burma Mindon Min was made king. John married Lila Rose Way in 1897. She was born in 1871 to parents George Way and Jane Coney who had married in 1870. Her mother was in fact born Felicia Jane Coney in 1841, and the 1851 census finds her listed as Cecilia Coney living at Monchton Up Wimborne with parents Ruben and Maria. Lila died aged 75 in 1946. I have not been able to locate John's death. From the census, they resided in Bournemouth with John noted as a house decorator/painter. Their children were:-

1) Albert born 1898, married Ethel M Hipkiss in 1925.
2) Elsie born 1901, died aged 24 in 1925.

Francis Hammett 1823-1849

Francis, son of Richard 1788, was born 1823 and baptised as Hamitt in Ringwood on the 24th August 1823. The same year witnessed building works start on Polesden Lacey in Surrey by Thomas Cubitt, the Gaols Act introduced as a result of prison reformer Elizabeth Fry's campaigning, and the Spanish Revolution failed. Francis married in 1846 at Tolpuddle to Jane Davison (baptised in Tolpuddle on the 12th August 1821 of Samuel & Diane Davidson of Southover, father a labourer). Francis was noted as a carpenter, his father Richard a mason, and Jane's father a labourer, before their witnesses of Richard Hammett (his father) and Martha Loveless (his mother's sister; his aunt).

The newlyweds would have only a few years together, as Francis died in Bere Regis on the 4th April 1849 aged just 25, and was buried in Tolpuddle a few days later on the 7th April 1849 by Thomas Warren, vicar.

From the 1851 census Jane is noted as a widowed pauper living with her parents and daughter. Jane married again in Tolpuddle in 1855 to Henry Foster, a widower and labourer (baptised Winterborne Whitechurch in 1819 of Eliza & Absalom Foster). His father was noted as Absalom Foster, a woodman, whilst Jane's was Samuel Davison, a soldier. Witnesses were George and Emma Davison (her brother and possibly his wife). The 1861 census sees them living at Whatcombe, Winterborne Whitechurch where he is a woodman, with his children who were Matilda 14, Christina 12, Sarah 10, Walter 8 and Jane's daughter Miriam 13 who was noted as Foster instead of Hammett.

Jane died aged 46 in 1868 and, whilst she resided at Morden, was buried in Tolpuddle with her first husband Francis. Their headstone reads:-

In memory of Francis Hammett who died April 4th 1849 aged 26 years. Also Jane his wife who died July 24th 1868 aged 46 years. This stone is erected by their only child.

Jane's father Samuel Davison was born in Coleraine near Londonderry in Northern Ireland. He was discharged a gunner aged 31 from the 7th Bat Artillery in the army in 1814. Having enlisted aged 22 (born circa 1783) in 1805, he served as a Private for nine years and one hundred and thirty-eight days, and was stationed in the West Indies. His description given was 5ft 7¾ tall, brown hair, blue eyes with a sallow complexion (The National Archives). Samuel Davison married Diana Balston in 1813 at Alverstoke, Hampshire. She was born in Tolpuddle and baptised there in 1786 of parents Isaac and Jenny. Perhaps she was working in Hampshire when she met Samuel who could have been stationed there with his unit. Then, once he was discharged, they went back to be nearer her roots in Tolpuddle and bring up their family. Samuel Davison was buried in Tolpuddle in 1863 aged 84, noted as being of Winterborne

Whitechurch, but presumably wanted to be laid to rest with his wife Diana, who was buried there earlier as Davison in 1862 by Vicar George L Nash (although both of them were listed under Davidson in the Government death registrations).

Francis Hammett and Jane Davison's only child who erected their headstone was:-

Miriam 1848 who never married. The census of 1871 sees her as a housemaid in Poole for Lucy Rowe, a Principal of a Ladies School. The next one in 1881 Miriam is in Christchurch a nurse to William Maples aged 81, a retired merchant. The year 1891 she is at the Boscombe Clinic in Bournemouth and is a trained sick nurse to Charles Gibbs Crawley, a retired Royal Naval Commander aged 78. The next census of 1901 she is living in Bournemouth and is a private sick nurse. Lastly, the census of 1911 finds Miriam a trained nurse in Tolpuddle with sisters Sarah and Clara Hammett. These two ladies were her first cousins once-removed, and with whom she was most probably visiting. Miriam died some five years later aged 69 in 1916 within the Christchurch registration district.

<u>Richard Hammett 1826-1895</u>

Richard, son of Richard 1788, was born on the 27th September 1826 Ringwood. The same year saw John Constable paint The Cornfield, on the railway line between Liverpool and Manchester the first tunnel was constructed, and in London Sir Stamford Raffles established The Royal Zoological Society. Richard would be baptised some years later on the 26th May 1833 in Tolpuddle by Vicar Thomas Warren. Many of his Hammett relatives had been masons, and this was a trade Richard. Richard married twice.

Firstly Richard married Ann Foot (1826-1866) at Tolpuddle in 1849 before witnesses Charles Pope and Elizabeth Mary Wiles. This was the same vicar who had baptised Ann in Tolpuddle in 1826, daughter of Michael Foot and Susanna Goddard who had married at St Mary and St James in Hazelbury Bryan in 1812. Ann died aged 39 in 1866, and was buried in Tolpuddle on the 10th March that year with the notation of being of Bryantspuddle (Briantspuddle). Her death was most probably child-birth related, as six days earlier in

Affpuddle Richard and Ann had had their newborn daughter Edith baptised, who had been born in the previous December of 1865.

Richard then married for the second time some six years later in 1872 at Tolpuddle to Emily Peck (1843-1918), before witnesses Charles Medway (his son-in-law to be) and Rosetta Hammett (his daughter who would later marry Charles Medway). Emily was born in Beverley, Yorkshire where she had been baptised on the 25th February 1843 at St John and St Martin, of parents Lucy Wains and William Peck who had married in 1838 in the Sculcoates district. Sometime between 1873 and 1876 Richard and Emily left Dorset for the county of Emily's birth.

Sadly Richard would later be admitted into the Beverley Union, and on the 26th February 1889 he was transferred from there to the County Lunatic Asylum, Beverley Parks, Walkington in Yorkshire. Aged 62, a married labourer with black hair and a little grey, grey eyes and suffering from epilepsy and hallucinations were all the words summing up Richard. Richard died aged 69 in 1895 from the exhaustion of epilepsy and Emily followed aged 75 in 1918, both events in the Beverley district (East Riding Yorkshire Council – NH6/64/6).

In the 1861 census Emily was living in Beverly as a general house servant to Robert George Boulton (1805-1877 Justice of the Peace and Doctor of Medicine) and his family, whilst Richard was in Tolpuddle with his first wife and family.

The following census of 1871 saw Richard still in Tolpuddle, living in Church Close Place with many of his fellow Hammett relatives as neighbours, but now a widower. His second wife to be, Emily, was transcribed as Peake instead of Peck, a cook residing at Fangfoss Hall, Fangfoss, Yorkshire in the company of a groom, housemaid and gardener, all of whom worked for George F and Isabella Duckett, noted as Baronet Deputy Lieutenant of Middlesex, late Major in the army. He was none other than Sir George Floyd Duckett, 3rd Baronet (1810-1902), with strings to his bow of military service, author of *Technological Military Dictionary* plus other works, and an archaeologist. His ancestor the 1st Baronet Sir George Jackson (1725-1822) naval administrator, judge, Member of Parliament (1786-1788 MP for Weymouth and Melcombe Regis) gave up his surname to that of Duckett. This was in accordance with his second wife's (Grace Goldstone) uncle's (Thomas Duckett) will, which allowed him to inherit the Hartham Estate in Corsham, Wiltshire, the Duckett family estate. This happened in 1797, six years after his Baronet was created.

Richard and Emily only ever appeared on one census together as a family, and that was in 1881. They were residing at Duck Lane in Beverly with Richard noted as a bricklayer.

In the 1891 census Richard is listed as an inmate at the County Lunatic Asylum in Beverly, also known as Broadgates Hospital. Meanwhile, Emily and the children are residing at Greens Passage in Beverly.

Life could not have been easy for Emily, with the responsibility of bringing up the children on her own whilst Richard was away ill. Richard had fathered twelve children with his two wives.

Those with his first wife Ann Foot were Michael Francis 1850-1850 (buried Tolpuddle aged 2 weeks old), Pamela Goddard 1851, Rosetta Foot 1853, Michael Foot 1855-1856, Susannah Goddard 1857, Alicia/Ellicia Anne 1859, Elizabeth (Betsey) Richards 1863 and Edith 1865.

With his second wife Emily Peck, Richard fathered children:- Alfred Francis (Frank) 1872, Louisa 1875, Richard Ernest 1878 and Ada Agnes 1880.

Pamela Goddard 1851. The same year as the publication of *Moby Dick* by Herman Melville, the abolishment of the Window Tax in England, and in America the introduction of the first baseball uniform. Pamela's middle name of Goddard was the maiden name of her maternal grandmother, often a tradition amongst families of yesteryear. Pamela married in 1881 in the Yorkshire district of Driffield to John Gibson Blakey, she 28 and he 24, before their witness Priscilla Ulliott. John was born in that area in 1856 to parents Thomas Barker Blakey and Mary Gibson, and given the middle name of his mother's maiden name. Both his parents died in Driffield in 1884 his mother Mary aged 73, and in 1886 his father Thomas aged 70.

Pamela's husband John was a gardener when they married. Later he was noted as a Redditch horticulturist, who in 1925 laid out the

Gardens of Remembrance there to honour the local men who gave their lives defending their country (Arts in Redditch internet site). Pamela died aged 77 in 1928 and John aged 76 in 1932, both in the Bromsgrove area. Pamela and John had children:-

1) Fred born 1881. Originally a pharmacy apprentice, he became a works chemist and later chief metallurgist to a company in Birmingham. He was also a Freemason, holding the post of Master of the Seymour Lodge in Redditch once. Fred passed away in 1951 at home in Abbey Road, Redditch aged 69, leaving a widow (internet site – thisisworcestershire archives.)

2) Sidney John born 1884. From the census entries he was a teacher's school apprentice and then an elementary school teacher, both in Redditch. He married in 1915 to Dorothy C Charman and they had a family.

Rosetta Foot 1853. The same year saw the birth of Vincent van Gogh the Dutch artist. In addition an escaped black American slave from America called William Wells Brown published in London his first novel called *Clotel; or the President's Daughter: a narrative of slave life in the United States* (William Wells Brown remained in England until his freedom was bought). Also, off the rugged coast of Barra one of the Hebrides in Scotland, an emigrant ship called *Annie Jane* was wrecked with the death of three hundred and forty-eight men, women and children, and one hundred and two survivors including the Captain. This vessel had left Liverpool Quebec bound with mainly Irish families on board setting off for a new life.

Following a tradition, Rosetta's middle name of Foot was that of her mother's maiden name. In 1877 Rosetta married Charles Medway (born 1852 Dorchester of parents James and Rebecca). This marriage produced no children.

From the various censuses, Charles worked for the Post Office in Dorchester where they resided. 1881 at Cornhill he was a stamper and Rosetta's sister Edith is with them. 1891 living at the Post Office, 53 South Street Charles is a sorting clerk, with them is his niece Florence Emily Jacobs, daughter of Frances Medway his sister who had married Charles Arthur Jacobs. 1901 still at the same address Charles is a posting clerk a telegraphic assistant. 1911 he is a retired Post Office pensioner and they are residing at 2 St Helen's

Road. They both lived long lives with Charles dying first in 1944 aged 91 and Rosetta in 1950 aged 97.

Susanna(h) Goddard 1857. The same year witnessed a novel by Thomas Hughes called *Tom Brown's Schooldays* partly based on his brother George Hughes, Queen Victoria made a decision to make the capital of Canada Ottawa, and in Tokyo an earthquake took one hundred thousand lives. Once again following with tradition, Susannah's middle name of Goddard was the maiden name of her maternal grandmother. I have been unable to trace Susannah after the 1871 census when she was living at Church Close Place in Tolpuddle with her family.

Alicia/Ellicia Ann 1859. The same year witnessed the opening in Edinburgh of the Scottish National Gallery. HRH Prince Albert opened the Royal Albert Bridge in Saltash, Cornwall, thus allowing the Cornwall railway to link into Devon and the rest of England, as previously this gateway was linked via a ferry. Also that year construction work started on the Suez Canal with the digging carried out by Egyptian workers and French engineers. The name Ellicia means *My God is Salvation*. As with her elder sister Susannah, I have not been able to trace Alicia after the 1871 census when she too is at home in Church Close Place, Tolpuddle

Elizabeth (Betsey) Richards 1863. The same year witnessed the birth of David Lloyd George (Prime Minister, who would later attend events in Tolpuddle), also in England thirty thousand lives are lost due to a scarlet fever epidemic. Whilst in America that year James Leonard Plimpton (1828-1911) of New York patented four-wheeled roller skates, which he rented out from his furniture shop and made skating lessons available along with medals for the winners, and opened America's first skating rink at Rhode Island. Perhaps Elizabeth's middle name was in honour of her father Richard, with an 's' added, for I cannot immediately identify this middle name of Richards.

Elizabeth married in 1891 Dorchester to Edwin Leach, (born 1864 Wincanton to parents Peter Leach and Elizabeth Sarah White who had married in 1845). Elizabeth probably died in 1918 aged 54, and Edwin in 1934 aged 63 (would have made his birth year 1871, but death registration errors are not uncommon), both in the Swindon area.

From the census information, Elizabeth had left Tolpuddle and gone north to Yorkshire with her birth family, but by 1891 she was back in Dorset. Here she was found to be living in Broadmayne, listed as niece to widow Elizabeth Croad 72, a retired innkeeper. Elizabeth Croad and her husband William had previously run the Black Dog Inn at Broadmayne, along with a farm of 180 acres. I have not been able to work out the exact relationship between these two Elizabeths, but perhaps the connection lies within the Foot lineage (Elizabeth's mother was a Foot before marriage).

By 1901 Elizabeth is married and living in Bridgewater with husband Edwin, a grocer's manager, and their children. 1901 they are at 6 Cromwell Street in Swindon where Edwin is a manager of a corn store with their twin daughters. 1915-1917 they are living at 2 Fleet Street, Swindon (as per their son Reginald's army recruitment details).

Their children were:-

1) Reginald Bertie born 1893. Served in WW1 with the Royal Engineers as Sapper 77039, promoted to Corporal in 1916, awarded the British War and Victory medals, which he signed for on the 31st August 1921, just months before his death on the 7th November aged 28. He had signed up in 1915 at Fenny Stratford Signal Depot, Bletchley, attended the signal school and proved himself to be a proficient office telegraphist.

Upon recruitment was noted as living at 2 Fleet Street, Swindon (his parent's address), was a sorting clerk telegraphist, unmarried, 5ft 10" tall, with a 35" chest, Church of England religion and next of kin his father Edwin of the same address. Reginald served abroad from the 12th January 1916 to the 29th October 1917 with the British Expeditionary Force, then was discharged on the 19th December 1917 as no longer fit for service, but to receive a weekly pension (The National Archives WO/364/5397).

Reginald suffered from tuberculosis and before his discharge had spent time in the Southern General Hospital, Dudley Road, Birmingham. Before his early death, his last address was 26 Culliford Road, Dorchester with his probate the 8th December 1921 made by his father Edwin Leach, a corn merchant, and valued at £404 13s 7d (roughly equated in 2012 to £16,747.63).

2) Dorothy Rose a twin born 1895. Not much more is known about her, other than in 1911 she is at home with her parents and twin sister and a dressmaker.

3) Dora Edith a twin born 1895. The only information I have gathered for her is exactly the same as that of her twin sister.

Edith 1865, but was baptised in 1866. The same year London bore witness to over five thousand deaths due to a cholera epidemic. Also that year the wholesale discount bank, also known as the banker's bank Overend Gurney & Company, collapsed owing £11 million, resulting in the failure of over two hundred companies. Whilst in Kimberley in South Africa diamonds were found. Edith married Fred Spencer (1868-1920 parents Alfred and Fanny) in 1892 in Yorkshire.

From the census, Edith appears to have moved around, from Dorset to Yorkshire, then back to Dorset again in 1881 where she is with her married sister Rosetta. In 1891 Edith is back in Yorkshire, living at The Vicarage, Langtoft, Driffield where she is a general domestic servant for Thomas Davies Tullock Speck, the vicar and his wife. In the July of the following year 1892 there was a great flood in Langtoft. Vicar Speck was still listed as residing there and perhaps Edith was too, before her marriage later that year to Fred Spencer. Fred was a baker and confectioner. 1901 sees them living in Great Driffield with their children and Edith's half-brother Richard Hammett a baker's assistant is their lodger. By 1911 they had moved to Beverley. Their children were:-

1) George born 1893, possibly died in 1938 aged 44 in the Hull area. He married Ada Elizabeth Howard (born 1896) in 1914 in the Beverley district. They had three children, two boys and one girl.

2) Alfred born 1894, married Hilda Midwood in 1927 in the Sculcoates area. They had no children. He was a pharmacist in Spalding in Lincolnshire.

3) Margery born 1898, died aged 15 in 1913, in the Beverley district.

4) Jessie born 1899, never married and possibly died aged 44 in 1943 in the Holderness area of Yorkshire.

5) A son/daughter who was dead by 1911, as mentioned on the 1911 census sheet.

Alfred Francis (Frank) 1872. The same year trains provided sleeping cars, further away in New York America Central Park was completed, and in Amsterdam Holland the Heineken brewery was born. Alfred was born in Tolpuddle and the first child born to his father Richard's second wife and was known as Frank. Sadly, from the 1901 and 1911 census information it would appear Alfred/Frank was a patient in the same Lunatic Asylum his father Richard had resided in as a patient. He died as Frank Hammett in 1943 aged 70 in the Holderness, East Riding area of Yorkshire.

Louisa Hammett 1875 (I have been unable to find a conclusive registration for her birth, but she was possibly registered as Louisa Peck September quarter 1876 Goole, Yorkshire, although her parents Richard Hammett and Emily Peck were married by then). The year 1876 also saw the arrival of the telephone, which Alexander Graham Bell invented, Mark Twain published *Tom Sawyer*, and rubber seeds are smuggled out of Brazil by Henry Wickham and taken to Malaysia, a deed that in time would bring an end to the Amazon rubber boom. In the 1881 census her surname, and that also for her family, was noted as Hammoth instead of Hammett, which is why sometimes it is hard to trace people via this source. Her trade from the various censuses is that of a milliner, dressmaker and costumier. I have not located either a marriage or a death for Louisa, but was informed by a relative of hers that she died in 1971.

Richard Ernest Hammett 1878. That same year in London, Cleopatra's Needle (one of a pair of ancient Egyptian obelisks) arrived from Alexandria (the other half of the pair was erected in New York's Central Park on the 22nd February 1881). Also the crowded paddle steamer pleasure boat *Princess Alice* collided on the Thames River just off Tripcock's Point near North Woolwich with the cargo vessel *Bywell Castle* resulting in the loss of over six hundred and forty lives. Whilst across the other side of the world the British attack Ali Masjid, a fort in the Khyber Pass, resulting in the Second Afghan War. Richard, like his father married twice.

Firstly Richard marred in 1904 to Ada Hodgson, who was possibly born in 1882, and died aged 47 in 1930. Richard then married in 1931 May Wilson. She possibly died in 1963 aged 75, whilst previously Richard had died aged 75 in 1953.

During his life Richard had been an errand boy for the Post Office, a baker's assistant (worked for his sister Edith's baker husband), and a gardener. He also served his country in WW1, enlisting aged nearly 38 at the end of 1915 with the West Riding Regiment under No: 29712. Later in 1918 was transferred to the Labour Corps under No: 406488. In January 1917 he arrived in Calais, then Etaples and received the Victory and British Medals. Richard's description was 5ft 8" tall, with a 35" chest, weighed 120lbs and was a gardener. He was discharged in April 1919 (The National Archives WO/363H/137).

It would appear Richard had no children in his second marriage to May, but had these children with first wife Ada:-

1) Clifford born 1904, married Mary J Thompson 1945.

2) Hilda born 1906, married Frederick Applegate 1939 and had children.

3) Mary born 1912, married 1935 Clifton Shackleton.

4) Emily born 1916, married 1937 Albert Holden.

Ada Agnes 1880. The same year also bore witness to the birth of future suffragette, Christabela Pankhurst. In the January of that year the telephone directory appeared for the very first time with about two hundred and fifty-five entries contained within it. Whilst on shores further away in Australia the outlaw Ned Kelly was hung on the 11th November at the Old Melbourne Gaol, resulting in him becoming a folk hero who stood up to the ruling classes. Ada was the last child born to Richard Hammett and his second wife Emily Peck.

Ada married in 1922 to Alfred Gutherless junior, who was born in 1886 of parents Alfred Gutherless senior and Annie Marie Simpson who had married in 1877. Annie died in 1906 aged 51 then Alfred remarried in 1910 to Clara E Freeman, who in turn died aged 73 in 1937.

Alfred Gutherless junior died in 1971, and Ada aged 83 in 1964. This couple's marriage appears not to have produced any children, possibly due to Ada being 42 when they married. From the various censuses, Ada was a nurse and domestic cook and Alfred a clerk in an accounts office.

FAMILY TREE OF JAMES HAMMETT'S UNCLE RICHARD 1788 -1852

Richard Hammett wed Elizabeth Welch

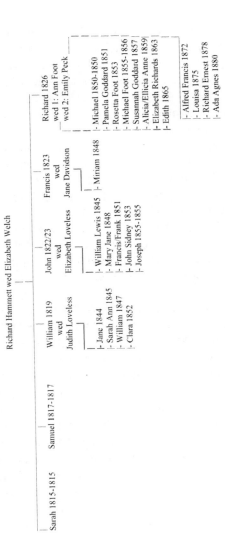

Sarah 1815-1815

Samuel 1817-1817

William 1819
wed
Judith Loveless

|- Jane 1844
|- Sarah Ann 1845
|- William 1847
|- Clara 1852

John 1822/23
wed
Elizabeth Loveless

|- William Lewis 1845
|- Mary Jane 1848
|- Francis/Frank 1851
|- John Sidney 1853
|- Joseph 1855-1855

Francis 1823
wed
Jane Davidson

|- Miriam 1848

Richard 1826
wed 1: Ann Foot
wed 2: Emily Peck

|- Michael 1850-1850
|- Pamela Goddard 1851
|- Rosetta Foot 1853
|- Michael Foot 1855-1856
|- Susannah Goddard 1857
|- Alicia/Ellicia Anne 1859
|- Elizabeth Richards 1863
|- Edith 1865

|- Alfred Francis 1872
|- Louisa 1875
|- Richard Ernest 1878
|- Ada Agnes 1880

FAMILY TREE OF JAMES HAMMETT'S COUSIN WILLIAM HAMMETT 1819

William Hammett wed Judith Loveless

| Jane 1844 wed Seth Puckett | Sarah Ann 1845 never married | William 1847 wed Annie Hopkins | Clara 1852 never married |

William 1847 wed Annie Hopkins:
- possibly Annie Louise 1873-1874
- William George 1874 wed Florence M
  - William 1919
- Augustus Timothy 1876-1902
- Lillie/Lilly/Lillian C 1883
- Edith D J 1885 wed Rolland Ebright Shuck |- Gladys 1911/12

Jane 1844 wed Seth Puckett:
- Mary Judith 1868 wed Thomas Job Fox
  - Leonard 1894, Clifford 1897,
  - Edith Annie Sarah 1870-1882
- Margaret Clara 1871-1892
- Harry William 1873 wed Martha Elizabeth Shave
  - Margaret 1902, Harryena 1909
- Lottie Jane 1875 wed Jacob William Gibbons
  - Annie 1900, Kezia 1903, William 1905, Freda 1908, Jeanie 1911, Arthur 1916
- Arthur James 1877-1877
- William Jabez Seth 1878 wed Cissie Agnes Ball
  - one boy, two girls
- Miriam Lillian 1881 wed Charles Edmund Hunt
  - Edmund 1907, Dorcas 1911
- Mabel Edith M 1883 wed Ernest Aubrey Roberts
  - no issue
- Bertie Augustus Frank 1886 wed Ann/Annie Yeatman
  - Mary 1917, Harry 1919, Margaret 1921

273

FAMILY TREE OF JAMES HAMMETT'S COUSIN JOHN HAMMETT 1822/23

John Hammett wed Elizabeth Loveless

William Lewis 1845
wed
Elizabeth Ann Lord

- Harry 1872 wed
  Hannah Elizabeth Turton
  |- Lewis 1899, Marjorie 1904

- Percy 1883 wed
  1: Daisy Ashdown
  2: Lillian Winnifred Bond
  |M2: two daughters

Mary Jane 1848
wed
William House

- Lizzie 1874 wed
  Samuel Riggs
- Lillian 1881 wed
  John Woods Tipper
  |- Evelyn 1910, Elsa 1914
- Eva 1883 wed
  John Woods Tipper
- William 1885 wed
  Daisy Martha Westmacott
  |- Violet 1912, Arthur 1917
- Herbert 1889 wed
  Jessie P Bowditch
  |- poss William 1913, Albert 1916,
  Gerald 1918, Sylvia 1919,
  Gwendoline 1923, Poppy 1925

Francis/Frank 1851
wed
Elizabeth Hussey

- Arthur 1874-1879
- Joseph 1876 wed
  Isabel Maud Joy
  |- Gladys 1903, Arthur 1908
  Kathleen 1910, Irene 1911
  Joseph 1915
- Sidney 1878 wed
  1: Mary Bessie Sims
  2: Ivy Beatrice Masterman
  |-M1: Mary circa 1911
- Elizabeth 1880
- Alice 1882-1882
- Ernest 1884 wed
  Jeanette Crocker
  |- Percy 1907, Cecil 1909, Bernard 1914, Sylvia 1917, Pamela 1921,
  Marie 1924, Anthony 1927
- Alice 1886
- George 1889-1892
- Ethel 1891 -1891
- Henry 1893

John Sidney 1853
wed
Lila Rose Way

- Albert 1898 wed
  Ethel M Hipkiss
  |- Elsie 1901-1925

Joseph 1855-1855

274

FAMILY TREE OF JAMES HAMMETT'S COUSIN FRACIS HAMMETT 1823

Francis Hammett wed Jane Davidson

Miriam 1848
Never married

FAMILY TREE OF JAMES HAMMETT'S COUSIN RICHARD HAMMETT 1826

Richard Hammett wed 1: Ann Foot

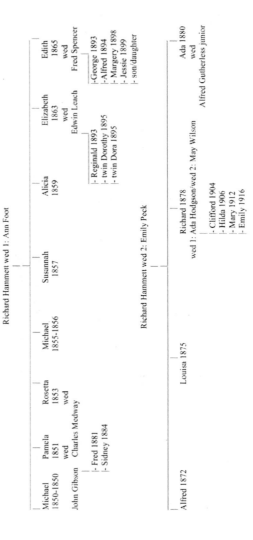

Michael
1850-1850

Pamela
1851
wed
John Gibson   Charles Medway

- Fred 1881
- Sidney 1884

Rosetta
1853
wed

Michael
1855-1856

Susannah
1857

Alicia
1859

- Reginald 1893
- twin Dorothy 1895
- twin Dora 1895

Elizabeth
1863
wed
Edwin Leach

Edith
1865
wed
Fred Spencer

- George 1893
- Alfred 1894
- Margery 1898
- Jessie 1899
- son/daughter

Richard Hammett wed 2: Emily Peck

Alfred 1872

Louisa 1875

Richard 1878
wed 1: Ada Hodgson/wed 2: May Wilson

- Clifford 1904
- Hilda 1906
- Mary 1912
- Emily 1916

Ada 1880
wed
Alfred Gutherless junior

PART II

Chapter 12

JAMES HAMMETT'S UNCLE JAMES AND HIS DESCENDANTS

James Hammett was born and baptised in Tolpuddle in 1801. That year the population in England and Wales was recorded to be 8.9 million, the third president in the United States was Thomas Jefferson and the first steam-powered vehicle carrying passengers was presented by Richard Trevithick. James was an agricultural labourer, who moved westwards settling in Somerset.

The Dorset Militia Pay List for 1825 (The National Archives WO/13/578) stationed at Dorchester noted a James Hammett from 11th May to 7th June, who lived at Dewlish, but was enrolled for the parish of West Knighton. He served twenty-eight days, twenty-five of them at the quarters and three on the march. I have assumed this to be the same James Hammett. At the same time, a son of his older half- brother John was also noted on the pay lists as serving, namely Dennis Hammet.

James married twice. Well, it is presumed he did from the records available. Firstly to a woman called Sophie, as she was noted as the mother on the baptism details of their daughters. But I have been unable to find a marriage for this couple. Sophie died in 1828 aged 28 and was buried by Reverend Waldy in Tolpuddle, placing her birth year around 1800. As James was noted as living in Dewlish in 1825, it is quite possible Sophie was from there too. There was a baptism in Dewlish on the 15th March 1801 for a Sophia Holloway Way the daughter of William and Elizabeth. William Way had married at Melcombe Horsey to Elizabeth Holloway of Tolpuddle. Perhaps this could be the same Sophie assumed to be the first wife of James.

James then married for a second time in 1833 at Dewlish to Ann Greening (transcribed Gruning), before witnesses George Park and William Vincent, and was noted as a widower. From census information and her age at death, Anne was born circa 1801 at Litten Cheney. I have not been able to locate a baptism for her, nor an earlier marriage. It would appear Anne had a baseborn daughter Harriet in 1823 from a previous relationship.

By 1841 James and Anne are living in Chard Somerset, where they seem to have settled.

The 1871 census showed James as a widowed labourer living in the Chard Union Workhouse in Old Chard, Somerset. His age was wrongly noted as 50, when it should have been 70, and his place of birth as Chard instead of Tolpuddle. The master of the workhouse was Edward Hoare 36 born Canterbury, Kent, the matron was his wife Ann Hoare 37 born Marlow, Buckinghamshire and their two children. The schoolmaster was George Rogers 44 born Ringwood, Hampshire, the schoolmistress Emily Edwards 27 born Hawkchurch, Dorset, the porter Jacob Brookes 23 born Trent, Somerset, the nurse Eliza Prosser 42 born Hawkchurch, Dorset and the cook Mary Ann Hadler 49 born Ashill, Somerset.

Anne had died as Ann Emmett in 1864, and was buried at St Mary the Virgin, Chard as Ann Hammett aged 63 of Old Town, Chard.

James probably left the Chard Union Workhouse in around 1873, being moved to the Wells Lunatic Asylum (also known as the Somerset & Bath Pauper Lunatic Asylum, and later the Mendip Hospital). Here the next year he died from senile decay in 1874 as James Emmett 75, a labourer from Chard, and was buried at the cemetery there on the 15th September 1874 in grave A13.

This Asylum was located in Bath Road, Wells, whilst the graveyard (The Old Mendip Hospital Cemetery) was off Hooper Avenue, Wells, and for the pauper lunatics. The ground there being consecrated in 1874 also had a chapel. Each grave was marked by a numbered cast iron marker. Unfortunately the National Health Service, which owned it, abandoned it in the early 1970's. The grave markers were pulled up and deposited in the chapel and the burial registers thrown away. So, it has not been possible to identify and photograph where the grave for James is. If not for the formation of the Friends of Mendip Hospital Cemetery Charity, this burial ground would have been sold off for development, and then lost forever. James would have been one of the first to be buried here as it opened in 1874 and he died that same year.

The year 1873 saw one hundred and one male and seventy-seven female patients joining this already established institution from other Unions. I believe James Hammett was amongst those one hundred and one men. This was due to the government previously granting four shillings per head for each pauper lunatic to be removed from the workhouse to the asylum. The asylum then witnessed this intake of patients increasing the numbers of inhabitants there to two hundred and seventy-three males and two hundred and seventy-nine females. Therefore bringing a total of five hundred and fifty-two inmates at the asylum for this time.

The Wells Lunatic Asylum, first opened on the 1st March 1848, was self-sufficient. On site were a bakery, butchery, laundry, a farm etc. These buildings of this former hospital are now known as South Horrington Village which was formed in the late 1990's when they were re-developed and transformed into some three hundred homes and sold off.

James and his first wife Sophie had two children who were Lavinia 1825 and Susannah 1827 who died in 1830. With his second wife Anne Greening there were no children apart from her baseborn daughter Harriett who was born in 1823 at Shipton Gorge. Harriett went on to have her own baseborn daughter Susan in 1843 at Chard. She later married Matthew Brooks.

Lavinia Hammett 1825-1854
Lavinia, daughter of James 1801 was born in and baptised in Tolpuddle in 1825. She appears to have gone back to Dorset in 1851 where she gave birth to her baseborn son in the Fordington Union Workhouse. Here he sadly died from secondary syphilis, which almost probably indicates Lavinia had suffered from it too.

Three years later in 1854 Lavinia died as Livinia/Levinia Hammett and is possibly buried in the churchyard at St George's. She was aged just 26, lived Mill Street, Fordington, noted as a servant with cause of death being cholera, which she appears to have suffered from for nine and half hours. With her was Ann Gawler also of Mill Street, whose signature was marked with an X, indicative of her not being able to write let alone sign her name.

In the September of 1854, Fordington had seen an outbreak of cholera, resulting in local deaths, four within one hour alone, and on another day six burials. There had been a previous outbreak in 1849, but the outbreak of 1854 was widely believed to have come about due to two local women in Holloway Row, Fordington taking in the washing for the seven hundred newly arrived Millbank prison convicts, housed at the nearby barracks.

These convicts had arrived in the August of that year from the London's Millbank prison, due to the cholera outbreak which had swept through there. The military barracks at Fordington was empty due to the troops being absent fighting the Crimean War, and therefore it was deemed a good idea to move the convicts down from London to Dorset.

With the laundry at the Fordington barracks being made to house retired guards, and as no women were allowed in the barracks, this had resulted in the laundry being sent out to be washed. The two women in Holloway Row given this task had hung the washing out in the street to dry. With the cholera disease in the washing it was thought to have spread airborne.

Historically Fordington, especially the Mill Street area, had had problems with sanitation and over-crowded living conditions. The narrow Mill Stream was all that stood between Mill Street and Holloway Row (Road).

It is not certain whether Lavinia lived with Ann Gawler as they both lived in Mill Street. The 1851 census for Mill Street, Fordington shows Ann Gawler aged 32, unmarried, a laundress, with her two children Charles 13 and Fanny 7. Also with her is a visitor Nathanial Gaulton 36 an unwed ostler (an inn stableman), whom she would later marry in 1855.

1861 Ann is still living in Mill Street but now is a married woman with husband Nathanial Gaulton. There too is her daughter Frances 16 who appears under the surname of Gaulton. Further research produced birth details for Ann's children. Charles was baptised in

1839 at St George's Church, Fordington by William Dodge curate, mother Ann Gawler lived Mill Street, a single woman. Maria Frances (Fanny) was baptised privately in 1844 by Richard Cutler the Chaplain of the Union Workhouse where her mother was from and presumably where she was born. She was then baptised by William Dodge at St George's.

Both Lavinia and Ann had spent time in the Fordington Union Workhouse and had borne children out of wedlock and lived in Mill Street. With Ann being a laundress, and possibly Lavinia too, perhaps this was how she became one of the many Fordington Cholera victims of 1854. Lavinia's only child was:-

1) **John William Hammett** born 14th June 1851 Union Workhouse Fordington, no father noted, and mother Lavinia's address given as the workhouse. Baptised as William John Hammett at Christ Church, West Fordington on the 26th June 1851 by the Reverend F Fisher (private baptism). This church was built in 1845 for the troops and situated next to the Royal Horse Artillery Barracks. Perhaps his father was a soldier. Lavinia was noted in this christening record as the mother with no mention of a father, and from the Union Workhouse. William had a very short life, dying as William John Hammett aged 3 months old in the Union Workhouse at Fordington, Dorset, of secondary syphilis, with his mother Levinia present. Levinia must have had the same condition and passed it onto her baby, very sad, and a few years later she would join him in death from cholera.

Susannah Hammett 1827-1830

Susannah, daughter of James 1801 was born in and baptised in Tolpuddle in 1827. She had a short life dying aged 3 in 1830, and was buried as Susan Hammett in Fordington. Her burial service was performed by the Reverend Waldy, who had also buried her mother (Bishop Transcripts – LDS Centre Hyde Park, Microfilm No: 1239251).

FAMILY TREE OF JAMES HAMMETT'S UNCLE JAMES

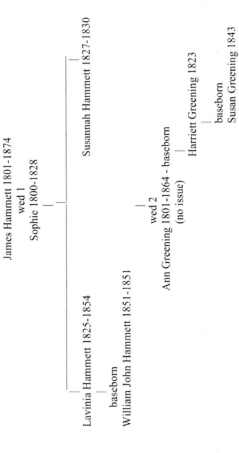

James Hammett 1801-1874
wed 1
Sophie 1800-1828

Susannah Hammett 1827-1830

Lavinia Hammett 1825-1854
baseborn
William John Hammett 1851-1851

wed 2
Ann Greening 1801-1864 - baseborn
(no issue)

Harriett Greening 1823
baseborn
Susan Greening 1843
wed
Matthew Brooks

PART III

Chapter 13

GRAND DEMONSTRATION ANNIVERSARIES AND TOLPUDDLE KX

Nearly one hundred and fourteen years after the Grand Demonstration of 1834, as described in Part II Chapter 4, on Sunday 20th March 1948 Tolpuddle came to London once again. This was to mark the anniversary of when the six Tolpuddle Martyrs were unjustly to suffer the horrors of transportation. Three hundred members of the Dorset County National Union of Agricultural Workers had come up from Dorset to march through the streets, retracing the same path as those who had marched in 1834. Leading was the London Workers Pipe Band, followed by the Tolpuddle branch banner carried by Mr Stark of Tolpuddle, then other various union banners, members and Labour Party folk. They stopped briefly at Trafalgar Square for a meeting, and also that day saw a performance of the Six Men of Dorset by Unity Theatre.

Another notable anniversary celebration in London occurred with the one hundred and seventy-fifth anniversary of the Grand Demonstration of 1834. This was marked by an event called Tolpuddle KX, with a series of events commencing in the week leading up to Saturday 25th April 2009 which was the main day. The title of Tolpuddle KX representing Tolpuddle Kings Cross, so named after the geographical location where it had initially taken place in the Islington area of 1834.

The crowds started to gather at about noon and assembled themselves around the clock tower in Caledonian Park. The then TUC deputy secretary Frances O'Grady unveiled a commemorative plaque affixed to the left side of the buttress of the clock tower, (on the right side of the buttress is another plaque for the tea-garden/market). This new plaque reads:-

Copenhagen Fields from this site on 21ˢᵗ April 1834 thousands marched in support of The Tolpuddle Martyrs who had been sentenced to transportation to Australia for forming a trades union.

There were songs from a choir, primary school children acted out a theatrical performance of the Dorset men's story, then union banners and their followers started to take their places in a procession for a march. Two women, Emily Thornberry MP and Frances O'Grady from the TUC, headed up the march by over five hundred people. Proceeding down the Caledonian Road and onto Edward Square, this made for a sight not to be missed.

At the destination of Edward Square various stalls and a central stage for the entertainment and speeches greeted the marchers, not unlike one hundred and seventy-five years before. Although there were not the crowds of 1834, this event was a success with a good turnout and was reported in the local Islington paper. Billy Bragg, who had attended many of the previous rallies in Tolpuddle, was one of the entertainers that day and, with the Mayor of Islington Stefan Kasprzyk in full regalia, this made for an impressive sight (event covered by Islington Tribune 01/05/2009 and Islington Gazette 30/04/2009).

The second banner in the marching procession of Saturday the 25ᵗʰ April 2009, was *In Memory of the Tolpuddle Martyrs.* It consisted of a tree with the six men's names noted and was carried by and marched behind by six of the Tolpuddle Martyrs' relatives. This represented six relatives for the six Tolpuddle Martyrs, or six-for-six. Various relatives had not only had a whip-round to fund the making of this banner, but also had collectively designed it. They had wanted a *family banner* to march behind in memory of their Dorset kinsfolk.

Mrs Hazel Werner, a descendant from both the Hammett and Loveless families of Tolpuddle (being related by blood to four of the Tolpuddle Martyrs, and by marriage to two of the others), had first suggested this idea to the rest of the relatives. Hazel then became responsible for overseeing the project and collecting the various funds required for the construction of this banner. Appropriately on the occasion of the one hundred and seventy-fifth anniversary the family banner was christened with an initial outing. Where better than the very location in Islington all those years ago when the population came from far and wide in support of the Dorchester Labourers as they were known then.

I was very proud to be one of those six people representing one of the Tolpuddle Martyrs on that day alongside Hazel and the other relatives. One of them was Kathy Claxton a direct descendant of James Hammett one of the Tolpuddle Martyrs. We all had a great day and even met and had our photograph taken with the local Mayor, Stefan Kasprzyk. Just as in 1834 the crowd was well behaved with no personage being escorted to the local police station in nearby Tolpuddle Street, a location where a few of the relatives could not resist having their photograph taken under the blue lamp and signage.

Both my husband and myself compiled a framed collage from the press coverage of Tolpuddle KX and photographs, along with a list of named relatives who contributed to this family banner. This was donated to the Tolpuddle Martyrs Museum in Tolpuddle and at one time it proudly hung on a wall inside the entrance to the Museum shop there.

The Islington area has historically attracted radical activism, as was witnessed in 1834. Later the Chartists would meet in the Jerusalem Passage area of Holborn. They were a movement of political and social reform with their Six Points of the Peoples' Charter. Thomas Paine (1737-1809) was the voice of the common man and a radical propagandist, who wrote in the Angel Inn (sited at the corner of Islington High Street and Pentonville Road) parts of his work *Rights of the Common Man*. John Stuart Mill (1806-1873), the most influential English speaking philosopher of the nineteenth century, addressed Reformists in Upper Street, Islington. Not forgetting Islington was the home of George Orwell and Karl Marx. An African ex-slave also lived here and was ordained Bishop of Niger at Canterbury Cathedral. His name was Samuel Crowther (1809-1891), who was born in Nigeria and first named Ajayi.

Copenhagen Fields was an open space on the hill not far from Holloway with a vista over London. Within this space was Copenhagen House, which opened during the 1620's, and was possibly a fashionable spa of those times. Various theories circulate, an inn built for Danish visitors when the King of Denmark came to James I's court in 1606, a Danish ambassador took up residence there during plague times, or it was named after an unknown Danish noble.

The 1750's saw this location become a tea garden and pleasure resort. In 1780 the landlady in occupation had the protection of troops from The Gordon Rioters who might damage her property on route to Lord Mansfield at Ken Wood. In the 1800's skittles, fives, dog fights and bear baiting were just a few of the activities which were enjoyed by those who frequented these premises.

By the mid 1800's, the house was damaged by a storm, which marked the end of the life of this property. Closure was unavoidable and came on the 21st March 1853 with a takeover by the Metropolitan Cattle Market. As in most cases with a new owner or occupier, changes were made, and in this case the main one would be the demolition of the house. On this site was built the Market Clock Tower, with Prince Albert opening it in the June of 1855. All that remains from those historic times now is the original clock tower. Attached to this structure is a plaque which reads:-

Copenhagen House – famous tavern and tea garden stood here from early 17th century to 1855. The Caledonian Market was held here from the 1870's until ceasing in 1939.

This ancient clock tower is now within the Caledonian Park in the Kings Cross area of London.

The Edward Square, mentioned previously, is situated just south of the Caledonian Park and was built in 1853 as a housing development with an enclosed square. This was partly opened to the public in 1888 and can claim to be one of the first London public gardens with the entrance accessed from Copenhagen Street. The Mitre public house is situated beside this entrance the wall of which displays a huge mural, depicting the events which took place in the Copenhagen Fields on the 21st April 1834.

The plaque on the railings by the entrance informs the reader that the mural on the gable end wall of the Mitre pub was painted by Dave Bangs in 1984 for the one hundred and fiftieth anniversary of the Tolpuddle Martyrs demonstration, with local people being used as models for the artwork. The artist for the wall panel was Kate

Blee, the gate panels were designed by children from Copenhagen and Blessed Sacrament Schools, the artist for the lettering on the wall enclosing the south lawn was Gary Breeze and the poem was written especially and donated by Andrew Motion, the poet laureate, an Islington resident. Weathering is unavoidable, as was the case with this mural, so it was repainted in 2008 by an artist called Karen.

The Tolpuddle Martyrs and Dorset further made an impression on that side of London as, located in an area just off the Hackney Road in Bethnal Green, in the borough of Tower Hamlets, the Dorset Estate is to be found. Located close to the now popular and famous Columbia Road Flower Market, a popular Sunday morning event with some saying the best place to purchase flowers and such like in London.

This modern estate was the first to have high-level blocks of flats, with the attention on reinforced concrete with height, designed by Skinner, Bailey and Berthold Lubetkin, the latter a Russian who had witnessed the Russian Revolution of 1917. After the Second World War when areas such as the East End of London had notably suffered massive destruction of buildings and housing during the war, there was a tendency to name these new constructions in honour of socialists, philanthropists and such like.

Therefore it is no surprise to find the Dorset Estate naming their properties after some of the Tolpuddle Martyrs and associated people. This area has no other historical link to the Tolpuddle Martyrs, which I can discover, but Copenhagen Fields, Islington being situated some distance away from this location, having that link and association.

Situated on the northern side of this Dorset Estate are two blocks of flats being Y-shaped, with eleven storeys, and named after George Loveless and James Hammett. To the south side there are four blocks of four storey flats named after a further Tolpuddle Martyr James Brine, with two further blocks named after Robert Owen (1771-1858 founder of the Grand National Consolidated Trades Union 1834) and (Dr) Arthur Wade (died 1846 a vicar and who like Robert Owen objected against the Tolpuddle Martyrs being transported). This estate was completed in 1957 and opened in 1958, providing two hundred and sixty-six flats for social housing. Close by is Weymouth Street which is another reminder of Dorset, the home county of the Tolpuddle Martyrs.

PART III

Chapter 14

THE TOLPUDDLE MARTYRS RALLY/FESTIVAL
AND RELATIVE DAYS

Annually, on the third weekend in July, the village of Tolpuddle in Dorset witnesses a total transformation in the form of an event. This was originally known as the Tolpuddle Martyrs' Rally, but later evolved into the Festival. The TUC (Trade Union Congress) is responsible for organising and orchestrating this ever-popular growing event.

The first rally they held was back in 1934, the centenary year of the trial and transportation of the Tolpuddle Martyrs. The Dorset County Chronical & Somerset Gazette for July 12th noted visitors to Tolpuddle were Lloyd George, Mrs Thomas Hardy (widow of Thomas Hardy, writer) to name but a few. Also in attendance then were some relatives of the Martyrs who were William Hammett of Dorchester, Miss Hammett of Tolpuddle, Francis Hammett of Dorchester, James Loveless, Mr and Mrs Puckett and family of Tolpuddle and John Hammett aged 84 a cousin of James Hammett and a cousin of the two Loveless brothers.

In nearby Dorchester from 30th August to 2nd September, the Dorchester Labourer's Centenary Commemorations were held. The official opening was on Thursday 30th August, with sporting events from ten different counties participating. There was a tennis tournament, athletes, football matches and a play was also put on. On Friday 31st August some of the events moved to Tolpuddle, where the unveiling of James Hammett's headstone in the churchyard took place. Many of his relatives attended this, including his son William and daughter-in-law and niece Mary Ann Hammett.

In addition, there was a dedication of the Memorial Cottages in Tolpuddle with an unveiling of a plaque. More sporting events occurred that day too.

Saturday 1st September saw the finals of all the sporting events, brass band concerts, another play and a pageant.

Sunday 2nd September the TUC had a demonstration in the afternoon.

(These daily events noted from an original commemorative bookmarker – Trade Union Congress, Walter M Citrine.)

Also that year saw the publication by the TUC of *The book of The Martyrs of Tolpuddle 1834-1934* being available for sale. This was the same book Mary Ann Hammett had contributed to. So the framework had been set for future rallies which later became festivals.

This annual weekend in July sees a programme of events which usually starts on the Friday going on throughout the weekend, with the Sunday being the main event day. Camping is arranged in the nearby fields adjacent to the TUC's properties, the Museum and the Tolpuddle Martyr's cottages. The main stage is sited close to the Museum shop frontage with a vista overlooking the front lawn and beyond the fields of Tolpuddle edging down to the River Piddle. There is another staged area in a huge marquee, aptly named the Martyrs' Marquee. There are numerous stalls selling refreshments, alongside the various unions, charities, political and campaign-based ones.

It is a family event, which also caters for children and teenagers. Entertainers, speakers and guests come from all corners of the globe, along with well-known home-grown ones. Some have become regulars, such as Billy Bragg, who performs *Power in the Union* and *The Red Flag* to name a few, and the late Tony Benn's captivating speeches.

Down the years Tolpuddle has played host to many a leading figurehead with Lloyd George in earlier times. Later ones who laid wreaths on the grave of James Hammett were James (Jim) Callaghan in 1968, Harold Wilson in 1971, John Smith in 1991 who even signed the village petition for the bypass (Dorset Evening Echo 22/07/1991) and Tony Blair in 1997.

The rally on the 17th July 1966 had two notable events. For the first time, members of the Agricultural Union of the Soviet Union attended, and, for as long as anyone could remember, it rained during the speeches. The speakers that year were Michael Foot and Lord Collison, with the march consisting of the various union banners alongside the Socialist ones in regard to the Vietnam War (The Times 18/07/1966 – The National Archives).

The festival year of 2010 still maintained free entrance to this festival. However, this came at a cost in the region of some £100,000 to put on, relying on donations and the support of volunteers (2010 Tolpuddle Martyrs' Festival programme).

The following festival year of 2011 saw for the first time entrance fees on all other days, apart from the main day of Sunday, which was still free. So far this is a trend which has continued with subsequent festival years.

In later years there has been the Tolpuddle Radical History School, which starts in Tolpuddle on the Thursday before the festival. Here attendees can learn about radical and trade union history. There is a fee to pay, which also includes entrance for the charged days of the festival. In addition there is the opportunity of setting up camp on that Thursday for an extra fee.

For some years now, relatives of the Tolpuddle Martyrs have collectively been meeting up at the festival on the Sunday in Tolpuddle. At one o'clock on the Sunday, in the churchyard of St John's in Tolpuddle, there is the wreath-laying ceremony at James Hammett's grave. He was the only one of the six Tolpuddle Martyrs to be buried in Tolpuddle, as the other five men all went to Ontario, Canada to live and so are laid to rest there.

It has now become the custom of some of James Hammett's many direct descendants and relatives, some of whom are related to all six of the Tolpuddle Martyrs, to lay wreaths, alongside representatives of the various unions, organizations and dignitaries. The late Tony Benn was usually amongst those who attended this service with a wreath in hand. The year of 2010 saw Billy Bragg place a wreath during that ceremony for the first time.

Afterwards there is a march through the village comprising of the various dignitaries, unions, visitors and, of course, those with family links to the Tolpuddle Martyrs. Collectively they all assemble with their many banners being carried, which make for a colourful vista. These banners include the family one for the Tolpuddle Martyrs which reads:-

In Memory of the Tolpuddle Martyrs.

Relatives of those men are proud to march behind this banner, which we all collectively designed and had made, on this special day in their ancestral village. Some even wear t-shirts matching the banner. It is Mrs Hazel Werner (mentioned earlier) we all have to thank for not only organising the making of the banner, but these t-shirts too.

In the year 2010 this march was accompanied by various musical bands, as it still is. They were The Northern Ireland Prison Officers Pipe Band, Great Western Jazz Band and Easington Band.

The circuit for this march assembles and begins on the road outside the Tolpuddle Martyrs Museum and goes through the village to the Methodist Chapel. Once here it turns back on itself to go back to the starting point outside the Museum again. Some years the procession has been so large that once those at the front have arrived back at their starting point, they are greeted by others still awaiting at the back of that procession line to start marching.

Once the march has been completed, all assemble back on the green before the main stage by the Museum and await the speeches from the various guests. This is then followed by the musical entertainment.

At the other end of the village at usually five o'clock in the afternoon, in the Methodist Chapel, the same one built by brothers William and John Hammett, and cousins of James Hammett, there is a service. This then brings closure to the day and event. The village also has a part to play in on this weekend, raising funds from the sale of refreshments in the old school house, and sometimes stalls on the frontages of the various local houses. The Martyrs Inn public house is also a hugely popular focal point for that weekend.

Each year the TUC produces different artworks for the front pages of their brochure for the programme of events on that weekend. Here are a few recent ones:-

2013 - world globe with George Loveless at one end reaching out to wife Betsy at the other end accompanied by words *Free the Tolpuddle Six, We Will Be Free.* This year premiered in Tolpuddle a travelling play by Townsend Productions, called *Tolpuddle Martyrs Story We Will Be Free.*

2012 - silhouette of the tree with the six men and words *Roots Of Solidarity.*

2011 - silhouette of the tree with the six men and words *Back To Our Roots.*

2010 - based upon the notice of the 25th April 1836 when a Public Dinner was held in London to celebrate the returning Tolpuddle Martyrs.

2009 - based upon an image from the 1934 celebrations of a man pointing to the words *Come to Tolpuddle.*

I cannot recall the exact year our own little individual family first attended the rally but it must have been in about the year 2000 and, to be honest, we have only attended on the main day of Sunday. Since that time, however, we have seen this event grow with attendance numbers up each year. I believe the camping pitches are sold out very swiftly too and have evolved to now have "posh" ablution facilities. Usually the weather on the Sunday has been kind, apart from the odd year. When the sun shines its golden rays on Tolpuddle that day, there is nowhere I would rather be.

In the past at nearby Dorchester on the Saturday before the festival Sunday the very courtroom, where the Tolpuddle Martyrs had their "loaded" trial, has been open to the public. Access has also been available then to visit the cells below this courthouse, including where the six Tolpuddle Martyrs were kept for three days before their trial and sentencing. Here along with other unfortunate souls, they were all housed in one large smoky, damp cell with a fireplace, which presumably was all they had for their heat and cooking. I am not sure at present if this arrangement is still available to the public. In 2013 the Shire Hall in Dorchester which covers the old crown court and cells was awarded heritage lottery support, thereby ensuring this important building is kept for future generations to visit. Although throughout the years, some of the poor souls on trial in that courtroom must have been guilty and deserving, others may not have been, including the six men from Tolpuddle.

On the Saturday during the festival weekend of 2009, a group of relatives of the Tolpuddle Martyrs, including some direct descendants of James Hammett, decided to meet up outside the Dorchester Courthouse. This included my little family.

Once inside this establishment, together we all embarked on a journey back in time. First we sat in the courtroom and listened to the guide who re-told the story of our relatives, a tale which over the years, for many of us, had become embedded within our genes and souls.

Looking up to the public gallery we imagined the loved ones of the six men from Tolpuddle who were our relatives, and who would have had to sit there throughout the whole trial in utter disbelief. To the sides of this room in a tiered galley would have sat the jury and more affluent people, not the great unwashed.

Later we were taken down the stairs, the very ones our six relatives had used from the cell to the courtroom. Here we had time to reflect in the very cell the men were kept in along with others at the time who also were on trial. This would have been a very crowed cell, with no privacy. In addition it was a damp place with a smoky atmosphere from the one fire there, which had no ventilation to speak of, and was their only source of heat and cooking.

Another meet-up with relatives of the Tolpuddle Martyrs was held the following year in 2010. This happened on one afternoon in the April of that year at the Lubbecke Way Community Hall in Dorchester. It was arranged by two sisters, Pam and Margi, who are descended through both the Hammett and Loveless lines. They are both therefore blood related to four of the Tolpuddle Martyrs, and by marriage to the two others.

Refreshments were on hand, including lovely home-made cakes, with donations to the Cystic Fibrosis Trust. The hall along with the furniture provided a comfortable environment for just such a gathering. In Tolpuddle on the festival Sunday when the various relatives have met up, there never seemed to be much time, with the various events going on. But there that day, all could have a seat and display, on the tables provided, their family history information along with much treasured photographs. Over that afternoon about forty-five relatives in total would pop in and out, including direct descendants of James Hammett Tolpuddle Martyr.

There was one guest, however, who was not a relative but a link to the past with the Hammett family. I have mentioned her previously within these pages. Her name was Mrs Freda Wade. I sometimes wonder if the ancestors are watching over events down here on earth, as I came across Mrs Wade by pure chance. She had made a contribution to the Dorset Living Memories project run by Age Concern. As she mentioned William Hammett, I was immediately drawn to her story and the rest, as they say, is history.

As a child Mrs Freda Wade recalled how her grandmother Edith Vincent, along with herself stopped to talk to William Hammett who was the son of James, one of the Tolpuddle Martyrs, back in 1934. Later Mrs Wade would escort a few of us to William's former abode where we posed for some photographs. Mrs Wade and her parents had lived further up the road from William in 1934, in Holloway Road. Their house 21 Harvey's Buildings/Terrace, had formerly been occupied by James Hammett's great-nephew Henry Hammett in 1901. This was a fact Mrs Wade had been unaware of.

This area of Dorchester was Fordington with the River Frome running nearby. It had been a poor area where the cholera outbreaks of the 1800's had occurred. This was an area with historical Hammett connections, including those for James Hammett's son-in-law Thomas Lester. Thomas had been noted in the 1871 census as residing at Mill Street, which is just the other side of the Holloway Road. Between these two roads there is only the narrow waters of the River Frome to part and separate them. The Community Hall in Lubbecke Way is situated just the other side of the King's Road, with Holloway Road and Mill Street running off it on the other side. That day we followed in the footsteps of our ancestral kinsfolk.

PART III

Chapter 15

COMRADES, A FILM BY BILL DOUGLAS

Over the years many films have been made about various historical events and figureheads, including the story of the Tolpuddle Martyrs, which was made in 1985, and titled *Comrades*. The following year of 1986 witnessed this film being shown at the London Film Festival, with the release of it a year later in 1987.

A film, lasting nearly three hours, recounted the story of the Tolpuddle Martyrs. The man behind this film was William Gerald Forbes (Bill) Douglas, who up until 1979 had never even heard of the Tolpuddle Martyrs. The absence of this knowledge was a void quickly filled when on a visit in 1979 to Dorchester he happened to visit the Museum there with a friend. This friend then drew his attention to a leaflet he had picked up regarding the Tolpuddle Martyrs with a suggestion that it had the potential for a film. The script for Comrades began that very year (information gleaned from booklet accompanying the DVD of Comrades 2009 – www.bfi.org.uk).

William Gerald Forbes (Bill) Douglas was born in 1934 not far from Edinburgh in Scotland, and died in 1991. He had a lifelong interest in the film industry and was an actor, writer and director. *Comrades* was to be his last film and what a powerful subject matter to be remembered by. No one else had up until then taken the film route of recalling The Tolpuddle Martyrs story and, so far as I am aware, no one has since. As with most films, it must be remembered, the script may vary somewhat from a few of the factual events and details.

The film was shot in Australia and also within the village of Tyneham in Dorset. Tolpuddle would not have been easy to shoot a period film in, having the occupation of a community within it and surrounded by too much of the modern world.

Tyneham on the other hand had never entered the modern world, as it had been left engulfed within the Dorset rural countryside by a time warp just before the Second World War. With the onset of war, the village of Tyneham was taken over by the occupation of the Ministry of Defence. Therefore this village was left just as it was back then without any sign of the trappings of a modern world.

Of course since those days the buildings in Tyneham had fallen into disrepair and sustained damage from the military with their various activities. But not all was lost, as the film industry could soon remedy such matters. With the aid of their talented specialist departments, they were soon able to create the desired effects and bring back to life on film a rural Dorset village, which then became Tolpuddle.

Filming for *Comrades* was also carried out in Dorchester and in the very courthouse where the Tolpuddle Martyrs had been on trial. For this establishment remains almost identical as it was back then.

My eyes did not view this film until more than twenty years after it had been released. I was pleasantly surprised to note from the cast of *Comrades* some well-known names.

Listed below are those names along with the rest of the players:-
GEORGE LOVELESS TM - Robin Soans
BETSY LOVELESS (wife of George) - Imelda Staunton
HETTY LOVELESS (their daughter) - Amber Wilkinson
JAMES LOVELESS TM (brother of George) - William Gaminara
SARAH LOVELESS (wife of James) - Katy Behean
THOMAS STANFIELD TM - Stephen Bateman
DIANE STANFIELD (wife of Thomas) - Sandra Voe
(also sister of George Loveless TM)
JOHN STANDFIELD (son of Thomas and Diane) - Philip Davis
ELVI (ELIZABETH) STANDFIELD - Valerie Whittington
(daughter of Thomas and Diane)
CHARITY STANDFIELD - Harriet Doyle
(daughter of Thomas and Diane)
JOHN HAMMETT (brother of James TM) - Patrick Field

BRIDGET HAMMETT (wife of John) - Heather Page
JAMES HAMMETT TM (brother of John) - Keith Allen
JAMES BRINE TM - Jeremy Flynn
JOSEPH BRINE (brother of James) - Shane Down
MRS BRINE (James and Joseph's mother) - Patricia Healey
JAMES FRAMPTON - Robert Stephens
MRS FRAMPTON - Joanna David
MR PITT - Michael Hordern
VICAR - Freddie Jones
MRS WETHAM - Barbara Windsor
CLERK - Murray Melvin
SAILOR - Michael Clerk
EDWARD LEGG - Mark Brown
MRS CARLYLE - Vanessa Redgrave
MR NORFOLK - James Fox
THE FOP - Arthur Dignam
NED LUDD (convict) - John Hargreaves
CHARLIE - Symon Parsonage
ABORIGINE - Charles Yunipingu
LANTERNIST
SERGEANT BELL
DIORAMA SHOWMAN
LAUGHING CAVALIER
WOLLASTON - all these eleven parts played by
RANGER Alex Norton
TRAMP
SEA CAPTAIN
McCALLUM
SILHOUETTIST
MAD PHOTOGRAPHER

As mentioned earlier, film scripts can differ from some of the actual facts. John Hammett was not a carpenter as portrayed in the film, but an agricultural labourer, and later in life a builder. He was not married at the time period this film was set and, when he was, his wife was not called Bridget, but Elizabeth. Bridget is not a name I have come across researching the Tolpuddle Hammett family.

However, his brother James, one of the Tolpuddle Martyrs, was married at this time period with one child, but there is no mention of his wife or child in the film. I feel it is important to point these facts out, as they are the truth, otherwise viewers of the film may be unaware of them.

PART III

Chapter 16

REFLECTIONS

When I first embarked on researching both the family histories of my husband and myself some sixteen to seventeen years ago, I never envisaged ending up here writing a book. Out of all the various branches of our numerous family trees, it was the Hammett one which was to take up most of my time and research.

This, of course, was not indicative of our other ancestors and relatives not being worthy or interesting enough. Many of them had played their parts in historical events or had interesting connections. In the past I have written and had commercially published articles, a few of which were on some of those very relatives.

But somehow with the Hammett family tree and Dorset connections it was different. I wanted to know what had become of all the members of that tree. Those who had been around in Tolpuddle in 1834, were they marked for life by the events then? What lives did the various descendants from the twigs on the Tolpuddle Hammett family tree have? Where did they end up in the world? Had they found their fortunes? Where did the ancestors of the Tolpuddle Hammetts hail from? These were just some of the questions mulling around in my mind.

My husband, as a youngster, had spent a week on holiday in Dorset with his classmates during a school holiday trip, and wanted to re-visit that part of the country. This coincided at about the same time I had been thinking of visiting my Hammett roots from Dorset. There was not only the ancestral village of Tolpuddle to visit, but a few other associated places within that neck of the woods. So it was we had what was to become our first of many family holidays there and have been in love with the county of Dorset ever since.

Dorset is a county with something for everyone, with such diverse scenery along with one of the most beautiful coastlines around. Layers of history are wrapped around this part of the world, revealing themselves in various guises accompanied by numerous tales, with the echoes of smugglers centuries old never far away. Over the years numerous people have found their creative juices awakened in Dorset from Enid Blyton's Noddy and Secret Seven, to the many novels by Thomas Hardy. The village of East Fleet near Chessil Beach became the village of Moonfleet in the novel by J Meade Falkner and later entered the film world. These are just a few of the many inspired and captivated by the charms of Dorset.

Now, back to the Hammett ancestry. It was firstly the Tolpuddle Martyr connection, which played a major role with more research. Digging deeper back in time, stripping back layers of years, research suddenly evolved into a learning curve, for us all. Certainly not one either my husband or I were ever taught at school. History lessons back in those days we recalled just usually covered the Romans, Saxons, some Industrial Revolution with the Spinning Jenny and such like. There had never been a whisper of the Tolpuddle Martyrs.

The hobby of researching the family history, particularly the Tolpuddle Hammett one, was something that went much deeper, using all resources available to gather and collect all sorts of information on people, places, events and then transporting it all back to the Tolpuddle Hammett family tree. At times this became an unquenchable thirst for more knowledge on this topic and associated family and people. It all sounds a bit far-fetched, but that it how it felt at times. It has, on my part, been a labour of love and at times, an obsession researching this family tree, my attention always immediately drawn to the name Hammett appearing along life's journey.

With this family tree I have attempted to put "flesh on the bones" bringing to life the various individuals from the Tolpuddle Hammetts with their Dorset roots. Of course the Tolpuddle Martyrs' side played a huge part, but in addition there were other people with a life story worth telling. Some of them touched on various major historical events, whilst others began their life in the workhouse only to end it there. Some were to die early or from accidents, which were reminders of how fragile life really was, and still is.

During my time researching the Tolpuddle Hammetts, I have come across various people who lay claim to be descendants or relatives of the Tolpuddle Martyr James Hammett. I sincerely hope by attempting to incorporate this family tree into written works, it will aid those who make these claims.

In addition to having the flame of the Tolpuddle Martyrs kept alive with the annual event in the ancestral village, this then became a focal point to meet up with distant connected relatives. Kinsfolk who, like myself, shared an interest of our past ancestors and relatives, many of whom would have felt the shockwaves of the year 1834 in one way or another.

This event became a diary entry each year and one not to be missed. It was where we could all meet, gathering up and bringing along newfound connected relatives along the way. Each year our numbers attending continues to grow, although some may be absent, living too far way to attend or not been able to for other reasons. These missing links in the chain are always there with us in spirit on that special day.

With our love of Dorset, we never needed an excuse to visit and many times have incorporated that weekend within our holiday. Together all the relatives unite and even designed a logo for the family marching banner and t-shirts. They contributed financially what each could and then one member oversaw the making of our joint efforts.

That member was distant cousin Hazel Werner, a Dorset lass and keeper of the banner when it is not in use. It is only right and fitting that the banner resides in Dorset, the home county.

A mine of all things Tolpuddle Martyrs came in the form of another distant cousin, Dawn Stewart. Like Hazel, she too is related to all six of the Tolpuddle Martyrs, for both these ladies are descended from the marriage of Elizabeth Hammett and Stephen Loveless. Dawn's interest in this topic came about as a young girl and she has been collecting all things connected to the Tolpuddle Martyrs since then, including some of us distant relatives.

I recall Dawn being one of the first relatives I was to connect with. This came in the form of being put in touch with her by a local author who resided in Tolpuddle at the time, the late Audrey Wirdnam. Audrey's works were:-

Pidela, an account of the village of Tolpuddle, Dorset from early times

and

Puddletown a Millennium Celebration 100 years of life and administration in Puddletown.

Jan Pickering, who was the Manager of the Tolpuddle Martyrs Museum for many years, I must thank for putting me in touch with Audrey initially. Jan also used to pass on my contact details to folks who visited the Museum and who thought they might have a Hammett connection.

Additionally leaving my contact details in the various visitor books in Tolpuddle at the museum and Church was to prove fruitful with the discovery of new relatives, including that of Hazel Werner mentioned previously.

Local Dorset newspaper appeals also were positive routes taken for the quest of seeking relatives who had not strayed too far from our joint ancestral roots. Some of those who responded were direct descendants of Tolpuddle Martyr James Hammett.

The use of the internet opened up a whole new world for researching family history. Here I could connect with people over the seas and far away, and that is just what happened. From Canada to the land where the Tolpuddle Martyrs were transported in Australia, and also back here in England, these locations housed more Tolpuddle Hammett relatives. Amongst them more of the many direct descendants James Hammett left behind with his lineage, totally unaware of their famous ancestor.

I must also make mention of the on-line parish clerk for Tolpuddle, Donna King, who resides in Canada and although not a relative of mine, she is related to the Loveless and Standfield Tolpuddle Martyrs. Her work is very much appreciated, as was the work of another lady, Irene Howgate, who sadly is no longer with us, having passed away.

Irene's ancestors were from the Dorset Loveless line, but could not be proved to be connected to the Tolpuddle ones. Irene compiled much research on all the various lines over the years, helping a great many people and was always there with one of her "blonde" jokes to lighten the day. Being a blonde myself, no offence was ever taken.

Treading the pathway of researching the Tolpuddle Hammetts over the years contact was to be made with various people in one way or another. Some of them were found to be relatives, whilst others were not. I was pleased to note that the majority of these contacts were mostly positive forces.

Over the years I have written many missives and exchanged emails with various organizations and people in the quest for further information or that missing part of the jigsaw for the family tree. One such person was Sir Julian Fellowes, to whom I originally wrote on my Fellowes lineage, who married into the Tolpuddle Hammett family tree. Searching for my mother's cousin I did a blanket search of the surname Fellowes. Some replied and others did not, however Sir Julian Fellowes kindly did. It may seem naïve, but initially the penny did not drop that this was "the" Julian Fellowes for his signature then was that of Kitchener-Fellowes, who is now known as Lord Fellowes.

Although Lord Fellowes and myself did not have a connection on the Fellowes side, for my Fellow(e)s relatives were originally from Northamptonshire and agricultural labourers who changed the name from Fellows to Fellowes, adding an "e", there was to be another link. Not a blood link, of course, but a connection with my Tolpuddle Hammett family tree.

It transpired Lord Fellowes had an ancestress who was the mother of Magistrate Frampton. This was the same Magistrate who had sealed the fate of the six Tolpuddle Martyrs, with his direct ancestry being from the lineage of an older half-sibling of Frampton's. What a turn up for the books, as they say.

I am proud not only to be descended from a branch of the Tolpuddle Hammetts, but also to be related to these Dorsetshire folks who stood their ground. Criminals and troublemakers they certainly were not for all they had wanted was a fair day's pay in exchange for an honest day's work. The whole village at the time would have been on that member's list of George Loveless or known someone who was. This is the true meaning of the expression of *All being in it together,* a statement which some modern day politicians have tried to adopt.

Some facts written about the Tolpuddle Martyrs and the Hammetts have not always been wholly correct, which I hope to iron out with this publication. I have used parish records, censuses, certificates and other aides in my research. In addition, some of the information has been passed down by the relatives, which cannot always be verified. It is worth mentioning these little pieces of passed down ancestral information, otherwise they could be lost forever.

This research is still ongoing and probably mistakes have been made of which I am unaware. I offer my apologies in advance if this is found to be the case. Above all, I hope you enjoyed this publication.

BIBLOGRAPHY

A Dorset Soldier, the autobiography of Sergeant William Lawrence 1790-1869 – Eileen Hathaway

Insurance Racketeers – Gordon Fellowes

Mad Dogs and Englishmen, an Expedition Round my Family - Sir Ranulph Fiennes

Mendip Hospital, an appreciation – Susan Marshall

Piedela, an account of the village of Tolpuddle – Audrey Wirdnam

Six Heroes in Chains – H Brooks 1929

The Book of the Martyrs of Tolpuddle 1834-1934 – Trade Union Congress

The Church Shown Up – George Loveless

The Martyr's Account, The Victims of Whiggery – George Loveless

The Story of George Loveless and the Tolpuddle Martyrs – Andrew Norman

The Tolpuddle Martyrs – Joyce Marlow

They Took Me For A Ride – Gordon Fellowes

Thomas Hardy's England – John Fowles & Jo Draper

Timeline of Britain – Gordon Kerr

Timeline History of the World – Gordon Kerr

Titanic: 14th-15th April 1912 the Official Story – Public Record Office collection

Tolpuddle an historical account through the eyes of George Loveless – compiled for the TUC by Graham Padden

Tolpuddle Martyrs – Marjorie Firth and Arthur Hopkinson

Victims of Whiggery - George Loveless

Who sailed on Titanic? The definitive passenger lists – Debbie Beavis

And any other publication(s) I have omitted to thank or acknowledge.

Lightning Source UK Ltd.
Milton Keynes UK
UKOW03f1822120814

236833UK00012B/141/P